BROADCAST TALK

The Media, Culture & Society Series

Series editors: John Corner, Nicholas Garnham, Paddy Scannell, Philip Schlesinger, Colin Sparks, Nancy Wood

The Economics of Television
The UK Case

Richard Collins, Nicholas Garnham and Gareth Locksley

Media, Culture and Society
A Critical Reader

edited by
Richard Collins, James Curran, Nicholas Garnham,
Paddy Scannell, Philip Schlesinger and Colin Sparks

Capitalism and Communication
Global Culture and the Economics
of Information

Nicholas Garnham, edited by Fred Inglis

Media, State and Nation
Political Violence and
Collective Identities

Philip Schlesinger

BROADCAST TALK

edited by
Paddy Scannell

SAGE Publications
London • Newbury Park • New Delhi

First published 1991

 SAGE Publications Ltd.
6 Bonhill Street
London EC2A 4PU

SAGE Publications Inc.
2455 Teller Road
Newbury Park, California 91320

SAGE Publications India Pvt Ltd
32, M-Block Market
Greater Kailash-I
New Delhi 110 048

British Library Cataloguing in Publication Data

Broadcast talk.—(Media, culture & society
series)
I. Scannell, Paddy II. Series
302.23

ISBN 0-8039-8374-3
ISBN 0-8039-8375-1 pbk

Library of Congress catalog card number 91-052965

Typeset by GCS, Leighton Buzzard, Beds.
Printed in Great Britain by Billing and Sons Ltd., Worcester

Contents

Transcription conventions

( )	If empty, indicates indecipherable utterance; otherwise, best guess at what was said.
(( ))	Verbal description of nonverbal behaviour.
(2.0)	Latency between or within utterances, in seconds.
—	Brief untimed pause within an utterance.
word-	Word is cut off abruptly.
(.)	Slightly longer untimed pause within or between utterances.
=	Latching together separate parts of a continuous utterance or indicating that B's utterance follows A's with no gap or overlap.
[	Point at which overlap occurs between speakers.
word	Stress added to a word or a syllable.
WORD	Extreme stress.
co::lons	Stretching of a vowel or consonant sound.
.	Terminal falling intonation.
?	Rising intonation.
/	Intonation rises somewhat, not as much as with ? intonation.
,	Brief pause at a syntactically relevant point in an utterance.
.hh	Audible inhalation.
hh	Audible exhalation.
heh	Laugh token.
'	Utterances marked lexically or prosodically as quotes.
!	Excited intonation.

Notes on Contributors

Graham Brand graduated from the Polytechnic of Central London in 1987 with a degree in Media Studies. He is now a freelance writer, producing comic strips for adults and children.

Steven E. Clayman is Assistant Professor of Sociology and Communication Studies at the University of California, Los Angeles. He is interested in the interactional foundations of mass communication with particular reference to news and politics and has published several articles on such topics.

John Corner is Senior Lecturer in Communication Studies at Liverpool University. He is on the editorial board of *Media, Culture & Society*, has written many articles and edited several books on the media, including *Documentary and the Mass Media* (Edward Arnold, 1986) and *Popular Television in Britain* (BFI, 1991).

Greg Garton graduated from Queen Margaret College, Edinburgh, in 1987, with distinction in communication studies and has subsequently written a doctoral thesis on verbal interviews in media studies.

Sandra Harris is a Professor and Dean of the Faculty of Humanities at Nottingham Polytechnic. Her field of research is sociolinguistics, especially institutional discourse, about which she has written numerous articles.

Ian Hutchby read Sociology at Middlesex Polytechnic between 1986 and 1990, and is currently researching a doctoral thesis on argument in talk-radio talk at the University of York.

Peter Lewis is a freelance writer and broadcaster, and a Visiting Fellow in the Department of Social Science, City University. He is co-author, with J. Booth, of *The Invisible Medium: Public, Community and Commercial Radio* (Macmillan, 1989), and is currently editing a global study of alternative media for UNESCO.

Martin Montgomery is Senior Lecturer in Literary Linguistics at the University of Strathclyde. He is the author of *Language and Society* (Methuen, 1986) and is particularly interested in critical approaches to the language of the media.

Paddy Scannell is a Senior Lecturer in Media Studies at the Polytechnic of Central London. He is co-author, with David Cardiff, of *A Social History of British Broadcasting,* Volume 1, Serving the Nation, 1922–1939 (Basil Blackwell, 1991). He is a founding editor of *Media, Culture & Society.*

Andrew Tolson is Senior Lecturer in Communication Studies at Queen Margaret College, Edinburgh. He has research interests in the uses of the interview as a form of mass communication.

1

Introduction: The Relevance of Talk

Paddy Scannell

I

Radio and television are live media. Like the telephone, the talk they produce exists in real time: the moment of speaking and the moment of hearing are the same. In the early years of both radio and television all transmissions were live. In both cases, the development of technologies for recording talk came considerably later, and although today many programmes are prerecorded, they are recorded in such a way as to preserve the effect of liveness. Studio talk shows, game shows, quizzes, discussion programmes and musical performances are not put together in the way that fictional narratives are, either for cinema or television. Recorded programmes are just that: *Wogan* and *Blind Date*, for instance, are not constructed shot by separate shot but in one continuous take. So the liveness of broadcasting, its sense of existing in real time – the time of the programme corresponding to the time of its reception – is a pervasive effect of the medium. The talk that goes out on radio and television is recognizably produced in actual institutional settings and intended for and addressed to actual listeners and viewers, listening and viewing in real-world circumstances.

As such this talk is intentionally communicative. The people speaking in the studio or other contexts do not appear to be either talking to themselves or locked in private discourse from which viewers and listeners are excluded. The effect of listening to radio and TV output is not that of overhearing talk not intended to be overheard. All talk on radio and TV is public discourse, is meant to be accessible to the audience for whom it is intended. Thus broadcast talk minimally has a double articulation: it is a communicative interaction between those participating in discussion, interview, game show or whatever and, at the same time, is designed to be heard by absent audiences.[1] The talk that takes place on radio and television has listenable properties intentionally built into it. A central concern in the study of broadcast talk is to specify the ways in which communicative intentionality is organized in the form and content of programmes.[2]

It is often said of broadcasting that it is a one-way medium, that the audience can't talk back, that there is no direct feedback. This is obviously true and the point is usually made in arguments about the power of broadcasters over their passive audiences. But against this two counter points can be made: the first is that in many face-to-face contexts the audience can't talk back – a religious service, a lecture or a concert performance are obvious instances. Two-way talk, in which participants have equal discursive rights, is only one form of talk though it should be thought of as the primary and prototypical form.[3] The second point to be made is that while the central fact of broadcasting's communicative context is that it speaks from one place and is heard in another, the design of talk on radio and TV recognizes this and attempts to bridge the gap by simulating co-presence with its listeners and viewers (Horton and Wohl, 1986).

Consideration of the spaces from which broadcasting speaks and in which it is heard is a precondition for understanding the communicative character of broadcasting and the talk it produces.[4] Talk on radio and television comes from many locations but there is one that is primary and that is the broadcasting studio. Most of the chapters in this collection concern themselves with studio-originated talk. The studio is the institutional discursive space of radio and television. It is a public space in which and from which institutional authority is maintained and displayed. The power of broadcasting, like that of any institution, lies in the way it can define the terms of social interaction in its own domain by pre-allocating social roles and statuses, and by controlling the content, style and duration of its events. A classic instance is the political interview, a genre of talk specific to radio and television, in which the broadcasters predefine what the talk is about, how it shall start, when it shall end and the parts to be played by the participants.[5] The same is true for game shows and quizzes, indeed for nearly all the talk that goes out on radio and television.

If the broadcasters are seemingly masters in their own domain there is, however, one omnipresent consideration that compels them to treat their arrangements as more than a purely internal matter and that is, of course, consideration for absent viewers or listeners. To consider the fundamental force of this point consider the consequences of deliberately ignoring the audience, of refusing to take its needs into account. There is a well-known historical instance in the UK: The Third Programme. Its historian, Kate Whitehead, noted 'a decidedly cavalier attitude towards the audience that prevailed amongst some of The Third Programme's founders'. George Barnes, the first Controller of The Third Programme, in an article for *The Listener* in 1946 describing the new service, promised (or threatened) that it would offer 'few "hearing aids" for listeners' (Whitehead, 1989: 16, 48). One unsurprising consequence of this lack of concern for listeners was that very few indeed actually listened. The Third Programme was the exception that proves the rule: if you want people to listen or to watch your programmes you must make them listenable to and watchable.

This seemingly simple proposition masks an issue of very great complexity, and one that it took broadcasters in the UK many years to resolve successfully. A central part of this process was the discovery of appropriate forms of talk for broadcasting (Scannell and Cardiff, 1991: 153–78). The talk that prevailed in early broadcasting in the UK was monologue rather than dialogue, in which selected speakers spoke at length from the studio to absent listeners on predetermined scripted topics. In 1928 Hilda Matheson, the first Head of

Talks in the BBC (British Broadcasting Corporation), conducted a series of experiments which led her to the view that it was 'useless to address the microphone as if it were a public meeting, or even to read it essays or leading articles. The person sitting at the other end expected the speaker to address him personally, simply, almost familiarly, as man to man' (Matheson, 1933: 75–6). Broadcasting could not speak to its audience as a crowd. It had to learn to speak to them as individuals. In this essential respect radio and television marked the end, not the extension, of mass communication where that is understood as a form of communication that constitutes its audience and speaks to it as a mass.

The pivotal fact is that the broadcasters, while they control the discourse, do not control the communicative context. The places from which broadcasting speaks and in which it is heard are completely separate from each other. Or, in other words, the settings in which listening and viewing take place are always beyond the control of the broadcasting institutions. Thus the communicative context within which broadcasting takes place does not confer on the broadcasters the authority and control over their audiences which the institutional setting combined with real presence bestows upon public speakers. Whereas the onus is upon the audience attending church, a political rally, a public lecture, a theatre or concert performance to affiliate to the situation and align their behaviour with performer(s) and setting, the situation in broadcasting is reserved. The communicators must affilitate to the situation of their audience, and align their communicative behaviour with those circumstances. The burden of responsibility is thus on the broadcasters to understand the conditions of reception and to express that understanding in language intended to be recognized as oriented to those conditions.

From the start it was recognized that listening and viewing took place in the sphere of domesticity, within the spaces of the household and normatively in the small, family living-room (Scannell and Cardiff, 1991: 356–80). How broadcasters attempted to produce programmes that fitted in to the domestic sphere and the daily round, that were appropriate to the conditions of reception, has a long and uneven history in relation to different types of output. But as it was increasingly understood that broadcasting, because it could not compel its audiences to listen or to behave as the broadcasters ideally wished, must adapt the form and content of its programmes to fit in with the circumstances of viewing and listening, attention focused on ways of achieving this. It was recognized that broadcast output, though articulated in the public domain as public discourse, was received within the sphere of privacy, as an optional leisure resource. Within this sphere, as Matheson noted, people did not expect to be talked down to, lectured or 'got at'. They expected to be spoken to in a familiar, friendly and informal matter as if they were equals on the same footing as the speaker. The voices of radio and television were and are heard in the context of household activities and other household voices, as part of the general social arrangements of households and their members. It is this that powerfully drives the communicative style and manner of broadcasting to approximate to the norms not of public forms of talk, but to those of ordinary, informal conversation, for this is overwhelmingly the preferred communicative style of interaction between people in the routine contexts of day-to-day life and especially in the places in which they live.

II

Talk has been defined as 'the casual exchange of conversation in the settings of day to day life' (Giddens, 1987: 99), as 'that familiar predominant kind of talk in which two or more participants freely alternate in speaking, which generally occurs outside specific institutional settings like religious services, law courts, classrooms and the like' (Levinson, 1983: 284). Until recently naturally occurring talk has not been seriously studied. Doubtless one reason for this, which has nice implications for the overall aim and attitude of this book, is that it was technically impossible to capture talk for analysis until the advent of recording devices developed in large part to meet broadcasting's powerful impulse to use naturally occurring talk in its programmes. The light-weight portable sound and videotape recorders – developed in the 1950s and 1960s for documentaries, news reports and interviews – made such talk available for use not only in broadcasting but for other purposes too. Since then linguists, anthropologists and sociologists have begun to use tape recordings of naturally occurring talk in order systematically to analyse its properties.

Theoretical studies of talk have been interested in it not so much for what it tells us about language as for what it tells us about the character of social interaction in institutional and non-institutional situations. The concern with actual utterances – what people say, and how, in particular social settings – focuses in the first place on the communicative features that constitute the grounds for their intelligibility and require of participants a commitment to cooperate with each other. The ethical basis of 'ordinary plain talk' is disclosed in Garfinkel's celebrated experiments with trust, in Schutz's 'reciprocity of perspective' and in Grice's conversational maxims. It should be stressed at the outset, to anticipate objections, that these theorizations of the communicative, cooperative basis of language as a fundamental kind of social interaction do not imply consensus theories of social relations. Rather, as Heritage puts it, such theories 'are *anterior* to the issue of cooperation versus conflict. At the end of the day conflict, just as much as cooperation, can only be conducted within an overarching framework of intelligibility' (Heritage, 1984: 70).

The extent to which individuals hold each other accountable and respons-ible for the maintenance of the self-evident nature of the world was powerfully demonstrated by Garfinkel's 'breaching' experiments designed to put the natural-seeming world in question (Garfinkel, 1984: Ch. 2). They showed the lengths to which people would go to maintain a perspective of normality on the situation and the degree of moral outrage felt when that perspective was violated. Over the years broadcasting has, on occasion, mischievously indulged in its own breaching experiments with audiences who have apparent-ly preferred to believe that the Martians have landed or that spaghetti grows on trees rather than disbelieve American network news or Richard Dimbleby on the BBC's *Panorama* programme (Dimbleby, 1977: 270–1). The notorious Orson Welles radio show is often taken as evidence of the power of the institution of broadcasting to brainwash audiences. But such a prank surely demonstrates rather the extent to which broadcasting is treated as a taken-for-granted – and therefore trusted – element in the routines of ordinary life. If it makes more sense to believe the impossible rather than doubt the institution, such power is also possessed – as Goffman has convincingly argued – by poker-faced individuals, salesmen and tricksters in other mundane contexts. The strategems and tactics of deception depend for their success on the fact that most of us, most of the time take the ordinary world on trust. In this century broadcasting has enormously enhanced that trust in the apparent world by making it apparent to all.

Garfinkel's experiments were designed to test empirically some of the key tenets of Schutz's theorization of the basis of day-to-day life. Any such theorization must face the fundamental problem of intersubjectivity: that is, be able to offer convincing accounts of how individuals can, in the first place, have common experiences and, in the second place, communicate about them. Without such theorization there are no grounds for any notion of a world-in-common to social actors. Schutz's solution was, as Heritage puts it, 'to state categorically that human beings can never have *identical* experiences of anything, but that this is irrelevant because they continuously assume that their experiences of the world are similar and act as if their experiences were identical-for-all-practical-purposes' (Heritage, 1984: 54). This insight was formulated as a 'general thesis of reciprocal perspectives' where individuals in routine social encounters are held to perform two basic idealizations: (a) the idealization of the interchangeability of standpoints and (b) the idealization of the congruency of the system of relevance (Heritage, 1984: 55). The former proposed that individuals take it for granted – and assume that others do so too – that if they put themselves in the other person's shoes they would experience it with the same typicality. It is not difficult to see that the filmic and televisual narrative techniques of reverse-field, matching eye-lines, etc. pragmatically depend on this assumption. The latter assumed that, for all practical purposes, individuals 'waive' the uniqueness of their own perspective while assuming that others do so too in the interests of mutual understanding.

The conversational maxims of the philosopher H.P. Grice have a similar fundamental bearing on the communicative ethos of talk. The maxims propose a set of four assumptions that underpin the conduct of conversation and serve as guidelines for the effective and efficient cooperative use of language. The maxims of Quality, Quantity, Relevance and Manner amount to a general cooperative principle: participants in talk should speak sincerely, informatively, relevantly and clearly. Of course it is evident that a great deal, perhaps most, of ordinary talk does not apparently conform to these principles. The force of the maxims operates at a more fundamental level and in conjunction with Grice's theorization of non-natural meaning, or communicative intentionality, which holds that a communicative meaning is one that is intended to be recognized as intended (Levinson, 1983: 16). This definition opens up for analysis the difference between what is said and what is meant, and leads on to a central concern of linguistic pragmatics, namely the analysis of non-semantic meanings in utterances via the remarkably powerful concept of implicatures (or implied meanings which hearers must infer by recognizing them as intended in the context of their utterance: cf. Levinson, 1983: 97–166; Brown and Levinson, 1987). In talk participants adhere to the maxims, even when they appear to ignore them or deliberately to flout them, largely through conversational implicatures.

The study of implicatures, central to linguistic pragmatics, has hardly begun to be applied to broadcasting though I am certain that it can account for many of the organizational features of radio and television discourse. The theory of communicative intentionality – which is not a theory of the motives of speakers (what they have in mind) but of the structuring preconditions of communication as social interaction (intentionality as common ground between speaker and hearer) – must in the first place be presupposed as a grounding condition for the activities of broadcasters *and* audiences. Audiences are required to make sense of, to make inferences about, the design, content and manner of radio and television programmes on the basis that their design, manner and content is intended for listeners and viewers to make sense of. The design, layout and lighting of the studio; the age, appearance, sex and dress of participants; the manner and style of how they talk to each other – all these give rise to warrantable inferences about the nature of the event there taking place, the character and status of participants and the relationship of event and participants to viewers or listeners. The *grain* of the voice (Barthes, 1977: 179–89) gives rise to inferences about the speaker, and changes in voice are an important means of creating implicatures. Voice is the irreducible mark of the spoken, of its physical, embodied presence and, for radio in particular, is crucial for listeners' assessments of the character of speakers and their alignment (or otherwise) with their performances. TV camera angles and movements clearly generate implicatures – about, for instance, the status of the relationship between speaker(s) in the studio and viewers in their homes. The camera monitors the faces of speakers and hearers in displayed television talk for corroborative evidence of participants' personality, state of mind and alignment (or otherwise) with what's going on.

In this the camera behaves as we all do in what Erving Goffman calls 'face engagements' and acts, on our behalf, to produce effects of co-presence. The concept of face was central to Goffman's lifelong concern with social occasions, 'the interaction order', how people behave in each others' presence. More than anyone, Goffman has focused on the self in relation to others (social identity) as something that is structured by and sustained in particular social settings: 'not men and their moments, but moments and their men' (Goffman, 1972: 3). From an early concern with self-presentation in everyday social settings, through to the fine detail of social encounters in public and private contexts Goffman came through, in his last work, to an analysis of talk as embodying and focusing the central concerns of the domain he had staked out for systematic examination.[6] 'Talk', Anthony Giddens remarks, 'is the basic medium of focused encounters and conversation is the prototype of the exchange of utterances involved in talk.' It is significant, he continues, that the preferred word for Goffman is 'talk' rather than 'language'. The latter suggests a formal system of signs and rules; the former suggests the situated nature of utterances and gestures embedded within the routine enactment of encounters (Giddens, 1987: 126).

Goffman's move into this field in the 1970s can be seen as one notable instance of the so-called 'linguistic turn' in recent social theory, aspects of which have been described above. This, 'at least in its most valuable forms, does not involve an extension of ideas taken from linguistics to other aspects of human activity, but rather explores the intersection between language and the constitution of social practices'. It is a turn away from linguistics, conceived as an independently formed discipline, towards examining the mutual coordination of language and praxis (Giddens, 1987: 78, 80). Nearly all the contributions to this book take recordings of talk on radio and television as their object of study. Talk is a richly occurring natural phenomenon on radio and television: talk in the context of the political news interview or news presentation, in early television documentaries, during elections, in television chat shows, in radio DJ programmes or phone-in talk shows. Its study can reveal much about the communicative character or ethos of broadcasting as an institution, about the quality of public life today as mediated through broadcasting and, more generally, about the structures of identity, performance and social interaction in today's society.

III

Broadcasting is an institution – a power, an authority – and talk on radio and television is *public, institutional* talk, an object of intense scrutiny, that gives rise to political, social, cultural and moral concerns. These are unavoidable matters of fact for broadcasters that affect general policy and the fine details of what actually can and cannot be said in this or that programme in this or that area of production. There are things that are sayable in documentaries or plays that are not sayable on news if the topic is, for instance, 'terrorism' (Elliott et al., 1986). Peter Lewis' discussion of referable words (Chapter 2) is a case study of the institutional management of 'language'. It would be all too easy to see this as simply typical of the BBC with its long track record, as Lewis hints, of being fussy about (bad) language. But such concerns about the limits of language-use are part of the politics of social interaction in a very pervasive sense (Andersson and Trudgill, 1990). Blasphemy from a bishop, expletives from a politician in public contexts cause shock and offence because they violate the situational proprieties of the occasion. It is inevitable that broadcasting must police the boundaries of (bad) language and that there should be controversy over where the lines are drawn. The conflict, in the case of BBC radio drama, turns out to be – as Lewis shows – a complicated struggle between the conflicting interests and attitudes of writers, producers, administrators and audiences.

In the 1950s television began to emerge as the dominant broadcasting medium. This, the period of its infancy, was when the techniques of the new medium were explored by the broadcasters and its possibilities discovered.

John Corner's study of the 'social encounter' (Chapter 3) in early television documentary marks the historical moment that the new medium ventured out of the studio and into the world to meet, not public persons, but ordinary people in order to introduce them to the growing viewing public. As such it is a choice instance of the difficulties of finding an appropriate communicative style both for participants in the programme and for the viewers on whose behalf this social encounter has been organized. Although broadcasting is necessarily oriented towards communication with its audiences, this does not mean, of course, that it always brings it off. The programmes Corner considers are nice examples of broadcasts that generate unease because their style is strained and the talk is awkward. The effort at sociability across class lines was still very much an effort in the novel context of television 35 years ago.

Production studies can tell us much about the hidden processes that organize the programmes-as-broadcast. They reveal the policies and politics of the broadcasting institutions and the assumptions made about programmes in relation to their audiences. But communicative intentions are embodied in discursive practices which must be described and analysed. The political news interview has received much attention in this respect. Less attention has been paid to how the news interview is situated in news programmes. Stephen Clayman's study of news-interview openings (Chapter 4) displays how these introductions organize for viewers a framework that enables them to make sense of what follows. That the introductions are for the benefit of viewers is shown by contrasting them with the interactional beginnings in informal contexts, such as casual conversation. This may be obvious but, as Clayman remarks, the aim of the analysis is to push beyond the commonplace to analyse the procedural logics by which these obvious characteristics are achieved and conveyed. Broadcasting reproduces the world as ordinary, but that seeming obviousness is an effect, the outcome of a multiplicity of small techniques and discursive practices that combine to produce that deeply taken-for-granted sense of familiarity with what is seen and heard.

Again, it may be obvious that politicians are evasive. It certainly is a generally held common-sense attitude. In 1964, British television viewers were for the first time invited to put questions to their political leaders in the run-up to a general election. Grace Wyndham Goldie, whose department dealt with the mail that flooded into the BBC, noted that there was a clear and simple demand for straight answers to the questions sent in. 'On the postcards, often underlined, were, again and again, words like "No hedging on this question please" and "Please answer Yes or No"' (Wyndham Goldie, 1978: 271). Sandra Harris (Chapter 5) considers how this effect of evasiveness is an embodied feature of the ways in which politicians answer questions in broadcast interviews. But more than this, *how* politicians answer questions is indicative of their communicative style, their projected image. Audiences make inferences about the character and competence of their elected representatives – of a Margaret Thatcher or Neil Kinnock – on the basis of common-sense evaluations of their performances, which include such apparently innocent matters as how they answer questions or, rather, *whether* they answer them.

Politicians' answers to interview questions may well be newsworthy events in their own right, especially at election times. The study of a response by Neil Kinnock to an interview question during the general election of 1987 shows how political talk on television can give rise to intense discussion in the press (and then on radio and TV) – talk about talk, glosses of what was meant or implied. Greg Garton, Martin Montgomery and Andrew Tolson analyse the pragmatic presuppositions that underpin the interpretations of the other parties, the press and broadcasters (Chapter 6). Their careful reconstruction of the unspoken assumptions in these glosses in an exemplary demonstration of how ideologies are embedded as unspoken, taken-for-granted common-sense assumptions in the publicly mediated discourses of contemporary politics.

Members of the public too have their say on political issues in a range of programmes on radio and television that access their views on contemporary life and affairs. The radio phone-in discussion is a particularly interesting instance of such programmes for it lies, as Ian Hutchby shows (Chapter 7), at the interface of the public and the private, the institutional and the interpersonal. Here common-sense understandings of the public world are produced by the interaction and exchange of private opinions in the act of 'going public'. Hutchby's analysis of how talk about news is collaboratively achieved in interactions between the studio host and callers in their homes or workplaces brings out very clearly how it is institutionally controlled while approximating to the character of ordinary conversation.

Hutchby's analysis further explores some of the complexities of the speaker/listener relationship which Goffman (1981) had problematized in his seminal essay on 'Footing'. The problematic relationship between speaker and utterance lies at the heart of Martin Montgomery's analysis (Chapter 8) of a famous example of contemporary British DJ talk – *Our Tune* – in which Simon Bates reads out, each morning, a letter from a listener. The complexity of this narrative genre lies in the uneasy relationship between the two narrators – what Montgomery calls the Epistolary Narrator (the letter-writer) and the Broadcast Narrator (Simon Bates). The epistolary form is a classic instance of private narrative transformed into public discourse. In the movement from subjective 'life experience' into objective 'life-story' the relationship between the tale and the teller changes, for Bates does not stand in the same relation to the ('real') events-as-narrated as the letter-writer. Nor, of course, do those listening to the tale. Montgomery unravels the tangled tensions of a narrative that lies across the boundaries of the public and the private in terms both of what it is about and how it is expressed.

The last two contributions to this collection have a common concern with the relationship between talk as performance and the production of identities in the public sphere of broadcasting. Both identify a self-reflexive playfulness – with language, with identity – as central characteristics of contemporary television and radio. Both presuppose a high degree of sophistication on the part of viewers and listeners accustomed not to take at face value the self-presentations and talk of performers in the public domain of the broadcast studio. I remember a somewhat aghast group of American students in Britain for the first time who had stumbled on *The Dame Edna Experience* on television one Sunday night. They could make no sense of it. Was it serious? Was *she* 'for real'? Andrew Tolson (Chapter 9) takes this programme as an index of the transformation of the character of the television 'personality' in the course of the last decade. In particular the category of the person (cf. Carrithers et al., 1985) as real and authentic is torpedoed by this show, with consequences for the character of the public sphere of broadcasting and the personality system which it sustains.

Jürgen Habermas, in outlining his influential thesis about the formation of the political public sphere in modern Europe, emphasized its specific, change-able historical character (Habermas, 1989). If broadcasting is a central locus for the contemporary public sphere, then it too must be understood historically (Scannell, 1989). I have argued that, in the British case, there has been a significant shift in the communicative ethos of broadcasting from an earlier authoritarian mode to a more populist and democratic manner and style – the key moment for this transformation being the late 1950s to the late 1960s (Scannell, 1988). Tolson criticizes this argument as too harmonious and unitary to be adequate as an account of the public sphere of broadcasting in the 'postpopulist' era of the 1980s. The Dame Edna show exemplifies the character of the contemporary broadcasting public sphere as remorselessly deconstructing 'that lynch-pin of the popular public sphere . . . the so-called "real person" who *speaks from experience'.*

The question of the broadcast personality is the subject of the last chapter in this collection. How is a recognizable, familiar personality created and maintained on radio and television? In addressing this issue Graham Brand and I argue (Chapter 10), following Goffman, that self-presentations on radio and television just as much as in everyday life are performances that may be – depending on their context – cynical, sincere or playful. The (ethno)methodo-logical problem considered is not simply the projection of an identity in a single social episode, but the management and maintenance of that identity over a lifetime. The problem is addressed in a case study of the career of Tony Blackburn, one of Britain's longest running DJs, and his self-presentation in his most recent programme, *The Tony Blackburn Show*. In particular Brand and I consider how identity in this case is an effect of talk – the talk of the programme presenter himself and in interaction with self-elected audience members who phone in during the programme.

IV

Media and Cultural Studies in the UK are still dominated by the encoding–decoding model of communication and a model of language based on Saussure. Mapped on to these is a text-reader theory, derived from literary studies of written 'texts', to account for the relationship between the products of radio and television and their audiences. The combined effect of these positions is to make it well-nigh impossible to discover talk as an object of study in relation to broadcasting.[7] The encoding–decoding model focuses primarily on the transmission of information from source to receiver and the problems of distortion in transmission. It reduces communication to a technical problem to be overcome, getting a 'message' across clearly. As such it imagines communication as a one-way process rather than as interactive, and ignores the expressive dimensions of communication, *how* things are said, why and for what possible effects. The problem is compounded by the preferred model of language which rejects the study of actual utterance (parole) for the study of language as an abstract system of signs (langue). Semiotics, the study of signs that has developed from Saussure, focuses on the meanings (ideologies) encoded in cultural products. It treats these objects as if they were written texts that may be read (decoded) naively or critically.

To think of programmes as texts and audiences as readers is to mistake the communicative character of much of the output of radio and television. In particular it fails to recognize the liveness of radio and television, their embeddedness in the here and now (their particularity) and the cardinal importance of context and audiences. All programmes have an audience-oriented communicative intentionality which is embodied in the organization of their setting (context) down to the smallest detail: there is nothing in the discourses of radio and television that is not motivated, that is not intended to generate inferences about what is being said by virtue of how it is being said. Most importantly, all broadcast output is, knowingly, wittingly *public*. That is, it is a self-conscious, self-reflexive performance produced for audiences who are situated elsewhere. Radio and television mediate the public into the private and the private into the public in the manner and style of their performances in a wide range of settings and for correspondingly diverse purposes. *How* that is accomplished, as this collection hopes to begin to show, is, to a great extent, through the on-air talk that is daily produced in the public, institutional spaces of radio and television and daily seen and heard in the private, domestic and work spaces of listening and viewing.

Notes

1. Studio-based programmes with live audiences have at least three and often four communicative circuits of interaction simultaneously in play: host and participants, host and studio audience, participants and audience, host and listeners or viewers.

2. In this introduction, and in this collection as a whole, no methodological distinction is drawn between radio talk and television talk – both are treated under the rubric of broadcasting. This is not, of course, to overlook the differences between radio and television talk that result from the absence of vision on radio. Radio drama (Drakakis, 1981: Rodger, 1982) deliberately exploits the 'blind' quality of the medium. Radio DJ talk routinely references the radio studio in on-air talk with listeners in order to contextualize where the talk is coming from (Montgomery, 1986) and radio commentary necessarily provides details of what listeners cannot see when covering live sporting or ceremonial events, for instance. The larger point is that the structures of talk-in-interaction on radio and television are, in all essentials, the same. Moreover, to think of radio and television *together* as institutions of broadcasting, is to rescue television as an object of academic interest from the embrace of film studies and the misguided tendency to treat it as essentially the same as film; i.e. as a visual medium with a visual 'language'. Television, technically, historically and analytically developed from radio and both are media of live talk. Television is radio with vision added.

3. Conversation, ordinary talk, is 'the prototypical kind of language usage . . . the matrix of

language acquisition . . . the central or most basic kind of language usage' (Levinson, 1983: 284–5). It has 'a "bed-rock" status in relation to other institutionalized forms of interpersonal conduct. Not only is conversation the most pervasively used mode of interaction in social life . . . [it] also consists of the fullest matrix of socially organized communicative practices and procedures' (Heritage and Atkinson, 1984: 12–13). Institutional forms of talk are studied in terms of the manner in which they depart from the norms and conventions of ordinary talk between participants with equal conversational rights. Thus, talk in many institutional settings (the classroom, the law courts, the surgery, the TV or radio studio) has begun to be studied by sociologists and linguists as providing fundamental insights into how institutional realities are routinely reproduced in and by the character of the talk that goes on in them (Heritage and Atkinson, 1984: 15, Note 9 for details of conversational analysis applied to institutions; Harris, 1988 for sociolinguistic studies of media language). This is a cardinal distinction and crucial to this book. Although broadcast talk is oriented towards the values of ordinary talk and its conversational norms, as public, institutional talks its manner and protocols are in certain respects different. Those differences reproduce broadcast talk as public, performed talk and radio and television as powerful social institutions.

4. All studies of language as utterance stress that it is fundamentally context bound. The *indexical* character of talk is emphasized in ethnomethodology and conversational analysis: speech-act theory, pragmatics and discourse analysis prefer the term *deixis*. Both study the ways in which setting and circumstances are used as resources by participants in the talk. The double context of broadcast talk (the time and place from which it speaks and in which it is heard) is fundamental to understanding its organization in relation to its audiences.

5. John Heritage and David Greatbatch have pioneered the application of conversation analysis to the broadcast political interview. For references see Steven Clayman's contribution to this collection.

6. For a review and assessment of Goffman's work, see Drew and Wootton (1988).

7. Barthes (1972: 77) and Hall (1980) are the ur-texts on semiotics and encoding–decoding for cultural, media and communication studies. For critical discussions of the code model, cf. Corner (1980) and Wren-Lewis (1983). Trevor Pateman (1983) criticizes the semiotic analysis of advertisements and offers a pragmatic theory of implicatures to explain what cannot be accounted for by the 'dummy' concept of connotation. The code model and semiotic approach to communication is subjected to a succint and trenchant critique by Sperber and Wilson (1986). For a general review of the limitations of structuralist approaches to language and the privileging of langue over parole, see Giddens, 1987: 73–108.

References

Andersson, A. and P. Trudgill (1990) *Bad Language.* Oxford: Basil Blackwell.

Barthes, R. (1972) *Mythologies.* London: Paladin.

Barthes, R. (1977) *Image-Music-Text.* London: Fontana.

Brown, P. and S.C. Levinson (1987) *Politeness. Some Universals in Language Usage.* Cambridge: Cambridge University Press.

Carrithers, M., S. Collins and S. Lukes (1985) *The Category of the Person.* Cambridge: Cambridge University Press.

Corner, J. (1980) 'Codes and Cultural Analysis', *Media, Culture and Society,* 2(1).

Dimbleby, J. (1977) *Richard Dimbleby.* London: Hodder and Stoughton.

Drakakis, J. (ed.) (1981) *British Radio Drama.* Cambridge: Cambridge University Press.

Drew, P. and A. Wootton (1988) *Erving Goffman. Exploring the Interaction Order.* Cambridge: Polity Press.

Elliott, P., G. Murdock and P, Schlesinger (1986) ' "Terrorism" and the State: A Case Study of the Discourses of Television', *Media, Culture and Society,* 5(2).

Garfinkel, H. (1984) *Studies in Ethnomethodology.* Cambridge: Polity Press.

Giddens, A. (1987) *Social Theory and Modern Sociology.* Cambridge: Polity Press.

Goffman, E. (1972) *Interaction Ritual.* Harmondsworth: Penguin Books.

Goffman, E. (1981) *Forms of Talk.* Oxford: Basil Blackwell.

Habermas, J. (1989) *The Structural Transformation of the Public Sphere*. Cambridge: Polity Press.

Hall, S. (1980) 'Encoding/Decoding', in S. Hall, D. Hobson, A. Lowe and P. Willis (eds), *Culture, Media, Language*. London: Hutchinson.

Harris, S. (1988) 'Sociolinguistic Approaches to Media Language', *Critical Studies in Mass Communication*, March.

Heritage, J. and M. Atkinson (1984) *Structures of Social Action*. Cambridge: Cambridge University Press.

Heritage, J. (1984) *Garfinkel and Ethnomethodology*. Cambridge: Polity Press.

Horton, D. and R.R. Wohl (1986) 'Mass Communication and Para-social Interaction: Observations on Intimacy at a Distance', in G. Gumpert and R. Cathcart (eds), *Inter/Media*. New York: Oxford University Press.

Levinson, S. (1983) *Pragmatics*. Cambridge: Cambridge University Press.

Matheson, H. (1933) *Broadcasting*. London: Thornton Butterworth.

Montgomery, M. (1986) 'DJ Talk', *Media, Culture and Society*, 8(4).

Pateman, T. (1983) 'How is Understanding an Advertisement Possible?' in H. Davis and P. Walton (eds), *Language, Image, Media*. Oxford: Basil Blackwell.

Rodger, I. (1982) *Radio Drama*. London: Macmillan.

Scannell, P. and D. Cardiff (1991) *A Social History of British Broadcasting*, Vol. I, 'Serving the Nation, 1922–1939'. Oxford: Basil Blackwell.

Scannell, P. (1988) '*Radio Times:* The Temporal Arrangements of Broadcasting in the Modern World', P. Drummond and R. Paterson (eds), *Television and Its Audience*. London: British Film Institute.

Scannell, P. (1989) 'Public Service Broadcasting and Modern Public Life', *Media, Culture and Society*, 11(2).

Sperber, D. and D. Wilson (1986) *Relevar*)xford: Basil Blackwell.

Whitehead, K. (1989) *The Third Progra* , *Literary History*. Oxford: Clarendon Press.

Wren-Lewis, J. (1983) 'The Encodir ding Model: Criticisms and Redevelopments for Research on Decoding', *Media, Culture and Society*, 5(2).

Wyndham Goldie, G. (1978) *Facing the Nation. Television and Politics, 1936–1976*. London: The Bodley Head.

2
Referable Words in Radio Drama

Peter M. Lewis

Not long after joining BBC North Region in the early 1930s, Olive Shapley assisted Geoffrey Bridson in a programme in which he hoped Newcastle and Durham miners would talk freely about their lives and work. Bridson was later to comment of BBC policy in this period:

> That the man in the street should have anything vital to contribute to broadcasting was an idea slow to gain acceptance. That he should actually use broadcasting to express his own opinions in his own unvarnished words was regarded as the end of all good social order. (Bridson, 1971: 52)

The miners did indeed begin talking freely in Bridson's live broadcast and after a few minutes Shapley was sent in to the studio with a placard carrying the blunt warning 'Do not say bugger or bloody!' Discussion languished until Shapley had to be recalled and normal talk resumed. Shapley recalls a 'terrible row' and Bridson nearly losing his job.[1] This was only one of a number of incidents which led to Reith's insistence on scripted discussions, a form which virtually excluded the working class from the airwaves (Cardiff, 1980). Later, in a series of pioneering features, Shapley tried to redress this imbalance by using the BBC's mobile recording unit to bring the voices of 'ordinary people' to the microphone. Even so, she admits, recording allowed her to 'cut out the buggers and bloodies'.

This early example of what has been, on the part of the BBC, a continuing attempt to control language, contains those key elements of censorship and self-censorship which are still sensitive issues within the Corporation today, not least in radio drama – my concern in this article.[2] I argue that in a medium where the word is virtually the sole vehicle of meaning, language and, in particular, the issue of 'language' (the BBC euphemism for swearing, expletives and the commoner forms of blasphemy) carries the whole weight of a struggle for control between listeners and producers, writers and producers, producers and senior management and ultimately between the BBC itself and government. At the risk of over-simplification, it may be helpful for a moment to make the metaphor explicit and imagine a peculiar five-sided tug-of-war. For the contestants – government, BBC management, producers, writers and listeners – a range of weighty and complex issues is at stake which motivate their respective stances and the need for each to win control. Yet the whole complex of relationships and tensions is reduced to a single 'rope' – language – which connects all the contestants so that tension between any two involves all the rest. This 'reduction' is partly analytical: I focus on 'language' in order to illustrate the relations of power between the different parties. But there is also some correspondence with what actually happens in the day-to-day exchanges between those concerned. Language – and especially 'language' – is indeed abstracted, literally bracketed, from its context and made to do duty for underlying political, social and psychological realities whose importance tends consequently to be overlooked. The discussion tours the different 'tug-of-war players', and examines some of those features of BBC organization which bear on their struggle – the importance of tradition and precedent in a bureaucracy and the role of meetings in reproducing them, the invocation of 'audience' to justify particular positions, the effect of slot and channel stereotypes ('typifications') and, crucially, 'referral up'. Under this procedure the responsibility usually accorded to producers may be voluntarily, or in certain cases, such as the use of 'referable words', compulsorily replaced by referral to higher authority (Burns, 1977).

Producers and writers

The Radio Drama Department receives some 10,000 scripts a year and, of the 500 original plays its broadcasts, between 70 and 80 are by new writers,[3] for many of whom these nursery slopes are a valuable introduction to television. The ability of the radio imagination to create expensive sets, costumes and locations, combined with the relatively low cost and simplicity of radio drama production compared with television, allows a degree of experiment and risk, as well as authorial control, impossible in the costlier medium. The single play is important in both media, but in television is giving way to the series which can attract co-production and/or the overseas sales needed to defray costs. The result is, as one radio producer has argued, that television plays speak with a 'corporate' or 'balanced' voice. Against this, he claims, radio drama is 'practically the last bastion of the individual's voice in the media' (Cooper, 1984: 10).

The individual choice exercised by writers is, however, constrained by the character of the slot and of the channel, for which the play is intended. For example, regular listeners to Radio 4 (and channel loyalty is a conspicuous feature of British listening behaviour; IBA [Independent Broadcasting Authority], 1986) will be aware of the differences between *Saturday Night Theatre* (described in BBC notes for intending writers as 'family listening' – BBC, 1981), *The Monday Play* ('demanding') and *The Afternoon Play* (with 'a strong narrative line [which] is an advantage for daytime listeners'). Anyone familiar with Radio 3 will not be surprised that plays on this channel are described as having to be 'works of considerable distinction in their own right, regardless of subject matter'. Some listeners might translate this as 'don't be surprised if the listening – and perhaps also the language – is tough going'. Should you by chance stray on to an unfamiliar BBC channel the tone of address will clearly signal its character. Marking the different slots within Radio 4 is harder but their differentiation is reinforced by presentation trails throughout the day, and amplified by play billings in the *Radio Times*. These different 'theatres of the air' have been running for a quarter of a century. Over time their repertoires have been transformed by a steady liberal osmosis and sometimes by deliberate intervention, but their differential relationship with each other, the socio-cultural universe they describe, has been preserved. Thus are the imaginations organized, not only of listeners and intending writers, but of the producers themselves.

For radio drama producers, the slot and channel character or stereotype is an important feature of the editorial process. Scripts must be characterized as potential material for this or that slot in order to simplify the task of dealing with the volume of incoming material. Each stereotype incorporates its appropriate audience type and functions in a similar way to the 'typification' Tuchman noted as a feature of news production (Tuchman, 1978: 58). Radio 3's obscurity was often the butt of humorous mockery during my research; thus a play in which unintelligible background speech was deliberately included as atmosphere was labelled 'good Radio 3 material', while for Radio 4's *Afternoon Play* there was a tendency to avoid 'downbeat endings' and jokey references to the need to avoid overt sex. Against this tendency the need not to be over-cautious in the use of language was defended by more general statements: 'we are not in the business of *not* giving offence. The most inoffensive play we could choose could still upset' and 'the relationship between writer and producer, and producer and audience is a delicately sprung balance. Unless we challenge the audience, the writers won't challenge us' (Regional Producers Meeting, 13 February 1987). Both assertions are of the kind that defy contradiction, but don't bring producers any nearer to the mirage of the distant audience.

As for writers, the perceived differences in the characters of the slot determine to a large extent the scripts sent in to the Radio Drama Department. A guide to writing radio drama by a former script editor is explicit:

> Of course you had some particular spot [*sic*] in mind when you decided on the play you were going to write. How else would you have known how long it was going to be? . . . It was through listening to the kind of plays broadcast at different times on Radio 4 or Radio 3 that you knew that the play you had in mind to write, in theme and treatment, suited this placing or that. (Ash, 1985: 60–1)

The readiness of the Drama Department, then, to accept new writers – indeed, the necessity of its doing so if it is to fill the schedules – carries with it the drawback that traditions and patterns are established among writers, producers and listeners which are exceedingly hard to shift. There is a policy tension for the Drama Department between satisfying an audience that has grown to understand and appreciate the existing slots, and developing a 'fringe theatre' which satisfies the desire of writers to challenge the frontiers of conventions as represented by those same slots.

Most BBC radio drama, though scripted, strives for a realistic model of speech that owes much to the portable tape recorder's 'discovery' of everyday speech patterns first made by Bridson and Shapley's successors in features and documentaries in the late 1950s (Rodger, 1982: 97ff). In the years that followed, writers for television and radio began to explore ordinary speech and the characters and situations where it could naturally be deployed. In

Armchair Theatre (ITV – Independent Television) and *Play for Today* (BBC TV), in drama documentaries like *Cathy Come Home* (BBC TV, 1966), and in radio drama, which launched some distinguished writing careers in this period, 'unvarnished words' along with hesitations and silence heralded a celebration of regional and working-class culture. A more permissive set of standards for language in broadcasting was but one element, albeit a major one, in a general climate of liberalization of society, and it was language, together with sex and violence on television, that attracted fierce criticism from defenders of traditional moral values such as Mary Whitehouse. Still today, and particularly in *The Afternoon Play* slot, what one critic has called the 'vicarage tea-party' type of radio drama rubs shoulders with a tougher strand of social realism, often produced in the BBC's regional centres.

One problem the Drama Department faces in a time of financial pressure occurs over the policy of repeats: there is an increasing tendency to try to boost small evening audiences with a second daytime hearing. For example, currently *The Monday Play* (Mondays 7.45 p.m.) is repeated on Saturday afternoons at 2.30 p.m. What was intended to be a 'demanding' slot has to double as a slot that can be heard in 'family time'. The television 'watershed' that permits 'language' and 'adult' topics after 9 p.m. when young children are presumed to be in bed cannot operate in the case of *The Monday Play.* The economic justification for repeats can therefore act as a pressure to 'clean up' plays broadcast in this slot. The decision by the Controller of Radio 4 early in 1988 not to give, on grounds of 'language', a Saturday afternoon repeat to Ken Blakeson's *Excess Baggage,* a play about Army wives, was exceptional but it highlighted this dilemma and attracted considerable press publicity (Radio 4, 22 February 1988). The BBC decided to counter the accusations of censorship stirred up by the affair by organizing a public seminar later the same year on the subject of 'Language in Broadcasting'. In what was for the Corporation an unusual display of *glasnost* the discussion ranged equally between panelists and producers, writers and critics and included explanations of their decisions by the Controllers of Radio 3 and 4.[4] The Drama Department had, not for the first time, discussed 'language' in its own private seminar a year before. There, one working definition offered was that

> 'Language' [means] those words and phrases which may potentially give offence to sections of our audience or indeed simply distract them from the main purpose of the play in question. (BBC internal memorandum, 18 April 1986)

The range of issues covered by the BBC's public seminar was very similar to those rehearsed internally: self-censorship, the problem of repeats, the dilemma posed by the conflicting needs to honour the 'contract of the slot' with the existing audience and yet attract new (younger) listeners with ideas and styles that challenged convention and might therefore offend. Conspicuous by its absence was any reference to the wider political realities of government pressure. Nor, despite a background note provided by the Head of Broadcasting Research, was there much clarification of the nature of those 'sections of the audience' who might be offended by 'language'.

Writers tended to take a less complicated view of listeners. Howard Barker

robustly affirmed that 'those who seek to inhibit emotion in drama through
the concept of obscenity betray a contempt for their audience'. Often cited but
never present at Departmental meetings, writers were for once able to speak for
themselves and their point of view was well represented by Barker's short
paper delivered from the panel (BBC, 1988: 26–9). Taking a position that, in
those days before the Rushdie affair, needed no qualification, he spoke of a
'democratic obligation' in writing tragic drama (which he opposed to mere
entertainment) to 'explore, describe and speculate on all areas of human
experience'. The few words in question, among the most highly charged in the
vocabulary, could not simply be abolished, and in his view the 'notion of a
false guardianship of values is . . . in effect, a bid for social engineering'.
Barker used 'words conventionally described as obscene . . . with calculation
and discrimination for their dramatic effect . . . sometimes with the deliberate
intention of creating the unease in the audience which is, for me, the condition
of experiencing tragedy'. He contrasted that unease with the limited range of
emotions deployed by entertainment which breeds apathy. Unease is inevitable if there is commitment on the part of actor and writer to truth and validity
in the representation of emotions. Barker could speak with authority on
censorship: his *Scenes from an Execution* only reached the airwaves after a
long battle over 'language' between the Drama Department and the then
Controller of Radio 3.[5]

Meetings and management

My record of Drama Department meetings is handwritten in notebooks since
permission to tape record was refused. The reason given was that quotation
out of context could be misleading. Underlying this explanation is probably a
fear that an outsider might misinterpret the verbal cut and thrust of meetings
in which a witty and sometimes cynical shorthand style of delivery is elevated
to the level of a performance, part of whose point is to show the speaker
operating effectively within his or her peer group. The discourse of performance is here at odds with a bureaucratic discourse. The conflict is important
and explains some of the editorial tensions between BBC management,
producers and outside writers. Producers have to be half creative impre-
sarios, half bureaucrats. Concentration on work in the studio may, as Burns
suggests, temporarily isolate a producer from the audience and from senior
management, but return to the office brings with it the chores of form-filling,
accounting for budgets, answering letters and responding to the queries and
demands of senior management. The latter, too, were once producers themselves; in the Radio Drama Department all continue to produce plays when
their administrative duties allow. Such is the BBC system, at least for those in
the editorial chain. (The appointment of Michael Checkland as Director-
General was exceptional in bringing to the topmost position someone from a
financial/accounting rather than a production background.)
  Radio producers not surprisingly are at home with verbal performance – in
the studio, on the telephone, in the BBC Club, over a drink at the George

public bar or a meal in a restaurant. In such a discourse a witty anecdote well told or the momentary lapse into accent or intonation to make an allusion rates equally with the ability to summarize a plot succinctly or evaluate the performance or potential of a writer. Tone and nuance, context and inter-text (what else is being produced or written at the time) are of the essence.

Much of this escapes the bureaucratic discourse, for bureaucrats need things written down. Minutes and memos cannot capture the play of speech any more than the subtleties of humour or musical mood. Banning jazz or 'crooning' ('emasculated singing of silly sentimental stuff') or 'any form of anaemic or debilitated vocal performance or over-sentimentality' (BBC WAC R34/281, 4 May 1943) was a problem for BBC bureaucrats in the 1930s and 1940s. 'Language' has the advantage of at least being definable: the forbidden words can be named and systems and precedents devised to contain or exclude them. So live talks ended up being scripted, and recording allowed undesirable speech to be edited out. In more recent times, the manipulative skills of chat show hosts together with time-delay devices have sanitized the phone-in. On the face of it, radio plays might be thought unproblematic: after all, once the script is in, the cards are as it were on the table. Yet for that very reason, use of 'language' in a play, being deliberate, seems offensive to bureaucrats, while to the author censorship is an outrageous violation of rights. The radio drama producer is in the middle and the schizophrenic nature of his or her position is brought out above all in the meeting, the site of that ambiguous interface between creativity and bureaucracy.

Meetings, as Giddens, drawing on Goffman's work, has remarked (Giddens, 1984: 64ff.; Goffman, 1963, 1974), play an important role in the maintenance of social systems across time and space. In an organization like the BBC, hierarchical systems of command and the importance of precedent in decision-making contribute to a process whereby successive accretions of daily routines and decisions *both* constitute the structure *and* take place within already established structural constraints. Following Goffman, Giddens stresses the work that all of us put into maintaining routines. Much of this reflexive monitoring has itself been delegated to routine, a barely conscious adjustment of performance in interaction with others. We routinely use 'frames' of behaviour and interpretation to make sense of different types of encounter, asking (and usually answering without difficulty) of any particular one 'What is going on here?' 'The routinisation of encounters is of major significance in binding the fleeting encounter to social reproduction and thus to the seeming "fixity" of institutions' (Giddens, 1984: 72). Talk is obviously of prime importance in sustaining encounters, but the non-verbal communication of clothing, gesture and spacing is also brought into play. Spacing is not only physical, as studied in proxemics, but social, and 'age (or age grade) and gender are the most all-embracing criteria of attributes of social identity' (Giddens, 1984: 85).

All these aspects of encounters were visible in the routines of the BBC radio drama staff I studied: class, gender, age were expressed in a code which was recognizably the same as the one described by Burns 10 years earlier:

a normative system composed of specific elements – of language, bearing, lines of talk and social skills – which are severally present in modern British society but which in the Corporation were combined to form an organised code of conduct and values. The code allowed for sizeable differences in attitude, opinion and aspiration . . . The manner was a way of defining the 'rules of the game' . . .'. (Burns, 1977: xiii)

The 'code', the 'rules' are understood by participants even if they are not normally mentioned. In certain frames of behaviour to do so would be 'bad form', impolitic or simply gauche. On other occasions, for example in the context of after-work chat in the Club, a code might be the subject of ironic or humorous analysis. Add to all this an almost tangible sense of Departmental history; only five people have occupied the post of Head of Radio Drama since the BBC began, a measure of the continuity of tradition. The weight of precedent which older members of the Department bring to bear in discussion is impressive, but it is sometimes experienced as oppressive by younger colleagues. One spoke to me of a 'feeling of being hedged in by years of definition . . . of them protecting their territory'. The us/them polarization inasmuch as it is a felt constraint, is part of the reality, but its implied criticism is perhaps unjust, for liberal initiatives from just such senior members of the Department. It is simply that the *longue durée* of Departmental history combined with the workings of a large bureaucracy conspire to act as a brake on innovation.

In the Drama Department, as in most others, meetings play a pivotal role in that the minutes recording them set in train important budgetary and administrative operations. But the manner in which social positions are expressed in the BBC means that *informal* encounters too are frequently vehicles for decision-making. 'By the way, you did cut, did you?' was the casual way censorship of referable words was requested by a Controller to a senior member of the Drama Department in connection with a play which the Department successfully defended and which went on to win an award. The verbal and non-verbal elements of encounters, routinized and reflective of power and status – the very displays that my subjects felt might be misleading – constantly reproduce the character of a department or channel.

In settings that ranged from the mandarin and intimidating, with overtones of Oxbridge High Table (Controller A's meeting), through the brisk jollity of long-time colleagues (Radio drama chiefs meet Controller B), to the relatively intimate private club atmosphere of the Drama Department, editorial decisions sifted material and directed it for broadcasting in the different 'theatres of the air'. In the course of all these, a verbal shorthand is routinely applied to refer to people (absent colleagues, authors, agents, other BBC departments and the hierarchy), plays, slots, channels and 'the audience' which carries a weighty cargo of assumptions.

Within the Radio 4 output the matching of slots and their audiences became crucial in Drama Department debates about 'language'. The daytime slots created the most problems: their larger audiences were attractive to producers and writers seeking to popularize a social message, yet at this time of day children were in earshot, and many older people were following a routine in which they expected Radio 4 to deliver them gently into the arms of evening television. Tensions were observable around this issue between younger producers and management, and between the regions and London.

'Referral up'

About one word in the language 'lexicon', however, there could be no debate.

> There is only one BBC policy; it is that the word 'fuck' may not be used on any network without referral through the Head of Department to the Network Controller. (BBC internal memorandum, 18 April 1986)

One producer, then in the North Region and with a distinguished record of 'gritty' plays, has argued that 'the main plank of censorship is not referral but self-censorship'. Under the above rule:

> as a script must be referred through your immediate superior, he may refuse to forward it to the Controller and so the chances are that the Controller may not get the opportunity to say yes because your superior may have said no first (though he cannot say yes). (Cooper, 1984)

Producers, especially those on a short contract, don't wish to gain a reputation for awkwardness, while Heads of Departments may have other battles, not this one, to fight.

Two instances of referral were aired in one of the quarterly meetings at which regional producers joined London-based colleagues for a day which included discussion on a set-piece theme (Regional Producers Meeting, Drama Department, 13 February 1987). 'Language' was the theme on this occasion and the instances were recounted by a producer who, being a relatively recent recruit from fringe theatre, was invited to lead the discussion as a useful fresh voice.

The first instance began with the recording of a *Book at Bedtime* in which the climax was the death of a protagonist. The producer was pleased with his actor's reading, but in subsequent editing, his attention was drawn to a 'word' by the Studio Manager who said 'You'll never get that in *Book at Bedtime.*' The producer referred it to his editor who said, 'I have no objections but will refer it higher.' The third in command in the Department also had no objections but referred it to the Head of Department whose opinion was that the sentence should be cut. 'At the time', the producer concluded, 'I felt those were the rules of the game. But now I feel extremely compromised because the judgements were both defensive and prescriptive. They were to avoid potential problems.'

The second example involved the excision of the words 'Jesus Christ!' from a *Thirty Minute Theatre* play (11.30 a.m. slot), described as gutsy social realism, about the North/South divide in Britain. In addition, some milder phrase was used instead of 'pissing in the wind'. The producer described his writer friend as 'not being able to believe his ears at this censorship. "Something is happening to me creatively," the writer complained.'

The Head of Department, in giving the meeting his version of the incident, said:

> There was a discussion. X [the producer] said there were one or two things in the play. *To protect you* I said 'Show me' and put circles round one or two things. I think that the play would have been much more popular had those words not been there. (Emphasis added.)

Before pursuing, as the meeting did, the general issues raised by these incidents, relatively trivial in themselves, it is worth noting, in connection with 'referral', that in the first incident, it is a technical colleague, a Studio Manager (SM), who starts the chain of doubt. An SM might well have more experience than a producer and in this case probably did. So whether out of sympathy for a new colleague, a desire to parade the experience, a concern for the Department's reputation or a wish to avoid a row that would reflect on his or her professional record (any enquiry would ask why this was not spotted at the editing stage), the SM intervened, crossing the technical/editorial divide, to offer comment. It is as if the business of 'protecting' the slot is diffused through different series and levels of staff. The combined effect is reactionary as shared experience and precedent mutually reinforce each other.

In the second incident, self-censorship is activated from above out of a concern to *protect* the producer: the effect is just as insidious however worthy the motive, and it is a long-term effect, resulting, on the next and subsequent occasions, in hesitation and doubt in the minds of both the producer (cf. Olive Shapley's editing) and the writer.

The writer in this case 'suffered trauma' (the words of his producer), and the point was taken up by another experienced colleague who made unfavourable comparisons with television drama, rehearsing a list of plays and authors that could not have been broadcast by BBC radio drama. The effect of censorship, he claimed, was that:

> many of our major writers are not writing hard-hitting stuff for us. It's irrational, utterly enervating, removes their confidence in the medium, and makes them doubt our estimation of their work . . . We have a reputation for not doing the toughest plays around.

An impatience with the limitations of Radio 4 as an outlet is an unspoken concern here. Few young people listen to the channel and despite the occasional play on Radio 1 or special events such as the Drama Department's Young Playwrights Festival, there were at this period not many spaces for the younger more radical producer to broadcast challenging work. Radio 3 should have offered some opportunity, but at the time of the research, relations between the Drama Department and the Controller of Radio 3 had reached an impasse. *Scenes from an Execution* had not been the only occasion of censorship and confrontation. The Controller had so frequently disagreed with the united view of the Drama Department that it had reluctantly come to the conclusion that there was no working relationship with him. In this Departmental management and producers were at one, but a year or more was to elapse before shifts at the top of the BBC brought in a new Controller. Meanwhile serious damage had been done to relations with writers and to the self-confidence of the Department.

The government and the BBC

The mid-1980s was undoubtedly a period in which financial and political pressure on the BBC was stepped up by a government intent on deregulation and privatization. The financial pressure was formalized by the Peacock Committee whose report in 1986, though it spared the BBC the indignity of advertising as a means of revenue, proposed the ending of the licence-fee and a move towards subscription. The new Broadcasting Act (1990), which has strengthened the competition for the BBC in both radio and television, is the natural complement of this strategy. Political pressure has been apparent in a wide variety of instances, but was strikingly symbolized during my research by the *Real Lives* affair culminating in the sacking of the Director-General Alasdair Milne in February 1987. Effectively now the BBC is on probation, with its income, the licence-fee, pegged at a level which forces it to make cuts, and with its Charter up for review in 1996.

In this kind of climate editorial pressures to play safe are intensified. Direct intervention by politicians and censorship by government is mostly confined to the bitterly contested area of news and current affairs. Fiction, except where it deals with political issues or matters of public reputation or controversy (and especially in the docu-drama or 'faction' form) is at one remove from these battles, and radio is anyway less conspicuous than television. Questions of morality and taste in this area of programming are left by politicians to public opinion as a court of appeal, and BBC treatment of the issue tends to reflect its current relationship with government on the one hand and, on the other, the state of public taste in the wider society of which broadcasting is a part and which it must represent.

Here the main pressure on the BBC comes from its audiences or rather the articulate minority which writes, telephones and contributes feedback to the programmes which invite it, mainly on Radio 4. This is the same section of the population which writes to Members of Parliament and to the press. In both quarters complaints are likely to be amplified: through questions in Parliament and through the correspondence columns of newspapers, many of which are involved directly or indirectly in broadcast competition with the BBC. In such circumstances, the inbred caution of policy-makers is tuned with special sensitivity.

A meeting between the three senior members of the Drama Department and the then Controller of Radio 4 (CR4), on 12 December 1985, provided an example. 'Language' came up in connection with possible repeats of two kinds. The first kind of repeat was of plays intended for *The Monday Play* slot that had gone out once on Radio 3 but which the Controller of Radio 3 (CR3) was not interested in repeating. One was Howard Brenton's *Epsom Downs*. CR4 had not heard it on its first transmission and asked therefore to hear a cassette, see critics' reviews, audience figures and RIs (Reaction Indexes).[6] The Drama trio described it as a 'remarkable piece of radio' made by collaboration of two of their best producers, but worried that there were 'three fucks' in it. As one of them said next day at the Department meeting, 'it is to be hoped they are obfuscated by the sound of horses' hooves'. The other play was

Howard Barker's *Scenes from an Execution* which, as we have seen, had been the subject of a battle between the Drama Department and CR3. The Department wanted to rebroadcast the play within the year as a *Monday Play*.

The switch of *The Monday Play,* with its 'tough' mandate, from Sunday evening to Saturday afternoon was the other kind of repeat which was a potential problem. CR4 remarked, 'we all know this could give us a tough time'. (His successor was to experience the truth of this prediction over the *Excess Baggage* affair.) He talked of 'the pendulum swinging back the other way' and twice in the meeting referred to the outside pressures of Mrs Whitehouse, the Prime Minister and Lord Hailsham who had recently delivered himself of a broadside about 'standards'. 'It's the language they're worried about, on radio anyway', he said. Whether the last 'they' referred to the BBC's Board of Management, the Board of Governors or the government was not clear. What is clear is that the message from above was being interpreted by those responsible for radio drama in two ways that complemented each other: (a) 'language' policy had to be justified by reference to a consistent approach for each slot, (b) an expensive form of radio had to be justified by demonstrating its breadth of appeal – or there was a risk of cuts.

The audience

Much is known about radio audience behaviour by the Broadcasting Research Department, and more no doubt could be discovered if the researchers were given an appropriate brief. Communication between producers and researchers is, however, sketchy, to say the least (Radio Academy, 1986: vii), and the intensity of the desire to know 'who are these listeners?' expressed in meetings is not matched by any apparent knowledge among the rank and file of the data already available.

The background note provided for the 1988 Language Seminar by the Head of Broadcasting Research was a succinct summary of what the BBC knows about radio listeners from its regular surveys and its special projects: for radio's differentiated and segmented audience most listening is a private affair and there is a close personal relationship between the listener and 'my' station or channel; there is relatively little (average about 20 minutes per day) listening by children and close to 90% of their listening is to Radio 1 and commercial radio where at present there are few 'language' problems.

> The radio listener, being a loyalist, is also a conservative. Transgression from tradition is deemed a personal affront. The trust and unwritten contract between me and 'my' station has been wantonly breached. Such grievous transgressions can arise from a wide variety of causes including minor or major changes in the day or time of transmission. The Broadcasting Research Department is not aware of a major undercurrent of concern about offensive language on any network. (Meneer, 1988)

It was pointed out at the Language Seminar that in the league table of complaints to the BBC, 'language' comes ninth with an average of 46 complaints a week. Poor scheduling (225 complaints a week), then poor taste, intrusiveness, factual error, policy, bias and English usage come before 'language'. The figure of 46 complaints a week must be set in the context of the year's output: 'if we sold tickets for every single play we do, to every single person who listens, we would be selling an average of 760 million seats a year' (BBC, 1988: 37).

I make no claim that the part of my research which focused on listeners gives a 'true' picture. The letters I received from listeners and the transcripts of my telephone interviews with a few of them deliver only another set of 'texts' for interpretation. To the extent, however, that they are independent confirmation of the general findings of BBC Broadcasting Research they have some value.

As a result of a notice placed in the *Radio Times*[7] inviting readers who listened to radio plays to write to me, I received 174 letters in reply. From these I selected a small 'panel' with whom I conducted in-depth telephone interviews to try to gain a picture of the social meaning of radio in their lives and of the interpretative process at work during play listening. The means of contact, using self-selected correspondents, lent itself to an ethnographic approach rather than controlled sampling for which I had neither the time nor resources. The BBC's Broadcasting Research Department's data were available to me and showed for the period in question (last quarter of 1986) and for the slot on which I was focusing (*The Afternoon Play,* Monday to Thursday, 3–4 p.m.) that three-quarters of listeners were women and that compared to the population as a whole the South East, ABs and older people were over-represented. The demographic profile of my 174 letter-writers (in so far as it was apparent or deducible from the letters) was by chance remarkably close to the listenership of *The Afternoon Play* itself, although, as *Radio Times* readers, the respondents were drawn from a minority of the play-listening audience.[8]

Only 22 (13%) of the 174 letters mentioned a dislike of 'language', or that 'language' was a reason to switch off. I had not specially asked about this (see Note 7) and respondents volunteered their criticism alongside positive comments. The general tone of the letters was of gratitude at being consulted, and pleasure at sharing the joys of a private hobby. A wealth of details was volunteered, providing a rich picture of radio listening which there is no space here to explore. More frequent than mention of 'language', was a dislike of plays dealing with social problems, especially those to do with Northern Ireland, and of shouting, 'background noise' (i.e. 'effects') and regional accents. The latter group of complaints has much to do with the conditions of listening (usually in parallel with other activities) and the poor technical quality of reception many listeners are prepared to put up with. The over-representation in the letter-writers of the South and South East where 'BBC English' is the norm partly explains the dislike of regional accents. The antipathy among what are mostly older listeners to plays about social problems together with the evidence about people's attachment to and use of a channel may be due to several factors that need more exploration.

1.   The censorship of news and current affairs coverage of Northern Ireland

means that drama, and especially radio drama, is one of the few available outlets for expression of issues in this area. An interesting coincidence makes the point: in the middle of the *Real Lives* crisis in 1985, an *Afternoon Play,* from the BBC's Northern Ireland studios, explored the relationship between two men, former schoolmates, a member of the IRA and a Protestant doctor *(Fogging,* by Arthur Deeny, Wednesday 31 July 1985). That the treatment of the issues, which drew no official protest, would not have been acceptable in a television documentary is an illustration of radio's relatively powerless cultural position compared to television.

2. The channel on which most drama is to be found, Radio 4, is also the channel where listeners hear most coverage of news and current affairs. Radio 4 listeners are also exposed to television and press coverage. Those who wrote to me repeatedly stressed that they looked to plays for relief and entertainment. This is the reaction of the listener who stays with a channel throughout the day and consequently looks to the drama slot to provide something distinctly different – i.e. 'not-news'. It is also the reaction of people whose work does not allow them to consume fiction in any other way. Mostly women, the demands of housework and caring for a family fill their days and evenings so that time for themselves – reading, or even watching television – is limited or non-existent. A number of my interviewees said that only plays on the radio, listened to while performing the quieter chores, could be enjoyed without guilt.

3. 'Problem plays' are likely to include the portrayal of strong emotions which in some listeners stir unwelcome echoes. Howard Barker's remarks are relevant here:

> The bland question so often put to writers 'Do you really need those words?' rings with a false innocence. The hidden meaning of this question is, 'Do you really need those feelings?' Attempts to restrict vocabulary are invariably attempts to restrict emotions. (BBC, 1988: 28)

So threatening to some listeners are these emotions that they sometimes hear 'language' in a play when it is not there (BBC, 1988: 37). For these listeners, and perhaps for those who are tired of news and current affairs and want their plays to be oases of supportive calm ('non-news'), 'language' becomes a typification that enables them to reject a play. From the letters written to me, it was clear that, like producers, most listeners employ typifications, in their case categorizing plays according to likes and dislikes. In those first moments of a play when hard listening work is required to gain one's bearings, typifications relieve the pressure of inter-pretation; and listeners in their own way *are* under pressure, especially if they are doing something else as well as listening. Their typifications cut across the slots and are more effective determinants of enjoyment than any labels or billings the broadcasters can devise.

Conclusion

We can now bring together the different types of 'purchase' which the 'tug-of-war' players have on language and attempt to locate the broadcasting problem within a wider political and social context. The view of aesthetic freedom expressed by Howard Barker, claiming almost a sacred right to the autonomy of authorship, is shared by many producers when, in their impresario role, they sponsor and represent the writer at editorial meetings. There are regional, age and sometimes gender divisions in internal BBC debates, but above all a pressure to justify the output 'in audience terms', which leads each party to invoke their concept of 'audience' in justification. For top BBC management, 'language' represents trouble it could do without, but inherently and at any time, not just the present fraught period of tension with government, the bureaucratic machine of the BBC must put limits on aesthetic freedom as it negotiates a position that keeps step with public taste and feeling.

The problem with language in broadcasting, as Tracey and Morrison point out in their study of Mary Whitehouse, is that it is:

> potentially a double assault – it is both the possible vehicle for what can usefully but crudely be described as alien ideologies, and it can simply of its very nature be offensive to the particular sensibilities of an individual viewer or listener. (Tracey and Morrison, 1979: 89)

Radio Drama Department managers are well aware of potential offence in both quarters:

> Just as the sense of personal involvement in radio makes violence, for example, more real and upsetting than it would be on stage or screen, so that same involvement makes the sense of outrage at a gross image more personal and upsetting. It is as if we had compelled the individual listener to utter a word or make concrete an image themselves which they would not normally allow to pass their lips or enter their minds. (BBC internal memorandum, 18 April 1986)

Here is an acknowledgement of the *individual* occasion for offence. Mary Whitehouse herself talked in 1974 of writers and producers in television as 'artists' who had failed to grasp 'the very nature of the medium in which they work . . . they manipulate not only the cameras but hearts and minds as well' (Quoted in Tracey and Morrison 1979: 97). Since then, a decade and more of academic debate on the audience's role in making meaning may incline us to reject Whitehouse's crude hypodermic theory of media effects, and grant that the Drama Department's formulation of the problem is realistic and responsible. Talk of 'responsibility', however, sends alarm bells ringing in the writers' camp: such words 'are nearly always employed by those who wish to add moral weight to the actions of the censor . . . far from being the reasonable action of responsible people, censorship can be arrogant, cynical, dangerous and often irresponsible' (Cooper, 1984: 8). The responsibility versus censorship dilemma is neither simple, nor does it divide the Radio Drama Department into neatly opposing camps. Each producer to some degree is both artist and bureaucrat and the collision of principles, in practice resolved by context and editorial judgement, is a constantly recurring schizophrenia. As McQuail concludes:

> It may be that the freedom, creativity and critical approach that many media personnel still cherish, despite the bureaucratic setting of their work, are ultimately incompatible with full professionalization. (McQuail, 1988: 149)

The recognition that words are *ideologically* loaded, that behind *individual* offence lies a terrain which is the site of cultural and political struggle, is what mobilizes the forces of right and left. Perhaps what above all distinguishes their respective positions is that whereas the left accepts that there has to be a 'struggle for the sign' and deliberately engages in it, the right sees language as an unalterable institution which must be defended as the very embodiment of the moral values in society. In embarking on her crusade in the 1960s Mary Whitehouse was out of step with her time. We might now sympathize with her demand for more accountability from broadcasters, but during the 1970s when the National Viewers' and Listeners' Association (NVALA) built up its campaign, most criticism of broadcasting came from the left. The years of the Thatcher administration saw the growth of right-wing pressure groups monitoring broadcasting for signs of offence, occasioned not only by political bias, but in moral affronts to family (Christian) values, and social threats to the lower middle-class way of life in the suburban households from which NVALA draws its members – and which is the heartland of support for Thatcherism.

For such a constituency 'bad' language is symptomatic of a wider, deeper malaise. Together with other attacks on language such as incorrect usage and pronunciation, it is part of that unholy trinity: language, sex and violence. Each must be kept within bounds – the first two within the family, the last reserved for the state in war and the maintenance of law and order. The sight and sound in the media of lack of control in these areas signal 'the collapse of all values and standards, the spiritual rottenness of modernity'.[9]

In the period in which the right was politically in the ascendant, the years of the Thatcher administration, the possibility that moral crusaders could take up individual complaints had to be taken very seriously by the BBC. But the moral and political concern with language overlaps with the BBC's own historical and self-appointed role as guardian of the 'Spoken Word'. In the first decades of the BBC's existence radio alone was its keeper. Even after the arrival of television and the loss of monopoly, the Home Service and its successor, Radio 4, continued to carry the mantle. From its origins under Reith, national radio spoke for a middle-class, London and South-Eastern section of the population, the section that, older now but no less vocal, still dominates the audience of Radio 4. Tolerance and intolerance on the question of 'language' is not arranged neatly along class lines but if 'language' carries a load of concerns about forbidden emotions and worrying social problems, then its use in broadcasts is a challenge to a comfortable status quo. The disparities of wealth and employment between North and South in Britain so visible to Bridson in the 1930s have been reflected in the voting patterns of recent years. If the heartland of the Conservative vote is also the greatest patron of Radio 4, it is understandable that there is a strain between the notion of 'my station' and the 'alien ideologies' that not infrequently accompany 'language'.

Notes

1. I am grateful to Olive Shapley for this anecdote recorded in an interview in January 1989.

2. The discussion which follows draws on data obtained during a period of participant observation in the BBC Radio Drama Department (from 1985 to 1987), in connection with a wider study designed to show how the traditions and routines of the BBC, the textual work of author and producer and the interpretations of listeners combine to construct the meaning of a radio play. The audience section of the study is based on analysis of 174 letters received from listeners, telephone interviews with a selection of them, and the contextualization of this evidence by reference to data supplied by BBC Broadcasting Research. I am grateful to Richard Imison, Deputy Head of Drama (Radio) for arranging access to his Department, and to Robin McCron, then Head of Special Projects, BBC Broadcasting Research, and to his staff for their assistance.

3. Figures given in a talk by Richard Imison at *What Price Radio and the Arts?*, Radio Academy seminar, Queen Elizabeth Hall, 24 March 1986

4. These were John Drummond (CR3) and Michael Green (CR4). In the descriptions and quotations which follow and which relate to Drama Department meetings in the period 1985–7, CR3 and CR4 refer to earlier postholders.

5. The central character in *Scenes From An Execution* was a Venetian artist, played by Glenda Jackson, whose refusal to respect the conventions expected in an officially commissioned painting was part of a strong-willed and uninhibited character. The original script contained some 'language' which CR3 insisted should be cut – 'we traded a few fissures and loins for two fucks' was how a senior drama producer remembered it later. The 100-minute play was transmitted on 14 October 1984, and was entered for, and won, the Prix Italia in a version shortened to 90 minutes in order to conform to the competition's limits on length.

6. The Reaction Index (RI) is a quantification of the measure of appreciation on a five-point scale noted in the weekly responses of the Listening Panel.

7. *Radio Times* 30 August–5 September 1986. 'Do you listen to radio plays? If so, what kinds do you enjoy, and what makes you choose to listen to any particular one? How much does your enjoyment depend on what you are doing at the time? Lecturer Peter M. Lewis, who is researching radio drama, would like to know. Write to him [address].'

8. One of the BBC's regular omnibus surveys included questions about the particular play whose production I was following and showed that only 5% of listeners to the play had read its billing in the *Radio Times* (Listening Panel Report for Week 3 [LR/87/13] prepared by Mike Smith, 17 February 1987).

9. Personal communication commenting on an earlier draft of this paper by Paddy Scannell. I am indebted to him for his help in arriving at a broader contextualization of the language issue in relation to the social history of the BBC.

References

Ash, W. (1985) *The Way to Write Radio Drama.* London: Elm Tree Books.

Bridson, D.G. (1971) *Prospero and Ariel – the Rise and Fall of Radio: A Personal Recollection.* London: Gollancz.

British Broadcasting Corporation (1981) *Notes on Radio Drama.* Script Editor, Drama (Radio).

British Broadcasting Corporation (1988) *Transcript of the BBC's Language in Broadcasting Seminar,* 14 June, London.

Burns, T. (1977) *The BBC: Public Institution and Private World.* London: Macmillan.

Cardiff, D. (1980) 'The Serious and the Popular: Aspects of the Evolution of Style in the Radio Talk 1928–1939', *Media, Culture and Society,* 2(1) 29–47.

Cooper, R. (1984) 'Censorship', *Broadcasting Bulletin of the Society of Authors,* Winter.

Giddens, A. (1984) *The Constitution of Soviety.* Oxford: Polity Press.

Goffman, E. (1963) *Behaviour in Public Places.* New York: Free Press.

Goffman, E. (1974) *Frame Analysis.* New York: Harper & Row.

Independent Broadcasting Authority (IBA) (1986) *Radio Research Digest.* Radio Division, November.

McQuail, D. (1988) *Mass Communication Theory: An Introduction.* London: Sage.

Meneer, P. (1988) *The Broadcasting Research View: Obscene and Blasphemous Language in Radio.* Note for BBC Radio's Language in Broadcasting Seminar, London.

Radio Academy (1986) *Radio Research: The Comprehensive Guide, 1975–1985* (Researcher Josephine Langham). London: BBC Data Publications.

Rodger, I. (1982) *Radio Drama.* London: Macmillan.

Tracey, M. and Morrison, D. (1979) *Whitehouse.* London: Macmillan.

Tuchman, G. (1978) *Making News: A Study in the Construction of Reality.* New York: Free Press.

3

The Interview as Social Encounter

John Corner

This chapter is a case study in the social history of television talk.[1] The particular form examined is documentary – a category which now embraces too wide a range of discursive forms for the development of any tight generic theory but one which nevertheless displays certain consistencies both of visualization and speech usage. These follow from documentary's characteristic concern for informing the viewer by 'evidencing' the world in its recorded *particularity.*

Essentially, I am concerned with questions of transition and development during the mid-to-late 1950s – a time when the nature of broadcast provision was significantly changed by the breaking of the BBC (British Broadcasting Corporation) monopoly and when so many shifts were occurring in British political and cultural life.[2] Within that frame, I have an interest in knowing more about the way in which the documentary output of the BBC and ITV (Independent Television) variously responded, in image and speech usage, both to the new centrality of TV as a medium of reportage and to cultural and social change. More narrowly still, among those discursive developments by which broadcasters sought to make documentary competitively engaging, the emergence of the location interview as a staple form of 'dramatized exposition' strikes me as being of particular importance.

The substantive focus, then, is provided by the early phases of television 'actuality' documentary and, more particularly, by those kinds of address to the viewer, modes of enquiry and visualizations of the social developed by ITV companies in their initial bid to compete against the BBC by providing what their senior executives often chose to call 'people's television'.[3] During this period, earlier registers of authoritative, public-service commentary and emerging formats for investigative journalism are mixed with fresh attempts at exploiting the domestic, personalized and sociable dimensions of the new medium in such a way as to provide documentary with egalitarian accents (though, of course, neither the motivation nor the social substance behind these accents can be taken for granted). Older cinematic traditions of the 'filmed essay' or public information film connect with developing styles of conducting and shooting interviews and with forms of location reporting in which a new directness and immediacy are increasingly sought despite the physical limitations of 35-mm film-making, especially when recording synchronized sound.

In what follows, I concentrate on three documentary programmes made and transmitted by Associated Rediffusion in the summer of 1956, the first full year of ITV. The primary emphasis is on the mix of visual and verbal registers and styles of address apparent at this stage in the development of TV's documentary discourse. Despite the hazards of cultural interpretation, I am also keen to discover what this formal mix might indicate about the social assumptions framing the documentarists' relationship with, on the one hand, the chosen topics, their contexts and the people whose images and voices serve to embody them and, on the other, with the members of the audience – their knowledge, values and expectations.

First of all, it may be useful to consider more closely some of those features and methods which constitute documentary's 'social address' and, given the relatively little analytical attention which TV documentary has received, to note some consequences of the shift from documentary within cinema to documentary within television, from documentary *films* to documentary *programmes*.

The social address of documentary television

Quite apart from the advantages which it eventually derived from changes in camera and recording technology, documentary television was almost from the start able to exploit properties and conventions of the medium which inevitably pulled it away from cinema-based styles of exposition.[4] Paramount here was the essentially 'domestic' character of a television service, coming into the living-rooms of the nation as part of a routine, regular provision and frequently viewed either in small family groupings or alone. Two related lines of advance led from this basic fact about the character of the system.

First, it became possible to produce documentary programme material within the larger format of a *series*. Here, continuity across the changes of topic could be provided by a regular presenter or presenters who would not only serve to give the series an identity, along with such things as title sequence, theme music, etc. but by becoming familiar to the audience would thereby perhaps generate something of the trust and the pleasure in expectation and recognition which familiarity can encourage.

Secondly, presenters were able to project a more informal relationship with the audience both by quite quickly assuming familiarity and by using to the full the advantages which television 'direct address' speech can bring to the discursive work of exposition (e.g. colloquial speech rhythms, expressive eye contact and the use of pronouns to set up relationships of complicity and identification within the process of viewing). In television, unlike cinema, the viewing space of the audience (home) can be intimately aligned with the institutional space of TV (the studio/station), promoting a sense of mutual interiority in respect of which excursions to the actualities of the 'outside world' can proceed as joint ventures. Thus an alignment of space as well as an alignment of time ('immediacy') can form the 'setting' for television address. Moreover, the fact that the majority of the presenter/narrators of TV documentary output were not experts or specialists (as in 'talks' broadcasting), but were *reporters* and *interviewers,* further heightened the potential for linking presenter and audience into an 'us'.[5]

Television documentary, though it developed a strong vein of impression-istic, aesthetically self-conscious and clearly 'authored' programmes (drawing here both on the 1930s cinema movement and on the pre-war tradition of radio features) had an increasing tendency to centralize the more 'journalistic' mode (to which a 1930s film like *Housing Problems* might seem the more appropriate datum) as well as the direct precedent of established radio practice. Given the typical themes of journalistic enquiry, and given the medium's potential, indicated above, for personalized, intimate discourses, it is not at all surprising that various forms of the *interview,* almost entirely absent from the 1930s cinematic tradition, should become the staple form of the new medium.

The BBC documentary-maker Norman Swallow comments on an early stage in the emergence of a new kind of social address in his discussion of the innovations begun by the BBC's *Special Enquiry,* first broadcast in 1952 and considerably influenced by the success of the American CBS (Columbia Broadcasting System) programme *See It Now:*

> The professional expert was replaced by the enquiring reporter, a man whose initial knowledge is no greater than that of the viewer on whose behalf he conducts the enquiry. He never dominates the programme, for most of its length he is only a voice speaking words that are slightly more personal than those of a film commen-tator . . . He moves from place to place, using his film camera as a reporter might use his notebook and pencil. He asks the questions that a sensible layman would ask . . . He was the fixed point of the enquiry, the man through whose eyes and ears the viewer absorbed the story.[6]

Elsewhere, I have explored in some detail the project of *Special Enquiry* as a new kind of television journalism in which the narrativized reportage of the 'man on the spot' was interspersed with the more conventional commentary-over-film and, less conventionally, with the accessed voices of 'ordinary people' in direct-to-camera testimony and opinion-stating. By the time a year or so of competition had intensified the need to build (or to keep) audiences by devising more entertaining approaches, the note of dutiful restraint suggested in Swallow's comments was no longer generally apposite. For yet newer versions of the 'personal' within the 'social' were being constructed, within newer rhetorics of documentary story-telling.

The 'sociable eye' of *Look in on London*

In exploring the shift towards more popular styles of documentary program-ming after 1955, I have chosen to focus on example from this series partly because three of the fifteen programmes made (identified as *Sewermen, Streetcleaners* and *Tramps)* have not only survived but can be hired, on a single 16-mm reel, from the BFI (British Film Institute).[7] Tracing the history of television's various mediations of 'the social' is beset by the problem that huge gaps exist in the archive of tele-recordings and filmed inserts available for study. Of course, many programmes were simply not recorded at all and went out 'live' to disappear for ever, while even material shot entirely on film was not often kept for very long. This makes it only too easy for a researcher to foreshorten programming developments and to overemphasize links or contrasts by generalizing from a strictly limited and potentially unrepresentative collection of surviving programmes.

Nevertheless, I believe that many aspects of the programmes selected relate both to general changes in documentary form in response to the need to compete for the expanding television audience and, more specifically, to an attempt by the ITV companies, with their newly recruited staff, to produce kinds of actuality material which contrasted appealingly and profitably with the more conventional BBC formats. The *Look in on London* series was made during an early phase of ITV's operation, subsequently dubbed 'The Retreat from Culture'. This phase, lasting for much of 1956, followed financial crisis in a number of companies resulting from initial advertising revenue being insufficient to cover costs. 'Serious' programming was dramatically reduced and the ITA's (Independent Television Authority) requirements for a 'balanced' schedule were temporarily waived. The emphasis on programmes low in cost and high in popular appeal is very clear from several sources.[8]

The programmes were 15 to 20 minutes long and, initially, were transmitted at 10.000 p.m. on Wednesdays (just before *Gun Law*), though later they were shifted to a Monday spot. The producer of the series was Caryl Doncaster, a documentarist with extensive BBC experience behind her. The programmes were directed and presented by Michael Ingrams, who had been successful in Associated Rediffusion's popular and pioneering news magazine *This Week,* also produced by Doncaster.[9] The basic idea was a weekly 'look' at an aspect of life in London, mostly organized in terms of different kinds of public service job and daily routine. The underlying model appears to have been a straightforward development from the social democratic explorations of much 1930s documentary – the object is once again to reveal the essential interdependence and engaging variety of the different elements in a fundamentally consensual social order. Two central themes from the 1930s are evident: revelation of the 'hidden drama' behind essential industries and public services, and the documentation of *social* problems (e.g. bad housing, vagrancy, low wages) independent of political or economic analysis.

Yet the programmes differ in a number of respects and often sharply both from cinema documentaries and from those earlier TV documentaries which I have either been able to see or to locate descriptions of. For a start, each programme's construction of the 'social' involves a much tighter focus on specific individuals encountered *in situ,* as it were, during the course of the weekly expedition. As well as primarily representing a (mostly occupational) 'type', these individuals are also investigated by the interviewer in terms of their more personal and private identities – in respect of family life, hobbies, leisure, etc. In this sense, then, the series provides much more of a 'people show' than most earlier documentary formats,[10] though given the scarcity of archive material, it would probably be inaccurate to place emphasis on its distinctiveness within contemporary developments.[11] Nevertheless, the programmes also have general informational business to manage (e.g. about London's sewage system, about refuse collection and disposal, about welfare provision for vagrants) and this they do largely by reverting to a relatively conventional use of commentated film of particular activities and processes.

A second, general respect in which the programmes differ from most earlier work is in the kinds of relationship which they are able to strike up with the viewer, chiefly by being able to realize those communicational possibilities of broadcast television mentioned earlier and by having the strand of individualized human interest and interaction just described. The invitation to 'look in' is here not only an invitation to knowledge but to entertainment (as a 'busker' type theme-tune, prominently featuring a banjo, makes clear). The accepting viewer adventures out 'on location' with the genial reporter as guide, to be taken into circumstances and encounters which, despite their being *recorded* on film, are mediated strongly within conventions of TV immediacy. These conventions were currently getting a new edge through developments in OB (Outside Broadcasting) – magically linking the comfort and security of domestic viewing with the happenstance and knowledge of 'out there' experience and activity.[12]

A broad sense of some of the more general social and presentational ideas which lay behind the devising of the programme can be got from the comments of its producer:

> In those days the image of the Beeb [BBC] was very upper class and stiff establishment. The voices, clothes and 'personas' of the interviewers were public school, and of course ITV, appealing more to the working man, changed all that.

And, again, on production intentions:

> We were also all young and believers in a classless, buoyant Britain, and a variety of accents. Above all, we wanted everything natural, and to get ratings and hold interest we pruned out ruthlessly and tried to start everything in an exciting manner.[13]

I shall develop these preliminary observations by examining a selection of transcribed extracts from the programmes. This should allow points and questions around three themes in particular to receive some depth of illustration. These connected themes are the relations between 'the public' and 'the private' set up by the programmes, the conduct of the 'enacted encounters' of the reporter-on-location and, finally, the governing assumptions at work in the programmes' overall address.

Public and private

As in the other surviving programmes in the series, the exposition of *Street-cleaners* is chiefly organized by movement between two basic types of material. There is the 'lively', human interest of encountering different kinds of people at work – an interest grounded in the 'location interviews' upon which each week's journey of discovery is based. Then, set within this, there is the direct delivery of information through voiced-over film, involving altogether more formal and distanced viewing relationships.

These two constituents of the documentary account are constructed within

differing rhetorics of the documentary 'eye'. The newer rhetoric places the
viewer as the invited, close 'onlooker' in relation to the enquiring activities
and social encounters of the guide/reporter, though an 'uninvited' camera
often discovers subjects in their activities just prior to the official arrival of the
programme in the person of the reporter. A typical sequence is from such a
scene of 'discovery' into which the reporter enters, through a medium shot of
reporter and subject/s, and into an interview exchange mixing variously
distanced 'two shots' with alternating close-ups of speakers plus occasional
cutaways to the reporter. The limitations imposed by the equipment at this
stage in the development of actuality shooting, together with the related
rehearsal requirements, combine to give a static, 'tableau'-like quality to the
encounters in comparison with later conventions of mobility and continuity in
the engaging and holding of the viewer as onlooker.

The sections of commentated film are strongly word-led, with the sequence
of images largely confined to the directly illustrative role of depicting places
and processes underneath a light descriptive account. This account is pep-
pered with 'remarkable facts', sometimes drawing revealingly on a programme's deepest social assumptions ('Each one of us throws away in a year
an equivalent amount of food to feed the average Indian for three months')
and occasionally modulating into tones of sub-Dimbleby sonority ('By next
year the old kipper bones, cigarette cartons, newspapers and the sweepings
from street, shop and home will all have changed into rich, brown earth').

In all three programmes examined, the project of discovery/exposition is
got off to a brisk start. Here is a transcription of the opening of *Streetcleaners*,
following the titles which, in the programmes discussed, locate the programme name on a placard somewhere within the establishing shots.

(CU [close up] shots of broom sweeping gutter; speech in VO [voice over].)

Who wields this broom?
Fred Robinson, Robbo to his friends. He keeps 1½ miles of Maida Vale in a state in
which you'd wish to find it – which is not the state you left it in.

The programme is hereby immediately launched upon an enquiry having
both a sharply personal dimension and an address to the viewer mediated via
the category of 'citizen', a category in which a degree of 'taking-for-granted'
of public services can be assumed and jokingly chided. 'We' do not know who
Robbo is, 'we' expect clean streets but leave litter. 'We', presumably, relate to
Maida Vale as the kind of area we might live in (perhaps a more problemati-
cally specific interpellation?). Notice, too, how there is offered an alternative,
more intimate rendering of the cleaner's identity – an early signal of the kind
of bridge which the programme, through its onlooking and overhearing
practices, wishes to construct between viewers' world and subject's world.

After this opening sequence, the programme (through the presenter/re-
porter) moves in to *arrest* the flow of the taken-for-granted activity in order to
open it up for viewer understanding; to explore its occupational and personal
as well as its public and organizational aspects. This requires the expositional
theatricality of the 'as-if-spontaneous' interview; seeming to be generated
abruptly out of the presenter's encounter with the working routines of the

chosen subjects and relayed to the viewer as part of the programme's ongoing, co-present enquiries. The first section of interview proceeds as follows. (Throughout this article I have used *I,* and *R,* to indicate, respectively, Interviewer and Respondent.)

(Medium shot of streetcleaner with a handcart sweeping gutter, reporter enters frame L.)

I.	Good afternoon.
R.	Good afternoon.
I.	You ever get tired doing this all day long? *(cut closer)*
R.	No, I don't get tired at all.
I.	Don't you?
R.	No.
I.	Don't you... doesn't it get a bit monotonous sweeping the same gutters?
R.	No, I got so used to it now.
I.	How long have you been doing it?
R.	Seven years.
I.	Oh, what were you doing before then?
R.	I was working for the Kensington Borough Council. *(CU face)*
I.	As what?
R.	As a dustman.
I.	Which do you like best, streetsweeping or dustbinning? *(CU reporter)*
R.	Well, I'd sooner be a dustman.
I.	Would you?
R.	Yes.
I.	Don't you get a bit of lumbago with all those... carting those heavy dustbins around?
R.	No, I got so used to it.
I.	Did you? What happens to you on this job? What sort of people do you meet?
R.	Well, I got half a cigarette here now what a gentleman give us to me the other day. *(CU hands and cigarette box)*
I.	Well, you've kept it.
R.	Yes, he always comes out the mansions every morning wet or fine and er takes 20 fags out, takes one out breaks it in half, gives one half to me puts the other back in his pockets.
I.	Ha Ha Ha every morning?
R.	Every morning wet or fine.
I.	Who are these chaps? *(Reporter's eyes shift to out-of-shot distance. Dustcart arrives)*

What seems immediately striking here is both the directness and, on occasion, awkward naivety of these initial questions about 'work'. This is all at some distance from the elaborately scripted (and often deeply condescending) fluency of many earlier kinds of documentary approach to working experience. Nevertheless, the terms on which this devised encounter between the representative of television and the streetcleaner takes place seem to shift uncertainly between a brisk, 'official' interrogation and the simulation of chat. No hand microphone interposes between presenter and subject and the presenter's posture is emphatically 'casual' (hands in pockets), contrasting with the other's nervous rigidity. The regular repetitions ('don't you', 'did you', etc.) and the sudden jump in level to an implausibly general cue-question ('What happens to you on this job?') also suggest both an early stage in the development of this type of TV interview performance and (perhaps) a relatively inexperienced interviewer. The problem may be seen as partly one of producing speech in an adequate *performance register*. This register mimics the syntax and cadence of a private exchange but, of course, it is throughout shaped by the requirements of staging a specific type of public display. For the interviewee, the tensions involved in maintaining a *performance* without straying out of his allocated *role* as a *spontaneous* speaker are considerable and I return to this question in relation to later examples.

The 'chance' arrival of the dustcart at the end of the sequence provides two more interviewees and the start of further anecdotal explorations of working life (memories of earlier times, coping with the smell, unusual things found in the rubbish, etc.). It is when the cart pulls away, leaving Robbo and the interviewer 'alone' again, that the programme moves to a very different level of the social. As the cleaner puts his gear back on his handcart, this exchange occurs:

(Reporter to streetcleaner, cart in between.)

I.   Off home now are you?
R.   Yes.
I.   I bet you need a good bath now after . . .
R.   I haven't got a bath
I.   You haven't got a bath?
R.   No, not where I am. It's a requisitioned house, it's condemned.
I.   Condemned?
R.   Yes, it's been condemned ever since 1939.
I.   And you've been in it all that time?
R.   Yes, and I'm still waiting to get into a council flat.
I.   Ah, you're on the list are you?
R.   I'm on the list. I'm on the Kensington Borough list and the LCC [London County Council] list and I'm still waiting.
I.   Oh and it's really bad is it?
R.   In a very bad condition.
I.   No, . . .
R.   It's unfit to live in.
I.   Is it?
R.   Yes.
I.   Well . . . er
R.   There's only me and my missus and we're eating and sleeping in one room.
I.   Could I come back and meet your wife?
R.   Yes, you're willing [*sic*] to come back and have a look at it and see what you think of it.
I.   Well, that's very kind of you, hm . . .
     Tell me, while we're going along *(they walk off)* what happens to all that rubbish, er?
R.   All the rubbish goes into the salvage van and goes down to Westminster to be 'chuted into the barge . . .
(Fade to film sequence with reporter VO.)

Here, once more, it is the apparently spontaneous route by which the information and the follow-up request are delivered that is crucial to the effect. Since the programme has not so far indicated that the question of the housing conditions of council employees will be part of its concern, this sudden turn in the direction of its attention appears quite astounding when read in the context of current documentary convention.[14] The fact that the move to this new aspect of the social is, as it were, *dramatized* as a scene of expectations confounded (leaving aside interesting questions about how it originated in the research and pre-take planning), *rather* than being introduced through some voiced-over link or to-camera comment, simulates precisely that sense of ongoing development (the presenter portrayed as being as surprised as the viewer) sought by the programme as a whole. Thus at the finish of the exchange, when yet another shift of focus and register leads into a sequence of commentary film on the processing of refuse (presented as a parallel phase to their conversations as they 'go along') the scene from which the fade-down is made presents the bizarre spectacle of a very urbane-looking man in a natty business suit escorting a streetcleaner (pushing his handcart) home! It is the highly personalized framings of the occupational and the social within which the programme works that permit this narratively continuous movement from the initial, *topic*-constituted typification (streetcleaning, a streetcleaner) to the more intensively individualized representation of *person* and personal circumstances. In this latter, the referenced *category* of the social becomes unclear (typical streetcleaners' circumstances? typical manual workers'? typical working class?).

Given this re-framing, from the occupational through the personal to the domestic, the sequences in Robbo's house betray some uncertainty of address. Awkwardly 'square-on' in shot and initially stilted in their attempts at a spontaneously colloquial route through to the kind of information sought, they depict Robbo and his wife being interviewed about the condition of their home, the weekly budget, leisure-time hobbies (they have no television) and even their happiness together. The mix of questioning here blends elements of jovial inquisitiveness about the personal (though the class tones and manner of the interviewer make this role a perhaps less comfortable and certainly a less convincing one to perform) with more serious investigative goals. An anticipated move to a new flat and speculation about the 'new life' which will follow provide a way of offsetting the strongly negative portrayal of Robbo and his wife's conditions. However, the programme does not attempt to develop (in the manner of, say, the classic 1935 film *Housing Problems)* an overt theme of social improvement by which depicted deprivation is reassuringly framed (in this respect, the 1935 film might better have been called *Housing Solutions).*

After another brief sequence of commentary film, this time concerning the use of London's refuse in land reclamation, we are returned to the streets again for a final comment:

(Reporter's VO: CU shot of broom sweeping gutter.)

And tomorrow Robbo's old broom will be busy again. This time we shall know who it is we are passing the time of day with. (*Passes Robbo at work, greets him and moves close to camera for direct address.*)
One more of London's millions who's no longer a stranger. (*Walks off, with a farewell wave to Robbo.*)

Here, at the end of the programme, the kind of social connections aimed for come out clearly in the suggestion of future familiarity. In the classic tradition of many earlier documentaries, 'we' are being put in touch with 'others' – the programme is promoting not only knowledge and vicarious social adventure but also a form of social relationship. The final line whimsically supposes some slow but steady process by which strangers are transformed into acquaintances through the programme's not only social but *sociable* address.[15] Though, clearly, Robbo is no more a 'stranger' to his friends and workmates then 'we' are to ours, the line carries an implicit notion – linking it back to the 1930s films – of the unnatural anonymity of the urban mass and of the need to strengthen connections of community. Creeping into this concluding comment there is perhaps a hint of a documentary ideal altogether more ambitious than that of disseminating popular knowledge. An ideal of ultimate parasociality, in which documentary introduces everyone (and their jobs) to everyone else. I shall discuss some further implications of this idea in the context of the series as a whole, but I would first like to turn to a brief but close examination of a principal feature of the programmes' expositional form.

Interview – encounter – enactment

As suggested above, the programmes, like others of the period, use new ideas about televisual documentary *form* to produce actuality material which is itself able to set up new kinds of relationship with audiences through its ways of accessing the social via activity within location *mise-en-scène*, quite apart from the relationships projected verbally by commentary and presentation. Yet this rendering of the social, freed from the limitations of studio treatments and with a newly democratic/populist sense of appropriate topics and framings, now had to construct naturalisms of behaviour and speech to exploit fully the possibilities for heightened immediacy and dynamism. Shooting styles, on-camera activity and speech registers sometimes display uneasiness and inconsistency in these initial phases of extending the range of documentary discourse.

Some indications of this have already been given, but a further example can be found in another programme in the series, *Tramps*. This attempts to explore aspects of the life of London's vagrant community and, eschewing the usual introductory address, it starts off abruptly with the presenter in a cheap-rate lodging house chatting to a seated group of men. One lodger's comments about a particular reception centre are soon interrupted by a shift to a filmed report ('Before you tell me about it, I want to take the viewers over to see it') in which we accompany the reporter into the centre via a brief conversation with the duty officer at the gate. This leads through to a meeting with the centre's warden which develops as below:

(Centre yard, warden in conversation with man, other men in background.)

Warden   . . . So don't be foolish and go out . . . leave the centre, stay until you've had your vacancy allotted to you. All right, my lad?
Man   Yes sir, thank you very much, sir.

Warden   Off you go.
        (Man walks off, reporter enters, they shake hands)
I.   Mr Hollis?
R.   Mr Ingrams I'm very pleased to greet you at our reception centre here.
I.   Thank you very much. I've had a bit of a look, bit like a barracks, isn't it?
R.   Very much so. Built in 1878 as an old workhouse. Rose by any other name . . . now a reception centre.
I.   Now suppose I walk in here today and tell you that I'm destitute, which isn't so far from the truth, what happens to me?
R.   You would be asked for particulars for yourself and sign a form to say you were destitute. Making a false statement would cause you to be prosecuted for making a false statement but all things being equal you would be admitted.
I.   And what then?
        (Cut to warden's VO; film sequence.)
        You would be directed to the bathroom where your clothing would be thoroughly inspected for vermin . . .

A number of things are of interest here. First of all, there is the very explicit manner in which the reporting is dramatized chronologically in the form of a visit – thus projecting, for viewer involvement, the sense of ongoing enquiry, a sense further reinforced by the facetiously self-dramatizing character of the initial questioning. The warden is first 'discovered' giving advice to one of the men and it is into this framing of unobserved onlooking that the reporter walks to be formally welcomed. Like a number of other occasions in the programmes when interviews with officials are featured, a problem of finding and sustaining appropriate registers of address arises. The interaction, though essentially a public act, feigns 'private' behaviour. Unlike the TV professional, the subject/interviewee may find that the mixed form of speech best suited to this cannot be easily produced, even after preparation and a run through. Thus we have the apparent awkwardness of a visually rendered one-to-one exchange in which the colloquiality of the reporter contrasts with the stiff, 'on the platform' formality of the respondent. From the start, the warden stays within the syntax and phrasings of 'official language', being perhaps reluctant to risk the loss of authority within the exchange which might follow a more personalized performance, quite apart from the difficulty of getting such a performance right. This is underlined by the move from his interview speech to his voiced-over commentary. The latter, though it continues in the basic register established in the interview, is clearly recorded at a different phase in the scheme of filming and, read from a script, it loses all semblance of conversational rhythm or spontaneity, having the itemization of institutional procedures as its primary concern.

Both the explicit referencing of a report as 'in process' and the uncertainty of respondent register are clearly apparent again in the exchange which ends a further section of question and answer following the warden's commentary. Here, a strong class inflection to the reporter's vocabulary is obvious too, as the programme subordinates itself to authority, whilst representing this as the seeking of *personal goodwill.*

(Reporter to warden in centre yard.)

I.   Now, I've a favour to ask of you. Will you give me a *carte blanche* to go round the place, look at everything and maybe talk to one or two of your ... er ... chaps?

R.   Certainly. You're most welcome to go round to speak to who you like and see what you like. If you require further assistance I shall be at your disposal.

It would be useful to have more programmes from this and other contemporary series available in order to see how far the represented relationships with officials and managers have general difficulties with sustaining the naturalism of 'on location' disclosure and the enactments of relaxed spontaneity upon which this is based. Unlike most of the manual and skilled workers interviewed in the programmes, officials may, in varying degrees, feel that they are put at risk by the scrutiny of the visiting television team. They may therefore have too big a commitment in projecting 'correct' impressions to develop the performance both of publicly informative comment and yet also of ostensibly situation-generated chat which the presenter seeks to elicit. It is also true that whereas the workers are frequently seen to be *interrupted* by the presenter in the course of their working routines (e.g. sweeping the gutters, clearing a sewer) thus preclassifying subsequent interview exchanges with them as variations on 'casual talk' (however uneasy or interrogatively weighted these may be), officials are seen to enter the space of the programme voluntarily and with their own professional identities and terms in play from the start. To put it another way, the programme is seen to 'happen on' the workers but to involve officials by prior arrangement.

To illustrate this point and the associated discursive conventions, a sharp contrast can be drawn between the above encounter and the initial section of *Streetcleaners* cited earlier or with this exchange from the programme *Sewermen.*

(In sewers, two men working, shovelling silt. The second of two interview sequences. Reporter to second man who pauses, hand on shovel.)

I.   What do you feel about night work?

R.   Well, it's just something you gradually get used to like. It's like everything else you adapt yourself to it.

I.   Have you been doing this work long?

R.   Well, close on four years.

I.   What were you doing before?

R.   Well, I was a milkman.

I.   Do you prefer this to being a milkman?

R.   Yes, I settled more to this than I did to the milk trade.

I.   That's ... that's an astonishing thing that you should prefer sludge to milk ... Tell me why?

R.   Well, for one thing it's ... I don't know ... it's just something that you just can't explain I think that that ... anyway I think as a milkman you're never done. We do know when we're done here at least.

I.   I see, the hours are the big thing are they? Is the pay better here than on a milk round?

R.   The actual flat rate, flat rate, of course the milkman gets more local commission and all that.

I.   Hmm, are you married?

R.   Yes.

I.   Does your wife prefer you doing these shorter hours with less money to longer hours and more money?

R.   This is more steady and more regular like you know, that's her general idea.
I.   So, she's pleased.
R.   Yes, really yes.
I.   Good.
(VO) Time for me to climb back to the outside world

Here, as in the *Streetcleaners* interview, the push through to the personal is
rapidly achieved via references to the nature of the job being performed and
the enquiry is conducted in what certainly now seems a disconcertingly brisk
style. The interviewee has little choice but to accept his allocated role as the
amiable supplier of 'particulars'. As with other interviews of this kind, an
anthropological character is given to investigator/subject relationships as a
result of the distance, assumed and then emphatically signified, between 'us'
(here, inhabitants of the 'outside world') and the particular and strange world
of work which we are bridged to by the programme's depictions.[16] At one
point, the idea of strangeness is given a condescendingly jokey treatment
through the suggestion that the interviewee prefers sludge to milk. This
specific rendering of strangeness is located within a larger strangeness typi-
fying the relationship between the programmes' own discourses and the whole
realm of working-class jobs, speech and recreation. Part of the series' character as social adventure, as well as its agenda of enquiry, derives from this
strangeness, raising questions about the class character of viewing relations
and of response among its contemporary audiences.

'Looking in': terms and contexts

My initial interest in these programmes was a teaching interest. Their differences, across a 30-year gap, from current documentary images and speech
proved useful in relativizing the conventions of documentary realism and in
opening up questions about the links both with changing social and political
relations and the developing technical means of representation. In particular,
this stage of the move towards greater immediacy, intimacy and continuity
(key ingredients of 'watchability') seemed important in respect of its *performance* requirements, which move closer to those of fictional realism. A rather
paradoxical gap thereby opens up between the terms of representation
(spontaneous, ongoing revelation projecting co-presence with the viewer) and
the determining, though largely hidden, terms of construction (organization
and preparation of the interviews, enactment of various entries, encounters,
farewells, etc., editing so as to construct a condensed chronology for the
account). This is clearly bound up with the idea of grounding exposition
diegetically (each week's 'trip') rather than organizing it explicitly through
themes and topics. Topic-structured programmes can employ a range of
different representational forms (e.g. studio direct address, filmed report,
archive compilation, studio and location interviews) without 'enactment'
being demanded beyond the normative convention of supposing interviewees
to be engaged primarily in interpersonal exchange.

The personalized, diegetic format of visit and encounter, capable of
incorporating through its presenter both serious and 'lighthearted' themes

must have been regarded at the time as one of the most promising ways of producing popular documentary given technical practicality (e.g. the constraints on any vérité approach). As suggested above, the simulation of OB [Outside Broadcast] 'liveness' and the general importance attached to getting television 'out of the studio' were probably strong influencing factors on the idea of approaching social enquiry through the naturalistic representation of 'finding out' as, itself, a sequence of interactive social episodes. This is in contrast with *Special Enquiry's* routine punctuation of its presenter-on-location reports by the accessed comment of interviewees addressing the topic separately from a range of different physical settings and at a 'time' outside that of the programme's own exposition. *Expositional* time-frames can of course accommodate such discontinuity much more easily than the time-frame of *Look in on London,* naturalized as it is around a diegesis of condensed *event* time – the time of social encounter, of visit, of 'tonight's adventure'. There is a contrast, too, with the use of interviewee voice-over so effectively pioneered in TV documentary by Denis Mitchell.[17] In this mode, places, people and social actions are viewed within the framing given by the speech of unidentified and often unseen participants, whose apparently unsolicited recounting of anecdotes and opinions provides a rich, informational address, grounding the film in 'subject' rather than 'observer' consciousness. However, the 'inner' character of speech thus elicited and used (the term 'think-tape' was coined to describe Mitchell's innovative use of the tape recorder for speech collection independent of the camera) provides neither the concise, factual responses of the 'enactment' method nor its drama of sociability.

The specific 'social optics' by which *Look in on London's* invitations are constructed inevitably relate to its broader cultural, as well as to its formal and technical contexts. Its (often awkward) movement between 'public information' and 'human interest' strands of enquiry stems in part from the fact that this is still the first phase of actuality-based social exploration by television. It is the sense of a largely unexplored social landscape on the one hand and a new and enthusiastic domestic audience on the other which informs the programmes' self-consciously bright and informal address and their notions of what, using the format, can engagingly be 'found out'. Within the terms of the social democratic perspective from which their expeditions into the city are mounted, there is clearly a lot of finding out to be done about certain kinds of people as well as about certain kinds of institution and activity. The ostensible *topic* of each programme therefore only loosely governs the local organization and treatment of the actuality material (including the interview-encounters), as is clear in the sequences from *Streetcleaners.*

Here, it is perhaps important to note that though the manner of enquiry frequently contains echoes of a genial chat style founded precisely on hierarchic division (such as one might find, for instance, between officers and men in the forces) the programmes *do* attempt to register 'work' in a way quite different from most earlier documentary versions of the social. Elements of working experience and of working lives (e.g. hours, rates of pay, conditions, leisure opportunities) often entirely absent from documentary framing are here located firmly within it. The clear class resonances of the encounters between presenter and workers and the confident middle-class versions of 'sociability' upon which the presenter's egalitarian adventures are based also interestingly point to the absence of professionalized 'classlessness' at this stage in the emerging repertoire of journalistic performance.[18] Comparison with earlier inflections of the class voice in documentary would, however, highlight the softening, accommodating effects of post-war social change. Just how marked or how naturalized these class factors would appear to the audiences of the time, is, of course, difficult to assess. The element of class confrontation (often signalled by dress as well as by speech) tends to be made more obvious by the style of interview representation, which uses continuous question and answer sequences and extensive 'two-shot' framing to elicit and present the information rather than the variety of more oblique, post-shoot devices which might now be used in the development of occupational or personal themes (e.g. interview used in fragments with interviewer out of frame and perhaps with questions removed; interviewees' comments used for short sequences of voice-over).

In a very useful survey of representations of the British working class in the period 1957–64,[19] Stuart Laing (1986) discusses the development of the 'affluence' ideology and of the idea that an increasing spread of middle-class values followed on from rising standards of living. He notes that '1956 was the key year for the consolidation of this image of an affluent Britain undergoing embourgeoisement'. It would be an important project to trace the emergent forms and conditions of such an imagery and its politics across contemporary broadcasting, especially in the areas of newly competitive popular provision.

Look in on London seems placed on the edge of the buoyant, Conservative, 'New Britain' discourses which Laing documents. Some of the assumptions behind its questioning and its projected appeal appear to be partly framed by that calculated depoliticizing perspective, with its notions of an established consensus and the shift to brighter times being brought about by market expansion. In that respect, its vein of class-confident populism can be seen as part of an experiment in new forms of ideological management. Nevertheless, as I have shown, it locates and represents its subjects within the framework of real differences in working conditions and living standards, within a society where 'welfare' is still a central and necessary term of concern. In doing this, it continues and develops a dominant, earlier strand of documentary discourse, connecting a public-service style surveillance of the social with a more innovative if also uncertain investigatory interest in 'the people'.

A selection from one series is clearly no basis for 'reading off' a general system of social relationships or even its typical modes of mediation and the provisional and perhaps very questionable nature of the comments I have thought it worthwhile to make is clear to me. Nearly everything remains to be done in the history of broadcast documentary, both in primary research and in producing a more secure theoretical and analytical grasp of developments. It has been part of my argument in this article that close scrutiny of the forms of televised speech, as they develop distinctive conventions of performance and projected social relationship, will be an important part of such cultural-historical enquiry.

Notes

1. An earlier version of this article was given as a paper at the 1988 International Television Studies Conference held at the University of London in July and organized jointly by the British Film Institute and the University of London Institute of Education. I am particularly grateful to comments made on the draft by Sylvia Harvey and Michael Pickering.

2. These questions, pursued across a number of genres, form the basis of the collected articles in Corner (ed.) (1991).

3. The terms within which ITV constructed its 'popular' provision, involving what was to be a major advancement of market principles into the sphere of public information have been the subject of much discussion in the light of recent (1990) changes in British broadcasting funding and regulation. In particular, debate has focused on the degree of cultural closure or, alternatively, of accessing of previously subordinated forms, involved in its commercial strategies. For a recent account, see the introductory essay and selected chapters in Corner (forthcoming).

4. One important exception to this is the strong early tradition of studio-based 'story documentary' work, which followed many wartime documentary feature films in leaking exposition through the dialogue and situations of an acted narrative. These programmes appear to have been displaced from the schedules when the technical limitations on obtaining relevant kinds of actuality material were reduced. For a detailed history of this and other strands of TV documentary before 1955, see Paddy Scannell (1979: 97–106) and Elaine Bell (1986: 65–80).

5. The emphasis on interviewing as a central feature of documentary presentation and the shift to 'actuality' from studio settings were also undoubtedly influenced by developments in radio features. No detailed study of the methods and forms of post-war radio journalism exists, but see Paddy Scannell's valuable discussion of pre-war output (Scannell, 1986: 1–26).

6. Norman Swallow (1956: 51). The quotation also indicates clearly that the transference of the documentary project from cinema to television did not bring many changes, if any, to its dominantly masculine character. Despite the domestic dimension both of the system and its conventions, the public sphere constituted by 'serious' television was nevertheless a sphere of male concern and debate whose information needs were served by male enquiry and presentation.

7. The *BFI Distribution Library Catalogue 1978* gives dates of 1956, 1957 and 1958 but the Associated Rediffusion files indicate that after 1956 all schedulings were of repeats.

8. See, particularly, Bernard Sendall (1982: 248–55, 326–9).

9. An account of the ideas behind this programme, which was quite quickly networked and became important to the development of TV feature journalism, is given by Bernard Sendall (1982: 355–6). The more lighthearted 'magazine' approach is clearly evident in *Look in on London*.

10. A remark of Norman Swallow is relevant here. 'What was missing from television documentary before the mid-fifties was, quite simply, people' (quoted in Scannell, 1979: 104).

11. Besides the direct development out of *This Week,* there might have been influence from the BBC's TV magazine programme about the capital, *London Town,* which began in 1949 and featured Richard Dimbleby. See Elaine Bell (1986) on this and also Jonathan Dimbleby (1975: 219–21) for an account of the programme's artful mixing of studio and actuality material.

12. Outside Broadcasts were prevalent in 1956. The BBC's very popular *Saturday Night Out* broadcast from a submarine and a helicopter and took a television set out as a present for the crew of the South Goodwin lightship.

13. In a letter to the author. More generally, the extent to which a 'classless, buoyant Britain' is seen to describe present or imminent circumstances rather than a goal for political struggle seems crucial to the kinds of accommodation which television makes with the burgeoning, Conservative theme of 'affluence' after the 1955 General Election. Through its funding, ITV is obviously more directly linked into this emerging economic and ideological configuration than is the BBC. The point is touched on again later.

14. Though a contemporary manual for writers wanting to work in television is interesting here. Talking of documentary material it notes, 'the programme should shock, surprise and even develop the occasional "twist"' and, on the organization and scripting of interview *responses,* 'I always try to make three main points, two interesting and one (if possible) surprising' (Swinson, 1960: 113).

15. Paddy Scannell (1988) usefully considers some general features of the 'sociability' of broadcasting.

16. The 'anthropological' view, with its implied social relations, has often been commented on in respect of documentary depictions of work. In the 1935 film *Coalface,* for instance, the fact that reference is made throughout to 'the miner' seems to reinforce a feeling that it is a (largely subterranean) *species* which is under scrutiny rather than a kind of employment.

17. Good examples of the (highly effective) use of this method in Mitchell's work are *In Prison* (BBC, 1957) and *Morning In the Streets* (BBC, 1959). Both are discussed in Corner (1991).

18. Though regional accents were occasionally to be heard. It was seen to be a strong point in favour of Robert Reid, the reporter for *Special Enquiry,* that he 'had a slight northern accent, [which] added to his earthy, no-nonsense appearance' (Swallow, 1966: 73).

19. Stuart Laing (1986: 17). For a tracing of related themes in the cinema, see also John Hill (1986).

References

Bell, E. (1986) 'The Origins of British Television Documentary: The BBC 1946–55', pp. 65–80 in J. Corner (ed.), *Documentary and the Mass Media.* London: Edward Arnold.

Corner, J. (1991) 'Documentary Voices', pp. 42–59 in J. Corner (ed.) *Popular Television in Britain: Studies in Cultural History.* London: British Film Institute.

Corner, J. (ed.) (1991) *Popular Television in Britain: Studies in Cultural History.* London: British Film Institute.

Dimbleby, D. (1975) *Richard Dimbleby.* London: Hodder and Stoughton.

Hill, J. (1986) *Sex, Class and Realism: British Cinema 1956–63.* London: British Film Institute.

Laing, S. (1986) *Representations of Working-Class Life 1957–1964.* London: Macmillan.

Scannell, P. (1979) 'The Social Eye of Documentary', *Media, Culture and Society,* 1(1): 65–80.

Scannell, P. (1986) 'The Stuff of Radio' pp. 1–26 in J. Corner (ed.), *Documentary and the Mass Media.* London: Edward Arnold.

Scannell, P. (1988) '*Radio Times*: The Temporal Arrangements of Broadcasting in the Modern World' pp. 15–31 in P. Drummond and R. Paterson (eds), *Television and Its Audience.* London: British Film Institute.

Sendall, B. (1982) *Independent Television in Britain. Volume 1: Origin and Foundation 1946–62.* London: Macmillan.

Swallow, N. (1956) 'Documentary TV Journalism', pp. 49–55 in Paul Rotha (ed.), *Television in the Making.* London: Focal Press.

Swallow, N. (1966) *Factual Television.* London: Focal Press.

Swinson, A. (1960) *Writing for Television.* London: Black (second edition).

4

News Interview Openings: Aspects of Sequential Organization

Steven E. Clayman

When broadcast journalists and public figures come together to talk about current affairs on the air, they ordinarily do so within the framework of a news interview. The news interview has been the subject of increasing attention recently by social scientists who have sought to describe and analyse the conventional speaking practices that characterize this form of broadcast talk (e.g. Clayman, 1988, forthcoming; Greatbatch, 1986a, 1986b, 1988; Harris, 1986; Heritage, 1985; Heritage and Greatbatch, forthcoming; for an overview, see Heritage et al., 1988). It is now apparent that the interview, far from being a neutral conduit for the transmission of information and opinion, is in fact a strongly institutionalized genre of discourse that exerts a pervasive influence on the conduit of journalists and public figures, and on the manner in which they form their talk with one another.

Thus far, most analytical attention has been focused on interviewing practices associated with questioning and answering, and on the interactional and institutional consequences of that system for taking turns. But news interviews do not begin with questions and answers. The questioning is preceded by an introductory segment which presents an agenda for the interview and articulates it with relevant events of the day. This is a study of the opening segment in live television news interviews. The broad objective is to understand how openings are organized by way of utterly routine but previously unexamined language practices, and to determine what communicative tasks are accomplished through these practices.[1]

In a variety of ways, the opening segment prefigures both the form and content of the interaction to follow. For example, interview openings have a sequential structure that differs from openings in more casual or 'conversational' interactions. These differences combine visibly to mark the encounter as something other than a spontaneously occurring interaction; more specifically, they help to make it recognizable as a prearranged interaction, one that is being orchestrated on behalf of the viewing audience. The first part of the chapter examines the basic sequential organization of news interview openings, and shows how it provides for the 'staged' quality that is such a familiar feature of this type of encounter.

The primary substantive task of the opening is to project an agenda for the interview, and to portray it as having been occasioned by some newsworthy happening. Thus, openings propose a temporal and causal relationship between events outside the talk (prominent occurrences 'in the world') and the present occasion of talk (the occasion of the interview). This is plainly a way of exhibiting the interview's newsworthiness, but it also has implications for the manner in which both the worldly events and the interview's agenda are articulated. As we shall see, the agenda for discussion is characterized in terms fitted to the events that occasioned it. At the same time, the precipitating events are formulated in terms relevant to the interview toward which they are leading. Accordingly, any connection between the present interview and exogenous events is *achieved* through coherent referential and descriptive practices within the opening.

The analysis that follows has further implications for our understanding of the organizational constraints on the production of news. While institutional and ideological factors have attracted the most attention as determinants of news, news discourse has certain intrinsic organizational properties of its own, properties which exert an independent influence on the content of news. These implications will be elaborated further in the concluding discussion.

Data

The bulk of the data was drawn from two nightly news interview programmes in the United States: ABC News *Nightline* and *The MacNeil/Lehrer NewsHour* on PBS. Each programme was taped in three one-week blocks, for a total of thirty episodes consisting of an equal number (fifteen) of each programme. The weekly symmetry of these blocks is broken by the absence of one day of taping – a Wednesday – which was replaced by taping on the following Monday. For each programme, ten episodes were videotaped, while five were audiotaped only. A second set of materials was taken from the networks' major Sunday interview programmes: *Meet the Press* (NBC), *Face the Nation* (CBS), and *This Week with David Brinkley* (ABC). All three programmes were videotaped on one weekend. The resulting corpus contains fifty opening segments. Some additional materials were gathered on a more haphazard basis.

Particular openings have been transcribed and reproduced for illustrative purposes. The extracts exemplify patterned regularities that, unless otherwise noted, hold without exception throughout the entire corpus. While the central findings are based upon an analysis of the openings themselves, some background information on the institutional setting, obtained from ethnographic observations conducted at the studios of two news interview programmes, is also introduced.

The opening sequence

The only part of the interview that is explicitly addressed to the audience is the opening. In it the interviewer delivers his or her remarks directly to the camera, rather than addressing the interviewees or other programme personnel. Moreover, this stretch of talk has distinguishable components that regularly unfold in a fixed order of occurrence. This is not to say that specific openings are identical in structure; variations may be observed.[2] Yet underlying these differences is a formal sequential organization that remains constant across the programmes examined, and across a wide range of topics and interviewees. The sequence and its components are briefly outlined. This method of initiating a state of interaction is then contrasted with openings in ordinary conversation, and it is shown that the differences are related to the non-spontaneous or 'staged' character of interview encounters.

Headline

Pre-headline Interviewers start off by encapsulating some newsworthy item in a general statement or 'headline'. Before launching into the headline, however, interviewers sometimes produce a preliminary or 'pre-headlining' item that leads toward the headline by setting up a puzzle of some kind. In example [1] below this pre-headlining task is accomplished by posing a question (lines 01–02), the answer to which is projected in the subsequent headline as the agenda for the upcoming interview (lines 03-04). ('I' below denotes 'Interviewer.')

> [1]   [*MacNeil/Lehrer* 13 June 1985a]
>
> 01 *I.*   How do authorities catch landlords or realtors who
> 02   discriminate against minorities?
> 03   There's an interesting proposal before Congress and
> 04   it's what we look at first tonight.

A preliminary puzzle may also be established by other means. For example, in extract [2] it is done through a series of provocative quotations (lines 01–04) which are initially unattributed, thereby posing a puzzle as to the author's identity. The solution is then provided immediately thereafter (05–07).

> [2]   [*Nightline* 3 June 1985]
>
> 01 *I.*   His comment on feminists: 'Send those chicks back to the
> 02   kitchen where they belong.' On Walter Mondale: 'A jar of
> 03   jelly.' And on the press: 'It's ridiculous for them to
> 04   say they speak for the American People.'
> 05   Throughout the years Patrick Buchanan has always been
> 06   controversial, but now he holds one of the most sensitive
> 07   posts on the Reagan White House staff.

Pre-headlines are plainly designed to capture the audience's attention and focus it on the next item – the headline proper. While not uncommon, pre-headlines appear to be optional, for interviewers frequently begin immediately with the headline itself.

Headline Headlines are packaged in two alternative formats. In the case of the *news announcement,* the interviewer straightforwardly reports some news item. Announcements may refer to a discrete event from the recent past (as in [3] below) or the near future [4].

> [3] [*MacNeil/Lehrer* 12 June 1985b]

I.   A major credit card forgery ring has been cracked by federal authorities.

[4]   [*MacNeil/Lehrer* 11 June 1985a]

I.   Tomorrow the Reagan administration makes another stab at getting aid for
       the rebels or contras fighting the Sandinista government of Nicaragua.

A more general social trend, theme or state of affairs may also be announced.

[5]   [*Nightline* 23 July 1985]

I.   Washington is split about what to do about South Africa and the debate is
       getting angrier.

Notice that the trend is marked as intensifying ('getting angrier').

The other major headlining format also involves the report of a news item,
but in this case it is framed as a topic for discussion. These are termed *agenda
projections,* for the news item is explicitly portrayed as the agenda to be
addressed in the upcoming interview. This is usually accomplished by preceding the news item with a preface like 'We focus tonight on . . .' (italicized
below).

[6]   [*MacNeil/Lehrer* 10 June 1985a]

I.   *We begin our focus sections tonight* with a closer look at today's announcement
       that the United States will continue to observe the limits of the never-ratified
       SALT II arms control treaty.

[7]   [*MacNeil/Lehrer* 12 June 1985a]

I.   *We focus first tonight on* the life and death of Karen Ann Quinlan, the young
       woman who became a symbol of one of the major issues of the 20th century,
       the right to die with dignity.

In [6] the embedded news item is a discrete event, while [7] contains a broader
theme, but both are presented as topics to be discussed.

Agenda projections may also convey information about the agenda by
identifying the participating interviewees. However, these are always used in
conjunction with some other headlining device. For instance, in [8] identification of the interviewees (03–08) follows a pre-headline (01–02).

[8]   [*Nightline* 24 July 1985]

01 *I.*   What's been accomplished in what the United Nations has
02   labeled the Decade for Women?
03   From the UN conference in Nairobi we'll talk with the
04   head of the US delegation, Maureen Reagan, with the head
05   of the Greek delegation, Margaret Papandreou, American-born
06   wife of the prime minister of Greece. And also, joining us
07   from Alexandria, Egypt, Jihan Sadat, widow of Egypt's Anwar
08   Sadat.

This leads to the final observation about the headline segment, namely that
it may be expanded to include multiple headlining devices.

[9]   [*Nightline* 4 June 1985]

01   From the A-bomb of 40 years ago to the most sophisticated
02   undersea weaponry of today, what has motivated Americans
03   to steal US military secrets for the Soviet Union?
04   Good evening. I'm Ted Koppel in Washington and this is
05   *Nightline.*

06   Our topic, the Walker family spy case and its role in the
07   continuing cloak and dagger war between the CIA and the KGB.
08   Our guests include a former deputy director of the CIA, and
09   from the federal penitentiary at Marion, Illinois,
10   Christopher Boyce, the so-called Falcon of 'Falcon and the
11   Snowman' fame, now serving 40 years for spying for the Soviets.

This elaborate segment contains a pre-headline (01–03), an agenda projection
with an embedded event (06) and theme (07), and another agenda projection
identifying the interviewees (08–11). Such combinations are especially common on *Nightline*, and appear to be connected with the fact that they are
opening the telecast itself, as well as a specific interview within it. Accordingly,
the host/interviewer and the programme title are also identified (04–05).

Story

After the headline comes a story segment that details relevant background
information. This segment exhibits the most variation in length and organization, and may contain taped reports prepared earlier. Stories are examined in
greater detail in later sections of this chapter. For now, it will suffice to
observe that the transition from headline to story may be marked in a variety
of ways. When the headline is an agenda projection, the transition is visible in
the shift from a statement of 'what we are going to talk about' to a discussion
of the events and circumstances themselves. In other instances (when the
headline is a news announcement) the transition may be overtly stated (06).

[10]   [*MacNeil/Lehrer* 11 June 1985b]

01 *I.*   As we reported earlier, the Reverend Charles Stanley was
02   re-elected president of the Southern Baptist Convention
03   today in a political struggle that happened not in the
04   world of politicians but in the ranks of the nation's
05   largest Protestant denomination.
06   Charlayne Hunter-Gault has our story. Charlayne?
07 *I2.*   Robin, it's been described as a holy war, but what it
08   really is is a fight between different factions of
09   Southern Baptists . . .

Overt story entry markers are generally used when the story segment is
lengthy, or when it entails a shift to another interviewer (as in [10] or to a
taped segment.

Entry into the story may also be marked in more subtle ways, through shifts
in verbal tense (usually from present to past) or temporal reference (usually
from the near-present to the past), or through a movement from existing states
of affairs to precipitating actions. The following illustrates a number of these
markers.

[11] [*MacNeil/Lehrer* 26 July 1985b]

I.   And there is still no deal on the overall budget.
  → All week long there have been reports of pressure and talk and new offers and
      potential breakthroughs . . .

Lead-in

The next segment prepares for entry into the interview proper, and centres around the task of introducing the interviewees. It has two components.

Pre-introduction   With occasional exceptions (see [15] below) introductions are generally preceded by an item that consists, minimally, of a preface such as the following.

[12]   [*MacNeil/Lehrer* 22 July 1985a]

I.   We hear first from . . .

[13]   [*MacNeil/Lehrer* 11 June 1985a]

I.   We pick up the debate now with . . .

These function to 'usher' the interviewees into the interaction. They may also convey advance information about the agenda at hand; in [13] for example, it is evident from the pre-introduction that the interview will take the form of a 'debate'. These same tasks may also be accomplished through more elaborate prefatory items such as the following, which provides advance information about the interviewee's identity preliminary to actually introducing her.

[14]   [*Nightline* 26 July 1985]

I.   In a moment we'll be joined by American journalist Lynda Schuster, who for the past year and a half has been eyewitness to the overwhelming problems that Argentina now faces.
       (Commercial break.)

I.   With us now live in our Miami Bureau . . .

Extended pre-introductions of this sort are particularly common when the opening segment is interrupted by a commercial break. Then the pre-introduction functions as a 'teaser', enticing the audience to stay tuned.

Introduction   In the final component of the opening segment, the interviewer identifies the guest interviewees to the audience. When multiple interviewees are present, they may all be introduced at this point; an alternative procedure is to limit the initial introduction to the first participant only, delaying the others until the point at which they are brought into the discussion. In either case introductions resemble the following (04–07), in which the interviewee's name is joined with other descriptive items.

[15]   [*MacNeil/Lehrer* 24 July 1985b]

```
01  I.   And that's one of the concerns that makes junk bonds as
02       troubling to some members of Congress as they are on
03       Wall Street.
04       Senator Pete Domenici, Republican of New Mexico, is one of
05       their most outspoken critics. He is the sponsor of legis-
06       lation that would sharply reduce the use of junk bonds in
07       hostile takeovers.
08       He's with us tonight from Capitol Hill.
09       Senator, what's the problem with using these things on
10       takeovers?
```

This particular introduction is somewhat atypical in that it lacks a prefatory item. However, the last sentence of the story segment (01–03) implicitly prepares for the introduction by shifting the topic toward 'members of Congress'. Moreover, the 'ushering-in' task ordinarily done in the pre-introduction is here accomplished after the identification segment (08). At any rate, the end of the introduction marks the completion of the opening segment, after which comes the first question (09–10).

Implications: the news interview as a stage encounter

When interview openings are contrasted with interactional openings in more 'informal' settings, such as casual conversation (see Schegloff, 1968, 1979, 1986; Jefferson, 1980), three features stand out as distinctive. These features combine to *visibly mark* the encounter as having been prearranged for the benefit of the viewing audience. First, many of the canonical elements of conversational openings are absent. In particular, there is no preliminary process through which speakers ordinarily exhibit their availability and readiness to interact (Schegloff, 1968, 1986). The problem of achieving coordinated entry into talk is a general one, and may be resolved through a verbal summons and answer sequence (Schegloff, 1968) or, in face-to-face interaction, through additional non-verbal processes employing gaze and bodily orientation to move toward interactional readiness (cf. Schiffrin, 1977; Heath, 1984). However, in news interviews no such process is observable; when the parties initially appear on screen, their physical comportment indicates that they are already 'primed' to interact. This pre-existing availability and readiness can be understood in light of the fact that interview participants arrive at the studio or are placed before remote camera links prior to air time; hence, they have already been aligned as interactants. And since they initially appear ready to proceed, but do not actually begin talking until they are introduced to the audience, the interaction appears to viewers as one that has been set up in advance expressly for their benefit.[3]

The second difference concerns the identification process. Speakers ordinarily take steps to identify those with whom they are interacting; indeed, mutual identification (by verbal or non-verbal means) is regularly the first order of business in conversational encounters (Schegloff, 1979, 1986). While news interview openings retain an identification process, it is transformed. The process is addressed exclusively to the audience when the interviewer (who is commonly identified earlier in the programme) introduces the guests. But the participants do not engage in any observable identification process among themselves. This modification can also be understood in light of prior social processes. Interviewees are sought, screened and invited to participate through a pre-interviewing process, and they agree to appear with full knowledge of the identities of those with whom they will be interacting. Moreover, the participants commonly meet briefly prior to air-time. This prior identification process permits the omission of such work on screen. Accordingly, the only identifications are addressed to the audience, further marking the interaction as having been prearranged for them.

Finally, interview openings must announce the topic of discussion in advance. This contrasts with topical organization in ordinary conversation, where topics are not predetermined (Sacks et al., 1974) but are instead negotiated – introduced, pursued and/or changed – within the interaction (Button and Casey, 1984; Maynard, 1980; Maynard and Zimmerman, 1984). News interview openings can stipulate their topics at the outset because they have been predetermined in accordance with relevant newsworthy events, a fact that becomes visible through the 'agenda-setting' shape of the opening sequence.[4]

It is commonplace to observe that news interviews are less than spontaneous, that they are to some degree 'staged' for audience consumption. The point here is that this staging has specific and identifiable consequences for the organization of interview talk and interaction. News interviews 'begin' in the context of prior interactional and institutional processes that have pre-assembled the relevant topics and participants. The opening that viewers witness is in this respect a false beginning. Consequently, when the on-air talk is initiated, some of the opening practices characteristic of conversational encounters become redundant and are thus omitted, while others become systematically specialized and transformed. The resulting shape of the opening sequence provides in part for the 'staged' quality that is such a familiar attribute of the broadcast news interview; it appears as something that has been planned in advance and is now being orchestrated on behalf of the viewing audience.[5]

Exhibiting newsworthiness: situating the interview within a sequence of newsworthy events

We have seen that the opening segment has a formal sequential organization that transcends particular programmes, topical agendas and interviewees. But this sequence is not produced as an end in itself. The opening is plainly designed to convey an agenda for the forthcoming interview and to situate it within an ongoing stream of newsworthy happenings. In this way, the occasion of talk is portrayed as a response to events and processes in the larger social world. Establishing this connection is a basic means of displaying the interview's 'newsworthiness', for it is through such discursive practices that the interview is linked to public occurrences in the wider society (cf. Lester, 1980).

As a first step in understanding how this connection is achieved, consider that an event/interview relationship may be straightforwardly displayed within the headline component alone. Recall that some headlines contain agenda projections that identify some outside event as a topic for discussion.

[16] [*MacNeil/Lehrer* 10 June 1985a]

I.   We begin our focus sections tonight with a closer look at today's announcement that the United States will continue to observe the limits of the never-ratified Salt II arms control treaty.

[17] [*MacNeil/Lehrer* 11 June 1985a]

> Tomorrow the Reagan administration makes another stab at getting aid for
> the rebels or contras fighting the Sandinista government of Nicaragua, and
> tonight we have a preview of the debate in Congress.

Agenda projections like these have two features that combine to exhibit an
event/interview connection. First, they establish an identity between some
exogenous event and the forthcoming topic of discussion. Notice that the focal
event need not precede the interview; in [17] the agenda is said to be a
'preview' of an upcoming congressional debate that will presumably be
touched off when the administration attempts to get contra aid 'tomorrow'.
But in both cases the interview is said to be about the reported happening.

Second, they contain temporal formulations that locate the event in relation
to the occasion of the interview.[6] Thus, in [16] the event is said to have
occurred in the recent past ('today'), while in [17] it is about to occur in the
near future ('tomorrow'). Such formulations clearly establish the timeliness of
the events, and they express that timeliness *in relation to* the occasion of the
interview. That is, rather than locate them on an abstract time-line (e.g.
'Wednesday' or '9 June 1985'), their location is expressed as some distance
from the present interaction (Schegloff, 1972: 116–17; see also Zerubavel,
1982). In addition, these particular examples also fix the present occasion
temporally ('tonight') and they do so through formulations that parallel and
thus hearably contrast with the timing of the precipitating event: 'tonight/
today' in [16] and 'tomorrow/tonight' in [17]. This imparts a sequential
coherence to these respective occurrences, portraying the present occasion of
talk as responsive to events in the larger social world.

An event/interview relationship may be similarly transparent in the pre-
introduction component. Some pre-introductions convey advance information about the topic, which often has to do with a timely event. The following
pre-introduction occurs after a story about differences between versions of the
budget offered by the House and Senate.

[18] [*MacNeil/Lehrer* 10 June 1985b]

> *I.*   We preview tomorrow's opening session now with two of the twenty-six who
>   must now find a way to bridge the differences . . .

Like the agenda projections examined above, this pre-introduction displays
an identity between the interview's agenda and an external event, temporally
locates the event in relation to the interview, and thus presents the interview as
having been occasioned by the reported event.

In other openings, however, the event/interview relationship is not established quite so explicitly. Headlines do not always contain agenda projections
with embedded events. Some agenda projections have more general themes
embedded within them (see [7] above), where the connection to any recent set
of events is not specified. Moreover, headlines need not contain agenda
projections at all; some simply announce a news item (see [3]–[5]) without
actually formulating it as a topic for discussion. Similarly, the pre-introduction need not contain advance information about the topic; some merely

'usher' the interviewees into the interaction (e.g. [12]; see also [14]). When these conditions are present, the interviewer announces a news item, elaborates background information and introduces the interviewees without ever actually *stating* that the interview will be dealing with the reported events. For example:

[19] [*MacNeil/Lehrer* 23 July 1985a]

I. President Reagan wants to change the way of the presidential veto. He wants the right to redline individual items in a spending bill rather than have to take it all or leave it all as he does now. It's called the line item veto, and it is so important to him that it was at the top of his lobbying agenda when he returned to the White House from the hospital this weekend. He has been on the phone the last few days trying to break a senate filibuster over it, but late today failed to pull it off. A move to end the filibuster came up three votes short; another attempt is expected tomorrow. The principal senate pusher of the legislation is Senator Mack Mattingly, Republican of Georgia. A principal opponent is Senator Lowell Weicker, Republican of Connecticut. Both are with us from Capitol Hill.

Yet even with this information, viewers can presumably recognize quite readily that the interview will indeed concern those events reported at the outset. This is made possible by the selection and arrangement of descriptive items within the opening. As we shall see, the interviewees are described in terms relevant to the events and themes reported earlier, while those events are characterized so as to be seen as leading up to the type of interview projected by the interviewee introductions. These various descriptive items are thus shaped to construct a coherent narrative in which the events and the interview emerge as elements of an interconnected sequence of happenings. The assembly of each element will be examined in turn, beginning with the interviewee introductions and working back to the precipitating events.

Introducing the interviewees

Consider, first, how interviewee introductions are put together. To understand this process is to grasp the principles of selection that govern the assembly of descriptive items within introductions. After describing these principles, we will consider how the resulting introductions function to set an agenda for the interview.

Person-description and introduction

Introductions consist primarily of person-descriptions, or utterances in which a person-reference term is coupled with one or more descriptive items (Maynard, 1982, 1984: 119–38). Thus, the interviewee's name and, frequently, title (arrows 1) are syntactically joined with other descriptive items (arrows 2).

[20] [*Nightline* 7 October 1986]

I. Joining us in our Washington bureau are
1→ Senator John Kerry of Massachusetts,
2→ a member of the State Foreign Relations Committee, and

2→ a critic of administration policy in Central America, and
1→ Congressman Dick Cheney of Wyoming,
2→ a leading proponent of aid to the contras,
2→ and member of the House Intelligence Committee.

A more complex person-description occurs when a person-descriptive item is itself described. In the following, the interviewee is first described as affiliated with an organization ('the Black Sash') (arrow 1), after which that organization is further characterized and described (arrows 2).

[21]   [*Nightline* 23 July 1985]

I.   With us now live also in our Washington bureau is Sheena Duncan,
      1→ president of a South African organization known as the Black Sash
      2a→ which, through three decades has come to symbolize white opposition to
            to apartheid in South Africa.
      2b→ Since 1976 public gatherings of members of the Black Sash organization in
            South Africa have been against the law.

Considered in isolation, these items simply described an organization, first (2a) as involving 'white opposition to apartheid', and then (2b) as one whose meetings have been outlawed. However, this occurs immediately after a person had been described as a member of that organization. In this context, organization-descriptions operate as an indirect means of further characterizing the person being introduced. That is, by describing the organizations to which the interviewees belong, such items are also descriptive of the interviewees themselves. Thus, as Maynard (1982: 196) has observed, in the last analysis it is conversational structure, or more generally the sequential structure of discourse, rather than grammar or syntax, that determines what is or is not a person-description.

Selecting descriptive items

What considerations govern the selection and assembly of descriptive items within introductions? To conceive of this as a problem requires some recognition of the fact that ordinary language descriptions in general are necessarily incomplete (Garfinkel, 1967: 35–53; Garfinkel and Sacks, 1970; Heritage, 1984: 150–7). Theoretically, acts of reference or description can always be elaborated indefinitely, but as a practical matter of course they must stop somewhere. This raises a problem of selection: given the indefinite extendability of any description, which features are properly chosen for inclusion?

    The answer, illuminated by a range of conversation analytic studies (e.g. Sacks, 1972, 1974; Schegloff, 1972; Drew, 1978; Watson, 1978; Maynard, 1982) is that selection decisions depend upon what situated activity is being accomplished in and through the description. The practice of describing is not a detached activity performed purely as an end in itself. Actual descriptions are always produced in some specific context for some practical purpose, and are addressed to an identifiable recipient. Particular descriptive items are selected in accordance with what is relevant in this situated context, for it is there that the description must accomplish whatever work it is called upon to do.

In news interviews, person-descriptions are transparently assembled in order to introduce the interviewees to the viewing audience. This activity occurs within a specific sequential context – the lead-in component of the opening sequence – which is transitionary between the prior detailing of newsworthy events and the subsequent interview. Accordingly, two contextual considerations seem especially relevant here, and they will be illustrated with reference to the following introductions (06–14 below). The preceding headline (01–02) reports that the talk will concern the 'state of emergency' recently declared by the South African government in response to escalating racial violence.

[22]   [*MacNeil/Lehrer* 22 July 1985a]

```
01   I.   Our major focus section tonight is South Africa and the
02        declaration of a state of emergency over the weekend.
03        We look first at recent events that have led to the
04        declaration.
05        (Taped story segment; 24 lines.)
06   I.   We hear first from the top South African official in the
07        United States, the ambassador designate, Herman Beukes.
08        (Interview with HB; 70 lines.)
09   I.   A different view on events in South Africa now from
10        Doctor Nthato Motlona, chairman and founder of the
11        Committee of Ten, an activist civic association in
12        Soweto, the black township near Johannesburg.
13        The group was formed in 1977 after riots swept
14        that township.
```

Notice first that these person-descriptions highlight facets of the interviewees' identities which are relevant to the focal event reported in the headline. In the first introduction, for example (06–07), the interviewee is characterized in terms of his occupation, which relates him to South Africa as that government's official spokesperson; he is thus identified as representing the primary agent in the focal event. (That the declaration of a state of emergency is a *government* action was conveyed earlier in the programme.)

The next interviewee (09–14) is connected to South Africa as a representative of blacks in that country, who as a category are also implicated in the focal event. However, much more descriptive work is required to accomplish this. He is initially described (10–11) as chairman and founder of an organization ('the Committee of Ten'). This description is then elaborated by a sequence of items, each designed to exhibit the relevance of this committee to South African race relations. Thus, the committee is described as 'an activist civic organization in Soweto' (11–12), which is followed by a description of Soweto (12) that identifies it racially and locates it near a larger South African city ('the black township near Johannesburg'), and another description of the organization (13–14) that elaborates on its involvement in black/white relations ('The group was formed in 1977 after riots swept that township').

Two contextual considerations appear to be operating in assembling these descriptive items, suggesting two principles of selection. The first governs the relevance of particular items. News interview introductions are designed to inform the audience of the interviewee's relationship to the upcoming agenda for discussion. And if previous arguments about an event/interview sequence are correct, the agenda should coherently follow from events reported earlier in the opening. The interviewee's identity should thus be formulated in a way that will align him or her to the focal matter, indicating the specific capacity in which he or she will be speaking to it. What is exhibited, then, is a topically aligned identity for the interviewee. This is clearly operating in the above introductions as only South African-relevant items are involved, and in particular those dealing with race relations there. (The only exception is in line (10) where the title 'Doctor' is employed, but titles have ritual significance which make them generally relevant on formal occasions such as this.) Accordingly, one principle governing the selection of descriptive items is the *topical relevance principle,* which operates as follows: select those components of interviewees' selves that are most relevant to the forthcoming topic as it is foreshadowed earlier in the opening (cf. Schegloff, 1972).

The second is an adequacy principle, which governs the elaborateness of each description. These descriptions are designed for an identifiable recipient: the viewing audience, which in this case consists mainly of the American public. Hence, in order for them to work as introductions, the topical relevance mentioned above must be made transparent enough so that most of the audience might be expected to grasp it. This appears to be what is at issue in the latter, more extended introduction above, in which the initial descriptive item (identifying Motlona as chairman and founder of 'the Committee of Ten') is systematically elaborated to specify its relevance to South African race relations. The trajectory of descriptive items thus implicates a second selectional principle, the *principle of recipient design:* make the interviewee's alignment to the topic explicit enough so as to be readily graspable by its intended recipient, which in this case is a typified sample of 'the American public' (cf. Schegloff, 1972; Sacks et al., 1974).

The operation of the second principle – recipient design – can be seen in the routine clarification of descriptive items when they might be presumed to be generally unfamiliar to the American public. The following extracts each contain an item (1) that is subsequently elaborated (2) (see also extract [21] above).

[23]   [*Nightline* 6 June 1985]

I.   We'll focus tonight on two of the issues raised by the ABC documentary 'The Fire Unleashed'. Nuclear reactors and nuclear waste. The tradeoff between risk and advantage.
         (*Background segment – 100 lines.*)
         (*Commercial break.*)

I.   With us now live at our affiliate KOAT in Albuquerque, New Mexico, Don Hancock, administrator of
    1→   the Southwest Research and Information Center,
    2→   a group dealing with energy and environmental issues.

[24]   [*MacNeil/Lehrer* 20 October 1986a]

I.   Our lead focus segment tonight is about Nicaragua, and what, if any, role the US government is or should be playing in the fight against the Sandinista government in Nicaragua.

(Background information – 8 lines.)
First, we turn to David Macmichael, who was an estimates officer on the
senior staff of the CIA from 1981 to 83.
He is now a senior fellow on
1→ the Council for Hemispheric Affairs,
2→ a Washington organization monitoring human rights and political developments in Central America.

Consider, for example, extract [24], where the acronym 'CIA' is readily
recognizable to Americans and is allowed to stand in its abbreviated form,
while the 'Council for Hemispheric Affairs' seems relatively obscure and is
thus clarified. By differentially handling these items, the interviewer audibly
treats them as having different degrees of familiarity.

The operation of the first principle – topical relevance – can be seen in the
methodical ways that interviewees are aligned as qualified to speak to the focal
matter. However, not all alignments are the same; they vary in the epistemological resources bestowed upon the interviewee. While alignments in general
indicate that the interviewees will be talking about previously reported events,
each projects a somewhat different type and level of expertise, and thus a
different treatment of the topic. In this regard, several alignment-types can be
briefly distinguished.

Participant–observer Interviewees may be shown to have first-hand knowledge of the focal matter. This may be conveyed by identifying them as
participants in the events or processes reported at the outset. For example, in
the following discussion of US–Soviet summitry, the interviewees are jointly
identified as having played 'key roles in East/West summit meetings in the
1970s' (07–08). Each party's specific summit experience is then outlined in
turn (09–13).

[25]   [*Nightline* 10 October 1986]

01 I. The practice of summitry; it's been going on for centuries,
02   but really, does the payoff match the pomp? . . . We'll go
03   behind the scenes of summit meeting strategy tonight as we
04   talk with two men who in past summits have been directly
05   involved in getting US and Soviet leaders ready.
06   *(Background segment – 100 lines.)*
07 I. Joining us now are two men who played key roles in
08   preparing for East–West summit meetings in the 1970s.
09   Former Soviet diplomat Arkady Shevchenko helped brief
10   Soviet Premier Leonid Brezhnev for the 1972 Nixon–Brezhnev
11   summit in Moscow. Former National Security official
12   William Hyland was involved in that summit and others with
13   presidents Nixon and Ford.

Alternatively, the interviewee may be said to be an eyewitness to the events
at hand.

[26]   [*Nightline* 26 July 1985]

I.   Twenty-five thousand people disappeared. Men, women, and innocent
       children, assumed murdered in a reign of terror in Argentina . . . Tonight, a
       unique inside look at an old ally but a new democracy, Argentina.
       (Background segment – 150 lines.)

I.   In a moment, we'll be joined by American journalist
Lynda Shuster, who for the past year and a half has been an
→   eyewitness to the overwhelming problems that Argentina faces.
(*Commercial break.*)
With us now live in our Miami bureau, *Wall Street Journal* correspondent
Lynda Schuster, whose area of expertise is Latin America and the
economy of Argentina.
→   Ms Schuster has recently returned from Argentina, where she witnessed
the climate of the ongoing trial and Argentina's economic situation.

Although her general expertise is also noted, special emphasis is placed on her
status as a direct witness. But whether identified as participant or witness, the
interviewee is aligned to offer comments as one with first-hand knowledge of
the subject under examination.

Certified expert   Interviewees may also be characterized as having specialized knowledge relevant to the focal news item. They are thus certified to
comment on it even though they may not have encountered it first-hand.
Expertise of this sort may be simply asserted (see line 05 below), but it is more
commonly displayed through descriptions of relevant organizational affiliation (06–07), publishing activities (08–09) and so on.

[27]   [*MacNeil/Lehrer* 14 June 1985a]

01   *I.*   Our first focus section is on the major news story of the
02   day, the hijacking of a TWA plane in the Middle East.
03   Joining us to try to shed some light on how this happened
04   and to piece together events there is
05   an expert on terrorism, Neil Livingston.
06   He is president of the Washington based Institute on
07   Terrorism and Subnational Conflict. Mr Livingston has
08   written two books on terrorism and America's ability to
09   combat it.

Advocate   Alignments may involve more than the interviewees' source of
relevant knowledge. They may also include each interviewee's opinion or
position on the focal matter (2, 3).

[28]   [*MacNeil/Lehrer* 13 June 1985a]

I.   How do authorities catch landlords or realtors who discriminate against
minorities? There's an interesting proposal before congress and it's what
we look at first tonight.
(*Background information – 8 lines.*)
1→ We have both sides of the argument now.
Phyllis Spiro of the Open Housing Council here in New York City
2→ supports federally funded testing.
William North, general counsel of the National Association of Realtors,
3→ opposes it.

When their perspectives are included (and they may be exhibited far less
directly than in this example, e.g. through party affiliations), the interviewees
are aligned as advocates prepared to defend a particular point of view. Here
the pre-introduction (1) also works to project advocacy identities. Frequently,

advocates come in pairs representing 'both' sides of the issue, and they are positioned to speak in an official capacity.

Each alignment-type projects a different treatment of story and, consequently, a distinct trajectory for the interview. The introduction of first-hand observers and certified experts foreshadows an *informational interview* where official insiders will provide background to the story. Alternatively, advocates project a markedly different *debate interview;* here the story is treated as a controversial issue such that divergent points of view will be exhibited and made to clash.[7] Significantly absent are non-official categories of interviewees; it is frequently observed that views outside the mainstream, as well as those of ordinary persons (e.g. those without official statuses or affiliations) are greatly underrepresented in news interviews (Nix, 1974; Hackett, 1985; Manoff, 1987). To some extent, this exclusionary process takes place behind the scenes, by selecting only official spokespersons as sources. However, every official is also a citizen, as well as a consumer, a taxpayer, a male or female, a homeowner or renter, etc. Hence, even after they have been chosen, some local work is required to establish the *official* facet of their identities as germane to the present occasion. And this occurs through the introductions, which bring relevant aspects of interviewees' selves to the fore, establishing a particular angle from which the topic will be addressed, and thus helping to constitute the lineaments of an agenda for discussion.

Repair

As final evidence of the topical relevance principle as an oriented-to feature of introductions, consider those introductions that are subsequently revised or repaired. Such repairs invariably address the *correctness* of a particular descriptive item, while accepting the relevance of that item and the general category of items to which it belongs.

In the following, repair is initiated by the interviewee (18–21) after the introduction has been completed and the first question is posed.

[29]   [*Nightline* 6 June 1985]

```
01   I.   We'll focus tonight on two of the issues raised by the ABC
02        documentary 'The Fire Unleashed'. Nuclear reactors and
03        nuclear waste. The tradeoff between risk and advantage.
04        (Background segment – 95 lines.)
05        (Commercial break.)
06   I.   With us now live at our affiliate KOAT in Albuquerque,
07        New Mexico, Don Hancock, administrator of The Southwest
08        Research and Information Center, a group dealing with
09        energy and environmental issues.
10        And in our New York Studios, Doctor Rosalyn Yalow, a
11        nuclear physicist who currently looks into the effects of
12        radiation on human beings for the Veterans Administration.
13        Doctor Yalow, in one of those little patented sound bites
14        that one hears in television news spots, we just heard you
15        a few moments ago saying that this problem of nuclear waste
16        is a soluble problem. Tell us about that, we need a little
17        encouragement this evening.
```

18   *RY* Well, first let me identify myself as not – my research is
19   not concerned with the effects of radiation on people.
20   My work is (radioimmunoassay), which is completely unrelated
21   to that.
22   *I.* My apologies.

The initial description of RY as a nuclear physicist engaged in research (11–12)
is squarely in line with the topic, announced earlier as 'nuclear reactors and
nuclear waste' (01–03). When RY revises this (18–21), she produces an
alternative characterization of her research, leaving intact her identity as a
nuclear physicist. Thus, while she clearly has an opportunity to repair the
introduction, she does not use it to invoke additional person-descriptions
highlighting other aspects of her self, choosing instead to replace an 'incorrect' descriptive item with an alternative taken from the same category of
items.

The following self-repair occurs later in the same interview, and exhibits a
similar orientation on the part of the interviewer. He is projecting the identity
of the next interviewee (a senator) in an extended pre-introduction, which he
subsequently revises (arrowed).

[30] [*Nightline* 6 June 1985]

> *I.*   . . . When we return, we'll broaden the discussion as we're joined by
>   Senator Jim McClure of Ohio, chairman of the Senate Energy and Natural
>   Resources Committee . . .
>   (*Commercial break.*)
> → *I.* First of all, a little correction very quickly. Senator John Glenn, Senator
>   Howard Metzenbaum, you need not call. I was wrong. Joining us live now
>   from Capitol Hill is Republican Senator Jim McClure, who is not from
>   Ohio, he's from Idaho, and he's chairman of the Senate Energy and
>   Natural Resources Committee and one of the backers of the 1982 Nuclear
>   Waste Policy Act.

Here the repair concerns the Senator's home state, and corrects the state
proposed earlier. But what remains constant through both the original and its
revision is the background assumption that it is his capacity as *senator* that is
the focus of attention on this occasion, and in particular his status as chair of
the Senate Energy and Natural Resources Committee.

Repairs thus operate in accordance with the same topical relevance principle, standing as further evidence of that as the fundamental principle determining focal aspects of interviewees' selves. Moreover, it is demonstrably
recognized and oriented-to by both interviewers and interviewees, because
regardless of who initiates repair, their revisions are conducted under the
auspices of that principle. Accordingly, who the interviewee is depends
fundamentally upon what he or she is present to talk about.

We now have a partial solution to the problem of achieving an event/inter-
view sequence. Introductions, because of the way they are built, project that
the interview will take up matters reported earlier in the opening. So even
when there is no agenda projection at the beginning, the introductions enable
viewers to infer that the interview will be dealing with, and hence was
occasioned by, previously reported events.

Assembling the precipitating news story

While introductions are fitted to the sequentially prior news item, the reverse process is also at work: the headline and story components are assembled in order to lead up to the interview that is about to take place. Rather than being a detached record of events, these items are methodically selected and combined to construct a particular version of events that will appropriately 'set the scene' for the discussion to follow. This will be demonstrated in two ways: first by comparing story formulations prior to informational interviews (those with observer and expert interviewees) versus those preceding debate interviews (those with advocate interviewees), and second by comparing pre-interview story formulations with those placed elsewhere in the news programme.

Story formulations preceding informational versus debate interviews

Pre-debate stories are always formulated to portray some unresolved disagreement or conflict, frequently concerning government policy. There are several ways of doing this. For one, a state of disagreement may be straightforwardly announced (arrowed).

[31] [*MacNeil/Lehrer* 6 October 1986b]

I.   Next tonight, we return to one of the hottest political issues of the day, drugs, and examine how politicians are dealing with it. With just four weeks left before the midterm elections, incumbent congressmen and senators are scrambling to come up with a new anti-drug program. And while there's near universal agreement that something should be done,
→   there is sharp disagreement on what exactly that should be.

Disagreement may also be exhibited by detailing the contrasting views that characterize opposing sides of the issue (see lines 03–07 below). Although it is noted these policy positions are similar in some respects (08–09), the similarities are backgrounded while the differences are foregrounded and highlighted.

[32] [*MacNeil/Lehrer* 10 June 1985b]

01 I. Tomorrow the hard part starts for twenty-six members of the House
02   and Senate. They are members of the conference committee which
03   must reach a compromise on the budget between a Senate version
04   that trims the cost of living increase for Social Security and
05   a House version that does not, a House version that freezes
06   defense spending and a Senate version that does not, and so on
07   down the seemingly poles-apart line,
08   although both do cut roughly the same amount from next year's
09   deficit, fifty-six billion dollars.

Finally, disagreement may be exhibited by formulating events in an 'action–reaction' sequence (cf. Maynard, 1988), where parties' moves and countermoves index their divergent views.

[33] [*MacNeil/Lehrer* 13 June 1985a]

01 I. ... The Reagan administration is pushing a new fund of some
02   four million dollars to help community groups set up such tests.

03   But the move is being fought by the National Association of
04   Realtors... We have both sides of the argument now...

Pre-debate stories thus exhibit a 'debatable' state of affairs, after which the
interview is presented as picking up on this ongoing clash of perspectives (04
above).

When disagreement is not apparent at relevant junctures, its absence is
notable and is commented upon by the interviewer. The following precedes a
debate interview concerning sanctions against South Africa.

[34]   [*MacNeil/Lehrer* 25 July 1985a]

          (*Discussing events since the South African Government declared a state of
          emergency.*)

01   I.   ... Today the story was the death of five more blacks and a
02   riotous clash with police outside Johannesburg, the arrest
03   total under the state of emergency going to 792, and
04   the move, led by France, to isolate the South African
05   government economically and diplomatically.
06   France took its sanctions call to the UN Security Council
07   late this afternoon and asked other nations of the world to
08   follow its lead.
09   South Africa is not a member of the UN General Assembly,
10   having been voted out some time ago, thus most of the words
11   heard today were those of condemnation. Here is an excerpt.
12   (*Cut to taped segment.*)
13   FA. (*Condemnation statement by the French ambassador.*)
14   DA. (*Condemnation statement by the Danish ambassador.*)
15   (*Return to the studio.*)
16   I.   The sanctions issue now as seen by two white South Africans:
17   Sheena Duncan, president of the anti-apartheid organization
18   known as the Black Sash, and John Chettle, director of the
19   Washington-based South Africa Foundation.

The story reports recent racial violence in South Africa (01–03) and the
reaction by the French government (04–08) calling for sanctions before the
UN. In the following taped segment, two UN ambassadors are shown making
statements on the sanctions issue (13–14). Both statements favour sanctions
and condemn the South African government; they display consensus rather
than conflict. However, this is noted in advance by the interviewer (09–11),
who provides an account to explain why only condemnations will be heard. By
doing so, he takes special steps to indicate that there are 'really' two sides to
this issue, even though only one is to be heard in the opening. He thus
continues to convey a situation of controversy consistent with the forthcoming
interview. And the lead-in to the interview (16–19) subtly projects a debate,
first (16) by referring to the topic as an 'issue', and marking the subjectivity of
the interviewees' views ('as seen by...'). While both interviewees are cate-
gorized as 'white South Africans' (16), invoking the common-sense expectation
that they might both be opposed to sanctions, one is described as president of
an anti-apartheid organization (17), and is thus defined as an 'atypical' white
South African, one who can be expected to favour sanctions. The ingredients
for a sanctions debate are thus assembled.

When the interview is of the informational variety, that is, when the guests serve as participants, observers, or experts rather than advocates, the story is formulated in very different terms. Pre-informational story formulations report discrete events while indicating little if any conflict or disagreement surrounding them. Indeed, subjective interpretations of matters are generally absent.

[35]   [*MacNeil/Lehrer* 10 June 1985a]

```
01   I.   We begin our focus sections tonight with a closer look at
02        today's announcement that the United States will continue
03        to observe the limits of the never-ratified SALT II arms
04        control treaty. A decision was needed because the US
05        strategic force is nearing a key treaty limitation, the
06        number of allowed multiple-warhead missiles, which carry
07        more than one nuclear weapon. SALT II allows each side
08        1200. The Soviets now have 1130; the US, 1190. The
09        sea trials of a new US Trident submarine would put the
10        US 14 missiles over the limit. That violation was
11        avoided by the President's decision to withdraw a Poseidon
12        submarine from service, which keeps the US level at 1198,
13        two under the SALT II limit. As we reported, today's
14        decision was made despite administration findings that the
15        Soviets have violated some of the terms of the 1979 treaty.
16        With us for a newsmaker interview is Kenneth Adelman,
17        director of the Arms Control and Disarmament Agency.
```

The headline here (01–04) is an agenda projection indicating that the discussion will concern a recent event: the US government's decision to continue to observe the SALT II treaty. The introduction (16–17) foreshadows an 'insider's' view of the event by identifying the guest as an administration official close to the decision; note that in addition to his status as an arms control official (17), the discussion is characterized as a 'newsmaker interview' (16). Hence, rather than a partisan debate over the decision's merits, or an independent assessment of it, this introduction projects a specifically technical and official discussion of its details. Consistent with this agenda, the intervening story segment (04–15) details the various technical conditions surrounding the decision; it outlines the treaty limitations (05–07), reports the number of warheads on each side (08), and explains why the decision had to be made at this time (09–13). This prepares for an insider interview dealing with the decision itself and the reasoning behind it. While the interviewer does note that the decision was made in spite of apparent Soviet violations (13–15), thus raising perhaps the spectre of controversy, this is not the focus of the story. Indeed, this item is placed last in a context where it can be heard as merely another condition under which the decision was made. Pre-informational and pre-debate story formulations thus have distinct systems of relevance, the former emphasizing the circumstances and implications of events, and the latter focusing on the situation controversy generated by or embodied in events.

Pre-interview versus news roundup story formulations

The argument advanced thus far would be trivial if it could be argued that the selection of an informational or debate format for the interview *and* its corresponding story formulation were determined by the objective essence of the events 'out there'. However, a comparison of pre-interview story formulations with alternative formulations placed elsewhere in the same news programme does not support such a contention. The *MacNeil/Lehrer NewsHour* can accommodate such a comparison, because the programme begins with a (roughly) 10-minute news 'roundup' or summary of the day's major stories. Hence, the pre-interview story formulation may be contrasted with its counterpart in the news roundup segment, thereby illuminating the manner in which story formulations are fitted to their sequential location within the programme.

To begin, compare the above pre-interview story concerning SALT II [35] to a corresponding story that appeared in the news summary.

[36]   [*MacNeil/Lehrer* 10 June 1985]

```
01   I.    The United States will remain in compliance with SALT II
02         despite violations of that unratified nuclear arms treaty
03         by the Soviet Union. President Reagan's decision was
04         announced today following weeks of speculation and advice
05         on what it should be. The decision means the United States
06         will remain under the nuclear warhead missile limits of
07         SALT II by dismantling an old submarine when a new Trident
08         sub is launched this fall. The announcement was accompanied
09         by a warning to Soviet leader Mikhail Gorbachev that the
10         Soviets must quit violating the treaty's terms. National
11         Security Advisor Robert McFarlane did the talking and
12         explaining for Mr Reagan this afternoon.
13         (Cut to tape of Robert McFarlane at a press conference.)
14   RM.   The pattern of Soviet violations, if left uncorrected,
15         undercuts the integrity and viability of arms control as
16         an instrument to assist in ensuring a secure and stable
17         future world. The United States will continue to pursue
18         vigorously with the Soviets the resolution of our concerns
19         over Soviet noncompliance. However, in the interests of
20         assuring that every opportunity to establish the secure,
21         stable future that we seek is fully explored, I am prepared
22         to go the extra mile to seek an interim framework of truly
23         mutual restraint. This is not an open-ended commitment in
24         perpetuity. We will evaluate Soviet compliance, Soviet
25         building programs, their performance in Geneva – all of
26         these things and, as milestones are reached in the future,
27         the decision may be different.
```

This formulation contains few technical details about the treaty or conditions surrounding the decision to honour it; the only exception is one sentence (05–08) explaining what compliance will mean. Thus, unlike the pre-interview version, there is no direct mention of the treaty's specific terms, nor the numbers of warheads on each side, nor why a decision was necessary at this time. Moreover, the question of Soviet violations, which is treated as only one of the various situational conditions in the pre-interview version, here takes a much more prominent position. From the very first statement (01–03) the decision is framed as having been made 'despite violations' by the USSR. This highlights the controversial nature of the decision, a property which is further emphasized by noting that the decision followed 'weeks of speculation and advice' (04). And in addition to the decision itself, this story reports another event that 'accompanied' the announced decision (08–10): an official warning to Gorbachev to 'quit violating the treaty's terms'. This is followed by a rather extended taped segment (14–27) showing the warning itself as it was issued at a press conference.

In short, this version portrays the treaty decision as a controversial public event, and links it to another public event (a warning to the Soviets) designed to counteract potential reservations. At the same time, technical details are minimized and downplayed. This is in marked contrast to the pre-interview version, where the focus is on the details surrounding the decision; hence the inclusion of specific circumstances and conditions under which the decision was made. The point is not merely that this version is different; rather, the nature of these differences highlight the manner in which the pre-interview version is fitted to its larger sequential location *vis-à-vis* the interview.

In the final example, the contrast between the pre-interview and roundup versions is similarly marked, although in this case even the roundup version is influenced – although to a lesser degree – by the existence of an eventual interview. First the pre-interview version, which begins (01–04) with a headline projecting a congressional debate over aid for the Nicaraguan contras, a debate sparked by Reagan administration initiatives.

[37]   [*MacNeil/Lehrer* 11 June 1985a]

```
01   I.   Tomorrow the Reagan administration makes another stab at
02        getting aid for the rebels or contras fighting the
03        Sandinista government of Nicaragua, and tonight we have a
04        preview of the debate in Congress. Last April the House
05        said no aid, but some minds appear to have been changed
06        by the subsequent visit of Sandinista leader Daniel Ortega
07        to Moscow. Last week the Senate approved an aid package of
08        38 million dollars. Tomorrow the House votes on two
09        different packages: one for 14 million dollars, the other
10        27 million. President Reagan tried to woo some more House
11        Democrats today with a letter promising to explore direct
12        talks with the Sandinistas and adding, we do not seek the
13        military overthrow of the Sandinista government. We pick
14        up the debate now with two Democrats, Congressman Lee
15        Hamilton from Indiana, chairman of the House Intelligence
16        Committee and co-sponsor of the 14 million dollar package,
17        and Congressman Dave McCurdy of Oklahoma, who as we saw was
18        one of the Democrats to support the larger contra aid
19        package and who met with the President at the White House
20        today.
```

The story leads toward this debate by reporting recent events that may alter congressional sympathies (04–07), identifying various positions within the House and Senate (07–10) and reporting Reagan's recent efforts to 'woo' members of Congress over to his side by promising direct talks with the Sandinistas (10–13). These events each include temporal formulations relating them to the present occasion, and are arranged to temporally zero in on it: 'last April' (04), 'last week' (07), 'tomorrow' (08), 'today' (11). All of this is fitted to the final introductions leading into the interview proper, which begin with a prefix ('We pick up the debate now . . .') presenting the interview as the next phase of this developing debate.

The roundup version, in contrast, has a completely different lead focus.

[38]   [*MacNeil/Lehrer* 11 June 1985]

```
01   I.   President Reagan said today he is exploring the possibility
02        of resuming direct talks with the Sandinista government of
03        Nicaragua. He said it in a letter he gave members of
04        Congress in a White House meeting. Both the letter and
05        the meeting are part of the administration's new effort to
06        get some kind of funds for the anti-Sandinista contra
07        guerrillas. The House is to vote on a 27 million dollar
08        compromise proposal tomorrow. Several Democrats who voted
09        against contra aid last month were at the White House today
10        and said they could support the new proposal.
11        (Taped statement of Congressman Dave McCurdy follows.)
12   I.   We will hear later from Congressman McCurdy and others in
13        a focus segment on the contra aid question.
```

Here the story lead (01–03) says nothing about Reagan's controversial efforts to get contra aid through Congress. Instead, the primary focus is on his publicly announced intention to resume 'direct talks with the Sandinista government.' This is only later put into the context of contra aid (04–07); only then does it become identified as an effort to influence Congress to provide aid. This contrasts with the pre-interview version, which focuses on Reagan's contra aid efforts and reactions within Congress from the beginning.

But while the roundup version has a different initial focus, it later shifts matters toward the anticipated congressional debate (07–10), and then runs a taped statement on this issue by one Democratic congressman (11) who is now prepared to support the President. This occurs just prior to an agenda projection within the roundup segment (12–13) foreshadowing the interview to come. Hence, this version eventually shifts toward the topic of the interview, and this shift is sequentially fitted to the agenda projection that closes the story. It would appear, then, that even the news summary at the beginning of the telecast may be subtly shaped by the fact that associated interviews are going to take place later on in the programme.

One implication is that the interview's agenda cannot properly be regarded as a straightforward response to preconstituted exogenous events. Indeed, it is misleading to conceive of occurrences as having a singular, determinate character prior to the occasion of talk, for those occurrences may be characterized in divergent and contrasting ways, each of them in some sense 'correct.' But as they are formulated within the opening, occurrences take on a particular shape and form because of the manner in which they are going to be talked about; they are selected and assembled in order to lead up to the kind of interview that is about to take place. The substantive and causal linkages between exogenous events and the present interview are thus *achieved* through discursive practices that constitute the opening segment.

Concluding remarks

This has been a study of some highly routine but thoroughly unremarkable speaking practices that organize news interview openings. Through these practices, the opening segment achieves specific institutional ends: (a) it marks the encounter from the outset as having been preassembled on behalf of the viewing audience, and (b) it sets an agenda for the interview, one that is linked to newsworthy events in the world at large. These are of course commonplace and obvious features of the news interview; upon witnessing an opening, anyone can presumably 'see at a glance' that the encounter has been staged for audience consumption, and that it was occasioned by prominent events in the news. But the aim here has been to push beyond the commonplace to analyse the underlying procedural logic by which these obvious characteristics are achieved and conveyed. To this end, we have outlined a formal sequential structure for news interview openings, and have specified the selectional principles that govern the assembly of items to fill specific 'slots' within the sequence. These procedures pervasively and recurrently organize interview openings, and they produce some of the most familiar qualities of news interview discourse.

While the immediate objective of this chapter has been to describe and analyse these language practices and their functions, the findings bear on one fundamental issue in media studies: how news is shaped by the institutional processes involved in its production. But the present study illuminates this issue from a decidedly different angle. Most research has focused on the routines of newsgathering, reporter–source relationships, ideological orientations and other behind-the-scenes aspects of journalistic practice to determine how these factors influence the content of news. In contrast, the focus of the current study are those practices of language and interaction which serve as the media through which news is packaged and presented to the audience. While the domain of discourse is no doubt responsive to prior bureaucratic and ideological processes, it is not wholly reducible to such factors; it has its own intrinsic organizational integrity (cf. Sacks et al., 1974). And as one corner of it, the news interview opening has organizational properties that demonstrably influence the content of news in two respects.

First, openings function to set an agenda for the interview; they both define and delimit the parameters of permissible discussion. This is significant for the social construction of news because, for a variety of technological and organizational reasons, news in both England the United States is increasingly being generated through processes of spoken interaction (Heritage et al., 1988). Thus, relatively spontaneous interactional encounters are coming to replace fully scripted news reports, and the growth of the news interview is one manifestation of this trend. In this context, news content cannot be fully explained without first understanding how topical agendas are established and enforced within such interactional encounters. The present analysis of the interview opening addresses one component of this process. It is important to avoid overstating the significance of the opening sequence; it does not create an impenetrable barrier within which participants are trapped throughout the course of the interview. However, it does establish a set of discussion parameters and makes them available to the participants as well as the audience of 'overhearers', thus creating at least the necessary conditions for their enforcement. Future research should follow the lead of Greatbatch (1986a, 1986b) to determine how topical agendas are managed within the interview, and consider further how the opening segment figures in this process.

While the opening segment articulates an agenda *within* the interview, it is possible to view that agenda as a product, originally, of newsworthy events in the larger social world. However, such events are complex and multifaceted, and may be correctly characterized in a variety of contrasting ways; they have no singular, determinate character. Out of the range of possible accounts, the opening constructs a particular version of events that will warrant the type of interview that is about to take place. Hence, as we have seen, stories preceding informational interviews differ from stories preceding debate interviews, and pre-interview stories in general differ from corresponding accounts that appear elsewhere in the news programme. The structure of the opening thus exerts an influence on the portrayal of events that ostensibly precipitated the interview, and any witnessable event/interview connection is achieved in part through such descriptive practices.

In a similar vein, researchers have observed, following Weaver (1975), that television news discourse has a sequential coherence that structures news content both within and across stories. Thus, stories for broadcast are organized into narratives with recognizable beginnings, middles and ends, and adjacent stories are combined into clusters according to common themes and topics. As a consequence, component stories appear to be selected and shaped to coherently fit within a thematic cluster (Altheide, 1977:75; Weaver, 1975; Paletz and Pearson, 1978). Discursive conventions of this kind appear to vary across cultural boundaries (Hallin and Mancini, 1984), and a somewhat different set of conventions seems to operate in printed news (Weaver, 1975; van Dijk, 1988). Nevertheless, together with the present study, these observations point to a largely unexplored domain in media studies: the routine, institutionalized language practices that serve to organize news discourse, and in particular the sequential conventions that govern the construction of coherent stretches of discourse. While this domain may seem rather mundane in comparison to the domain of ideology, and perhaps trivial in comparison to large-scale institutional forces, it is nevertheless a significant dimension of newswork, a dimension with its own organizational practices and constraints. Our grasp of the institutional frameworks of news production will remain incomplete until the domain of discourse is more thoroughly explored.

Notes

I'm grateful to Doug Maynard for reading and commenting on an earlier version of this paper. This research was supported in part by grant MH14641 from the National Institute of Mental Health.

1. For a more specialized analysis of a single, dramatic opening, see Pomerantz (1989).

2. *Nightline*, for example, has more elaborate openings than *The MacNeil/Lehrer NewsHour*. This is due in part to the fact that in the former the interview's opening is coterminous with the opening of the programme as a whole and is expanded to deal with that task, while the latter programme opens with a news summary or overview of the days events, this summary preceding the specific interview segments.

3. This should not be taken to imply that this absence is a necessary feature of prearranged encounters. For example, on celebrity talk shows in the US guests are commonly brought onstage as they're introduced, enabling the audience to witness their physical movement toward one another and into a state of talk. This creates at least the veneer of an interaction that appears to be 'just beginning', even though such encounters are known to be planned, and the parties may well have spoken to one another prior to air-time. What is being proposed here is that the participants' previously exhibited availability and readiness to interact *enables* them to dispense with the ordinary processes of entry, and that by doing so they visibly *mark* the interaction as following from some prior set of arrangements. (For a further discussion of the relatively 'informal' or 'conversational' character of chat shows versus news interviews, see Greatbatch, 1988.)

4. Greetings and 'how are you' are also notably absent, but this will not be dealt with in detail here. However, Whalen and Zimmerman (1987) have noticed similar absences in citizen calls to the police. They demonstrate that it is through such absence that the participants exhibit an orientation to the focused 'institutional' character of the interaction. This may achieve a similar end in news interviews as the participants address one another as incumbents of particular identities. Furthermore, since the interview opening that appears on television is really a 'false' beginning, greetings and 'how-are-yous' would seem to be technically redundant at this juncture and thus may be expendable. Other work may also be achieved by these absences, including an orientation to the question/answer turn-taking system characteristic of interview talk (Greatbatch, 1988). That is, by omitting greetings, 'how-are-yous,' and other canonical interactional sequences, parties display strict adherence to the restriction that they produce only questions and answers within their turns.

5. For an analysis of other ways in which news interview talk is organizationally designed as 'talk for an overhearing audience', see Heritage (1985).

6. Temporal formulations are sometimes absent within agenda projection/headlines, but this appears to occur only when the timeliness of the embedded event has already been established earlier in the programme (e.g. in a prior news summary), or when it is taken to be something that 'everyone' knows, as with certain major stories that have already received widespread coverage.

7. News personnel orient to these different categories of interviews, and they select interviewees in accordance with predetermined format considerations (Gladstone, 1986; Hill, 1987; Clayman, 1987: 150–1).

References

Altheide, David L. (1977) *Creating Reality: How TV News Distorts Events*. Newbury Park: Sage.

Button, Graham and Neil Casey (1984) 'Generating Topic: The Use of Topical Initial Elicitors', pp. 167–90 in J.M. Atkinson and J. Heritage (eds), *Structures of Social Action*. Cambridge: Cambridge University Press.

Clayman, Steven E. (1987) 'Generating News: The Interactional Organization of News Interviews.' Doctoral Dissertation, Department of Sociology, University of California, Santa Barbara.

Clayman, Steven E. (1988) 'Displaying Neutrality in Television News Interviews', *Social Problems*, 35(4): 474–92.

Clayman, Steven E. (forthcoming) 'Footing in the Achievement of Neutrality: The Case of News

Interview Discourse', in Paul Drew and John Heritage (eds), *Talk at Work*. Cambridge: Cambridge University Press.

Drew, Paul (1978) 'Accusations: The Occasioned Use of Members' Knowledge of "Religious Geography" in Describing Events', *Sociology*, 12(1): 1–22.

Garfinkel, Harold (1967) *Studies in Ethnomethodology*. Englewood Cliffs: Prentice-Hall.

Garfinkel, Harold and Harvey Sacks (1970) 'On Formal Structures of Practical Actions', pp. 338–66 in J.C. McKinney and E.A. Tiryakian (eds), *Theoretical Sociology*. New York: Appleton Century Crofts.

Gans, Herbert (1979) *Deciding What's News*. New York: Vintage Books.

Gladstone, Valerie (1986) 'MacNeil and Lehrer and the Art of Talking', *Dial*, May: 16–18, 45.

Greatbatch, David (1986a) 'Aspects of Topical Organization in News Interviews: The Use of Agenda Shifting Procedures by Interviewees', *Media, Culture and Society*, 8(4): 441–55.

Greatbatch, David (1986b) 'Some Standard Uses of Supplementary Questions in News Interviews', pp. 86–123 in John Wilson and Brian Crow (eds), *Belfast Working Papers in Language and Linguistics*, Vol. 8. Jordanstown: University of Ulster.

Greatbatch, David (1988) 'A Turn-Taking System for British News Interviews', *Language in Society*, 17: 401–30.

Hackett, Robert A. (1985) 'A Hierarchy of Access: Aspects of Source Bias in Canadian TV News'. *Journalism Quarterly*, 62(2): 256–65, 277.

Hallin, Daniel C. and Paolo Mancini (1984) 'Speaking of the President: Political Structure and Representational Form in US and Italian Television News', *Theory and Society*, 13(6): 829–50.

Harris, Sandra (1986) 'Interviewers' Questions in Broadcast Interviews', pp. 50–85 in John Wilson and Brian Crow (eds), *Belfast Working Papers in Language and Linguistics*, Vol. 8. Jordanstown: University of Ulster.

Heath, Christian (1984) 'Talk and Recipiency: Sequential Organization in Speech and Body Movement', pp. 247–65 in J.M. Atkinson and J. Heritage (eds), *Structures of Social Action*. Cambridge: Cambridge University Press.

Heritage, John (1984) *Garfinkel and Ethnomethodology*. Cambridge: Polity Press.

Heritage, John (1985) 'Analyzing News Interviews: Aspects of the Production of Talk for an Overhearing Audience', pp. 95–117 in Teun A. van Dijk (ed.), *Handbook of Discourse Analysis, Vol. 3: Discourse and Dialogue*. London: Academic Press.

Heritage, John C., Steven E. Clayman and Don H. Zimmerman (1988) 'Discourse and Message Analysis: The Micro-Structure of Mass Media Messages', pp. 77–109 in R. Hawkins, S. Pingree and J. Weimann (eds), *Advancing Communication Science: Merging Mass and Interpersonal Processes*. Sage Annual Reviews of Communication Research, Vol. 16. Newbury Park: Sage.

Heritage, John and David Greatbatch (forthcoming) 'On the Institutional Character of Institutional Talk: The Case of News Interviews', in D. Boden and D. Zimmerman (eds) *Talk and Social Structure*. Cambridge: Polity Press.

Hill, Doug (1987) 'Ted Koppel's *Nightline:* It's Now *The* Arena for Quizzing Today's Newsmakers', *TV Guide*, 10 Jan: 4–9.

Jefferson, Gail (1980) 'On Trouble-Premonitory Response to Inquiry', *Sociological Inquiry*, 50(3/4): 153–85.

Lester, Marilyn (1980) 'Generating Newsworthiness: The Interpretive Construction of Public Events', *American Sociological Review*, 45(6): 984–94.

Manoff, Robert Karl (1987) 'Quick-Fix News: MacNeil/Lehrer Play it Safe', *The Progressive*, 51(7): 15.

Maynard, Douglas W. (1980) 'Placement of Topic Changes in Conversation', *Semiotica*, 30: 263–90.

Maynard, Douglas W. (1982) 'Person-Description in Plea Bargaining', *Semiotica*, 42(2/4): 195–213.

Maynard, Douglas W. (1984) *Inside Plea Bargaining: The Language of Negotiation*. New York: Plenum.

Maynard, Douglas W. (1988) 'Narratives and Narrative Structure in Plea Bargaining', *Law and Society Review*, 22(3): 449–81.

Maynard, Douglas, W. and Don H. Zimmerman (1984) 'Topical Talk, Ritual, and the Social Organization of Relationships', *Social Psychology Quarterly*, 47: 301–16.

Nix, Mindy (1974) 'The Meet the Press Game', pp. 66–71 in G. Tuchman (ed.), *The TV Establishment*. Englewood Cliffs: Prentice-Hall.

Paletz, D.L. and Pearson R.E. (1978) ' "The Way You Look Tonight' ': A Critique of Television News Criticism', pp. 65–85 in W. Adams and F. Schreibman (eds), *Television Network News: Issues in Content Research*. Washington, DC: School of Public and International Affairs, George Washington University.

Pomerantz, Anita (1989) 'Constructing Skepticism: Four Devices Used to Engender the Audience's Skepticism', *Research on Language and Social Interaction*, 22: 293–314.

Sacks, Harvey (1972) 'An Initial Investigation of the Usability of Conversational Data for Doing Sociology', pp. 31–74 in D. Sudnow (ed.), *Studies in Social Interaction*. New York: Free Press.

Sacks, Harvey (1974) 'On the Analyzability of Stories by Children', pp. 216–32 in R. Turner (ed.), *Ethnomethodology*. Harmondsworth: Penguin.

Sacks, Harvey, Emanuel A. Schegloff and Gail Jefferson (1974) 'A Simplest Systematics for the Organization of Turn Taking for Conversation', *Language*, 50: 696–735.

Schegloff, Emanuel A. (1968) 'Sequencing in Conversational Openings', *American Anthropologist*, 70: 1075–95.

Schegloff, Emanuel A. (1972) 'Notes on a Conversational Practice: Formulating Place', pp. 75–119 in D. Sudnow (ed.), *Studies in Social Interaction*. New York: Free Press.

Schegloff, Emanuel A. (1979) 'Identification and Recognition in Telephone Call Openings', pp. 23–78 in G. Psathas (ed.), *Everyday Language: Studies in Ethnomethodology*. New York: Irvington.

Schegloff, Emanuel A. (1986) 'On the Achievement of "Routine" ' *Human Studies*.

Schiffrin, Deborah (1977) 'Opening Encounters', *American Sociological Review*, 42(5): 672–91.

van Dikj, Teun A. (1988) *News as Discourse*. Hilldale, NJ: Lawrence Erlbaum.

Watson, D.R. (1978) 'Categorization, Authorization and Blame-Negotiation in Conversation', *Sociology*, 12: 105–13.

Weaver, Paul (1975) 'Newspaper News and Television News', pp. 81–94 in Douglas Cater and Richard Adler (eds), *Television as a Social Force: New Approaches to TV Criticism*. New York: Praeger Publishers.

Whalen, Marilyn and Don H. Zimmerman (1987) 'Sequential and Institutional Contexts in Calls for Help', *Social Psychology Quarterly*, 50: 172–85.

Zerubavel, Eviatar (1982) 'The Standardization of Time: A Sociohistorical Perspective', *American Journal of Sociology*, 88(1): 1–23.

5

Evasive Action: How Politicians Respond to Questions in Political Interviews

Sandra Harris

One of the funniest episodes of the BBC2 series *Yes, Minister* included the following exchange between Jim Hacker, as a then Cabinet Minister, and a television interviewer:

I.   Now Minister – are you laying the foundations of the police state?

JH.   You know – I'm glad you asked me about that question

I.   Well Minister – could we have the answer?

JH.   Well yes of course – I'm just about to give it to you – if I may – uh – yes – as I said I'm glad you asked me that question because [pause] it's a question [pause] a lot of people are asking – because a lot of people want to know the answer to it – and let's be quite clear about this – without beating about the bush – the plain fact of the matter is – that it's a very important question indeed – and people have a right to know

I.   Minister – we haven't yet had the answer

JH.   I'm sorry – what was the question?[1]

Like so much in the *Yes, Minister* series, the satire in this extract trades on the widespread and not very flattering public perception of politicians and the workings of Whitehall. This particular episode plays on one of the most prevalent qualities which the public at large attribute to politicians as a generic breed – evasiveness, symbolized here by the manifest failure of Jim Hacker to give a straight answer to a straight question.

What are the roots of this widespread belief among their constituents that politicians are evasive? *Do* politicians fail to answer interviewers' questions? Are some politicians more evasive than others? If differences do exist among individual politicians, are these related in any way to 'political style', to the image-making process through which all major politicians must at some time define their versions of policy-making substance?

A number of recent researchers have commented on the tendency of mass communication studies in the past to concentrate on the substance and production of media messages, taking little or no account of interactional and stylistic features, of how that 'substance' is assembled and generated dynamically in actual media 'talk' (Greatbatch, 1987; Clayman, 1988, 1990; Clayman and Whalen, 1989). Given that much of what most of us actually experience of politics consists of the highly visible competing discourses of politicians, it has become clear that political style cannot be considered merely as a neutral 'medium' for the exchange and transmission of ideas. To analyse the structure and content of political discourse apart from the interactional medium within which it is generated seems increasingly unrealistic (see Heritage et al., 1988).

It thus seems appropriate that the apparent 'evasiveness' of politicians should be satirized in the form of a political interview, since such interviews have become high-profile speech events and a crucial testing ground for politicians. Indeed, in the American context also, Clayman and Whalen (1989) maintain that in recent years such interviews on television have 'emerged as a central vehicle for the dissemination of news and public affairs information' (p. 341).[2] And in the British context, Patrick Hannan has argued that:

> Certainly the way we perceive our leaders and the way they present themselves to us has been radically altered by the political interview on radio and television... The interview is one of the most important ways in which the political debate is conducted. It's a key way in how *they* communicate with *us*.[3]

The development of the broadcast interview, and especially the political news interview, into an important means of journalistic enquiry and the increasing tendency of interviewers to aim at challenging, interesting and often controversial discourse has been much remarked on both by British media interviewers themselves (e.g. Day, 1961, 1975, 1991; Dimbleby, 1975; Walden, 1985) and by academics such as Wedell (1968), Kumar (1975), Burns (1977), Whale (1977) and others. The increasing tendency of interviewers to aim at producing controversial discourse in the adversarial mode has undoubtedly changed the character of the broadcast interview in the UK since the 1950s and the advent of ITV (Independent Television), when interviewees, especially if they were major politicians, were arguably treated with greater deference.

More recently, however, Robin Day has maintained that in the 1980s there has been a further change in the character of the British political interview. Once again, he has suggested, interviews have tended to become a source of 'propaganda' for politicians, not because interviewers are deferential and fail to challenge them on major issues, but because in a much more obvious way they are not answering interviewers' questions:

> On both sides of the political fence there is now a tendency to use an interview – whether on radio or television – simply to say what you want to say – to repeat what you have to say – to ignore the questions – to repeat your statement irrespective of whether it bears any relationship to the – to what most people would regard as the truth and uh let the interviewer cope with it – the interviewer can only cope with it by – by uh – he can't suggest the person concerned is telling an untruth – there's a limit to the amount he can go on asking the same question – and in fact that technique – under that technique the answers are made longer and longer so that the question is forgotten.[4]

This raises a number of interesting issues. Not only do political interviews play a significant part in the political process but they also provide a reasonably consistent framework of questions and answers, inasmuch as natural language situations can ever be consistent. Such a framework makes it feasible to assess some of the ways real politicians respond to questions and the various linguistic options open to them during an interview. Clearly, it is possible to provide a response to a question that is not noticeably aberrant but which is not an answer. To what extent are politicians' responses constrained by the syntactic and semantic properties of an interviewer's question, or are they free, as Day suggests, to ignore the question with impunity? Are interviewers able to force politicians to provide answers to specific questions, and perhaps more importantly, to supply particular answers?[5] In other words, is it possible to define that evasiveness which is so often attributed to politicians by the public more precisely and in terms that are empirically defensible?

In order to provide answers to some of these questions, the remainder of the chapter attempts to do the following:

1 describe how the relationship between questions and answers can be analysed on the basis of syntactic and semantic features and coded into a framework which distinguishes between a direct answer and one which is not direct. This will involve classifying 'responses' to questions as a restricted set of possible options;
2 apply the framework to a data base consisting of seventeen political interviews;
3 discuss the implications of the results in terms of the variable performance of major politicians, most particularly Margaret Thatcher and Neil Kinnock, and politicians in general as compared to other respondent groups;
4 qualify the interpretation of empirical data in the light of the high degree of contextual motivation involved in the recordings which comprise the data base and the complex nature of 'political style'.

Questions and answers

Considering its increasing importance in both the media and the political process, it is not surprising that the broadcast interview has been the focus of recent research (see Jucker, 1986; Cohen, 1987). Probably the most extensive work has been done within the general framework of Conversation Analysis (see Greatbatch, 1986, 1987; Heritage, 1985), and there is no doubt that this work has been fruitful. While the main focus has been on the 'news interview' as a motivated deviation from ordinary conversation, the most relevant work for the purposes of this chapter is on the use of 'agenda-shifting' procedures by interviewees. David Greatbatch rightly points out the control over the management and organization of topics which is afforded to interviewers by virtue of the role of questioner. He also maintains that, with the development of the adversarial interview over the past 30 years or so, interviewers have been able to 'resist' and sanction interviewees' agenda-shifting manoeuvres (Greatbatch, 1986: 454) in such a way that audience perceptions and expectations have been reshaped.

What this means essentially is that interviewees are now held accountable, not only for refusals to answer a question (which are, after all, still relatively rare) but also for attempted agenda shifts and indirection. This happens in several ways, according to Greatbatch. First of all, the interviewer is likely to resist such strategies on the part of the interviewee in a variety of ways. And, secondly, Greatbatch maintains that audiences are now conditioned to notice when an interviewee is being evasive in his/her responses and hence what he calls 'agenda-shifting' manoeuvres reflect unfavourably on the interviewee. What is missing from the work within Conversation Analysis is any attempt to define just what constitutes an answer or to examine more rigorously and precisely the relationship between questions and 'responses'.[6]

Blum-Kulka (1983) does attempt to define the relationship between questions and answers and thus approaches the dynamics of political interviews in a rather different way. Using a framework based primarily on Burton's (1980) work on discourse and drama, she argues that interviewers rate politicians' responses to questions as either 'supportive' or 'non-supportive' according to specific criteria: (a) cohesiveness; (b) topic coherence; (c) presuppositional coherence; and (d) coherence at the level of speech acts. Responses which are lacking in either cohesiveness or coherence are judged as 'non-supportive' by the interviewer who designs his/her next turn with a reformulation which acts as a 'challenge' to the interviewee. Blum-Kulka's framework is a useful one, and goes some way towards illuminating the relationship between interviewers' questions and politicians' answers in political interviews. However, it is perfectly possible for responses to maintain a considerable level of both cohesion and coherence without necessarily 'answering' the question. Topic coherence, in particular, is very difficult to define precisely enough to be helpful in distinguishing between an 'answer' to a question which is direct and one which is evasive.

In a recent study of 'news interviews', Jucker (1986) maintains that it is difficult to determine on syntactic grounds whether a politician has given a direct answer to a question. He cites the following as evidence:

AAA. but what about imports from within the EEC into this country
BBB. I think imports from within the EEC we can't do all that much about and it's the rules are very complicated and some people er try to get around these rules by various devices
AAA. fiddles of various kinds
BBB. I think that might be extending it a bit but that could well be said to be true (Jucker, 1986: 141).

Focusing on the second interviewer question, Jucker argues that it is impossible to assess what constitutes a direct answer to this 'question', since it is moodless in form and has no unambiguous response set. (Jucker maintains it is comparatively easy to determine the response sets of 'wh' and 'yes/no' interrogative questions.) However, to exclude non-interrogatives which clearly function as pragmatic questions (such as the above) would mean discounting a large part of the data from the analysis.

My own view is that it is not so difficult to assign response sets to certain of these non-interrogative questions as Jucker suggests. Certainly it is the case that a substantial number of interviewers' questions are not interrogative in form, about a quarter of the total (23%) in my data,[7] and it would be undesirable to exclude them. However, in pragmatic terms, most moodless

and declarative utterances which occupy a question slot in political interviews
are put forward for agreement or disagreement by the interviewee, i.e. either
'yes, that is the case' or 'no, it isn't' or some intermediate point on the scale of
probability. 'Yes/no' questions thus have a well-defined response set, and it
seems to me perfectly possible to treat most moodless and declarative
questions as versions of 'yes/no' interrogatives.[8] Indeed, it seems to me that
Jucker's own example can be handled in precisely this way. 'Fiddles of various
kinds' asks the interviewee to agree or disagree, and his answer is, in fact, a
highly qualified 'yes'. In any event, there are in my data comparatively few
cases of moodless quetions but a large number of examples such as the
following:

> (I: Interviewer; Pol: Politician; TUL: Trade union leader.)

> 1. *I.*   so you're saying – Prime Minister – in effect that he should go out and look
>   for it
>   *Pol.* no – I'm saying we try to mobilise all efforts

> 2. *I.*   and that's your answer to the counter-attack
>   *Pol.* there can be no other answer

> 3. *I.*   and you didn't know that hundreds of NGA men in Fleet Street were
>   going to walk out of all those newspapers – and you're the General
>   secretary
>   *TUL.* I – I said that I anticipated there would be a spontaneous reaction and this
>   is precisely what happened

These seem to me relatively easy to classify in terms of whether they supply the
requested agreement/disagreement (Examples 1 and 2) or avoid supplying it
(Example 3).

The linguistic literature on questions is immense and is mostly irrelevant to
my present purpose. Since, like much discourse which takes place in institutional contexts, the political interview involves a basic question/answer
framework where turns are largely pre-allocated, the problem of identifying
questions in the data is greatly reduced. Certainly the common-sense perception of the listening public is very much that the role of the interviewer is to
ask questions and that of the interviewee to answer them. With this in mind, it
is probably simplest to define questions pragmatically as requests to provide
information rather than syntactically as interrogatives, though most interviewer turns in my data (77%) do involve some form of interrogative. But, as
Jucker suggests, it is useful to regard the various syntactic and semantic types
of utterances which are employed by interviewers as pragmatic acts directed at
eliciting information and, as such, the majority can be identified as 'questions'
for all practical purposes.

This is not to suggest that the question/answer framework in political
interviews is never problematic or that breaches do not occur, as the following
example illustrates:

> BW: Brian Walden (interviewer); JC: James Callaghan (interviewee).

> *BW.* why can't we have – a clear answer on the two points I keep putting to you
>   about unilateral uh uh – about unilateral nuclear disarmament and Britain's

conventional deter – its own deterrent and – secondly – uh the American ⌈nuclear bases

JC.   ⌊(   )

BW. are you telling me because everybody knows and because it's embarrassing to the Labour Party I don't want to discuss it

⌈(   )

JC. ⌊no that's what you're saying – that's not what I'm ⌈saying

BW.   ⌊but you

keep saying ⌈that everybody knows your view – I can't work your

JC.   ⌊(what what I'm)

BW. view out from this interview

JC. I'm sorry you can't but I think you'll be the only one who can't work it out – because I think that everybody knows what my position is – I've made it clear ⌈and and

BW. ⌊where did you make it clear

JC. oh I've made it clear in speeches over the last 40 years – and I still – that's that's where the position still stands ⌈and

BW.   ⌊oh well then on that basis I know exactly what you think – you do not think the Labour Party is wise to suggest the closing of American bases and do not think they should give up Britain's independent nuclear deterrent

Although Brian Walden's first two utterances are interrogative in form, their primary illocutionary force is not to elicit information but to act as an accusation that James Callaghan is refusing to provide an answer. The accusation is built into the 'why' question as a presupposition and then reformulated as a proposition embedded in a polar interrogative frame ('are you telling me') before Callaghan has a chance to respond. Walden's next utterances seem to overstep the bounds of interviewer 'neutrality', disrupting the structure of pre-allocated turns and acting as personal assertions in what has essentially become an argument in which participants state opposing views. Indeed, it's interesting to note that this particular interview broke down altogether shortly after this point and became itself a newsworthy item when it was prematurely brought to an end by the interviewer. Furthermore, the public response to this interview was strongly unfavourable to Brian Walden, suggesting that there are fairly strict limits on the extent to which an interviewer can force a politician to provide what he (the interviewer) considers a satisfactory answer to a particular question.[9]

Indeed, when disputable propositions are either embedded in questions or in assertions prefacing a question, the illocutionary force of a question as a request for information can be open to challenge.

FE: Fred Emery (interviewer); JB: John Biffin (interviewee).

FE. now I know Mr Brittan is apparently going to make a statement in the Commons at half past ten about this – but Downing Street has confirmed that this letter was sent – and there are reports that Mr Brittan indeed knew about it – before his statement to the contrary – now the question is this – I want to put to you as a very experienced cabinet minister – are there any circumstances you can think of – such as confidentiality – which would justify any minister apparently concealing a matter such as this from the House

JB. well – you are making the accusation of concealment

FE. no I'm not making it – I'm asking you

JB. well – I'm sorry then – I misunderstood the tone of your voice

In this extract, it is the illocutionary force of the interviewer's 'question' which is explicitly disputed. That questions can and do act as accusations seems clear,[10] with the interviewee faced with the choice of tacitly accepting the accusation as true by answering the question or challenging the interviewer.

This brings us directly to a consideration of the relationship between 'questions' and 'answers' on which any analysis of politicians' evasiveness in interviews must be based. In order to tell whether a politician has in fact answered a question, it is essential to make a distinction between responses and answers. If we define a 'response' as whatever follows a question, it is clear that a large number of utterances may be acceptable as responses which do not necessarily count as answers. Two criteria are relevant here. First, Schegloff (1972) proposed the notion of *conditional relevance*, by which he meant that given the first part of an 'adjacency pair' (and he argues that question/answer is clearly an adjacency pair), the second part is expectable and its non-occurrence will be noted by the hearer. However, the notion of conditional relevance is only minimally helpful when defining evasiveness in the discourse of politicians, since nearly all responses to interviewers' questions can be seen as conditionally relevant in some sense, but not all provide answers. In addition, since interviewer questions are often both lengthy and complex and can be prefaced by a series of assertions, it is quite possible for the interviewee to avoid giving a direct answer while still maintaining conditional relevance. As Levinson suggests,

> What the notion of conditional relevance makes clear is that what binds the parts of adjacency pairs together is not a formation rule of the sort that would specify that a question must receive an answer to count as well-formed discourse, but the setting up of specific expectations which must be attended to (Levinson, 1983: 306).

It is these 'specific expectations' in political interviews that I shall attempt to define more precisely and in linguistic terms.

Secondly, the notion of *situational appropriacy* is also applicable to political interviews. A response may well be conditionally relevant but not situationally appropriate. For example, the following exchange in the context of a political interview is unlikely to occur, although 'no' is certainly a conditionally relevant response to the interviewer's question:

I.   can we move on – Prime Minister – to the sort of criticisms that have been made of your style of leadership and – and government and um – uh – there have been many criticisms – one for example in *The Economist* – which is a paper which is favourable to the Government – which has described your style of leadership as being – uh petulantly authoritarian – which is characteristic of your your Government – now when you read criticisms like that – do you recognise this as being a comment on the way you are running the country
Pol. no

But in the context of a political interview we expect politicians to elaborate, even when asked questions which request a 'yes/no' response. Highly elaborated responses in this context are situationally appropriate and serve specific functions, since a politician is primarily concerned to use the question/answer framework to get his/her message across to the overhearing audience rather than attempting merely to influence the questioner. Hence, in this situation all politicians are likely to produce highly elaborated answers, and 'yes' + elaboration is equally common to 'no' + elaboration.

Description of coding framework

Using the basic syntactic types of questions ('wh', polar and disjunctive) and defining a question as an incomplete proposition, it is possible to devise a coding procedure which classifies 'responses' (whatever follows a question) into three broad categories, each one sub-divided again. The three broad categories are: Direct Answers, Indirect Answers and Challenges. Direct Answers are roughly equivalent to what Philips (1984) calls 'copy types' and Challenges to her 'non-copy types'. Indirect Answers are an intermediate type, which Philips (using a legal context) does not explicitly classify but which occur frequently in political interviews.

I have considered all utterances which follow a question as a response to that question for purposes of the classification. Thus a 'response' may vary from a few words to a lengthy series of utterances. This is not without its difficulties, as will become apparent in the discussion of the results. The data base consists of seventeen political interviews, mostly with major politicians, recorded between 1984 and 1987 on both radio and television (see Appendix 2, pp. 96–7).

Coding framework

I. Direct answers

A. Responses containing explicitly expressed 'yes' or 'no', 'of course', 'right', etc. *or* 'copy' type answer involving deletion in response to question requesting polarity choice *or* the selection of one disjunct.

Examples

1 *I.*   are you saying that you will still resolutely continue with what you believe to be right even if it's unpopular
   Pol.   oh yes – that is why I'm here

2 *I.*   was that a connection you were deliberately making and do you make it
   Pol.   no – I said violence and intimidation must never be seen to pay – never

3 *I.*   well Mr Steel – do you think that as was suggested – in the introduction – Mrs Thatcher has lost her political touch
   Pol.   well I think she has lost her political touch

4 *I.*   fair enough but you didn't actually answer the question – which is had you been Prime Minister at the time would you or would you not have permitted those airplanes to take off from British bases
   Pol.   oh I wouldn't permit it

B. Responses which supply a value for missing variable in response to a 'wh'
    question.
    Examples:
    1 *I.*   now why does the leader of the Labour Party draw encourage-
                 ment from the writings of an Italian Communist like Gramsci
                 whose uh – writings were canvassed in the ideological debate –
                 uh – in the 1950s and 1960s
       Pol.   because he was right – he was right in at least the degree to
                 which I quoted him

    2 *I.*   Prime Minister can we start with the – uh – decision today by
                 the European Parliament – what is your feeling about their
                 refusal to pay Britain's rebate
       Pol.   I thought it was absolutely despicable

    3 *I.*   but why do you want to do it again [run for Parliament] –
                 assuming that they want you
       Pol.   well I've been in Parliament for 33 years – I've been in Cabinets
                 for 11 years – I've had a certain amount of experience as a
                 Minister – I very much enjoy the task of representation in
                 terms of constituency work – that truthfully is what I miss
                 most – the case work and going to Bristol two or three times a
                 week – I miss that very much – I think it's a contribution that
                 I can make

II. Indirect answers
A. Responses which involve inference (either selection of some intermediate
    position between 'yes' and 'no' *or* either 'yes' or 'no' can be inferred from
    the answer) *or* a value for a missing variable can be inferred in response to
    a 'wh' question.
    Examples:
    1 *I.*   I've been told that religion is very important to you – is this a
                 factor in your immense public courage
       Pol.   I think there are times when it would be difficult to carry on
                 unless one had faith – um – and I have and I am very grateful I
                 was brought up that way and that I think enables you to see
                 what matters from what doesn't – because in the last resort you
                 either have the choice to act with courage or without it – and I
                 think the fact that you have faith enables you to have that much
                 more courage in the face of any situation

    2 *I.*   do you call on all those who support you – whether in your
                 union or not uh to avoid mass picketing in a way which can
                 cause violence
       TUL.   well Sir Robin I can say that uh every trade unionist who turns
                 up to demonstrate in support of our members is issued with a
                 leaflet which requests him uh to avoid the violence – to avoid
                 being provoked into violence – and certainly not to attack
                 anybody or any property.

3 *I.*   are you going to have to pay and is it going to be worthwhile
            paying a little bit more to this year's European budget – which
            the row is about

   Pol   I don't think so

4 *I.*   are you convinced that there won't be some kind of – there
            won't be a U-turn but there may be some kind of adjustment
            made which will win favour from all the electorate

   Pol.   there may be – the public – there may be but the public – the
            public are not going to be fooled by any last minute tinkering

B. Responses from which neither 'yes' or 'no' (nor a value for a missing
    variable) can be inferred but which maintain cohesion, topic coherence,
    presuppositional framework and illocutionary coherence.
    Examples:

1. *I.*   is it or is it not your point of view that the police got a bloody
            good hiding

   Pol.   it is my view that the young people of Tottenham acted in
            self-defence against a police provocation that had been going
            on for a number of weeks

2 *I.*   how much would you spend both in terms of money and in time
            re-nationalising all the companies that by that stage the Tory
            government will have sold off

   Pol.   the priority that we've got as we approach that government is
            to put investment and employment right at the top of the
            agenda – every kind of expenditure has got to be considered in
            that context – and that's the discipline which I impose upon the
            next government and which the next government accepts so
            consequently where that process of rationalisation securing – uh
            re-establishing public control over important industries fits
            into that emergency programme.

III. Challenges

A. Responses which challenge one or more of the presuppositions of a
    question.
    Examples:

1 *I.*   what's the future if uneconomic pits continue to be around –
            won't that in the end undermine the mining industry

   TUL.   well – as you know Miss Chalmers it must be that you're
            listening to your own propaganda because for the last 40
            minutes I've been explaining to you that the NCB in Britain is
            the most efficient and technologically advanced industry in the
            world

2 *I.*   are you saying Neil that the uh nightmare or the Labour night-
            mare – if you like – of Britain becoming a sort of land-based

aircraft carrier – for want of another word – are you saying this
has at last come true

   Pol.   it isn't a Labour nightmare

3 *I.*   I ask you Prime Minister why you haven't applied real consumer power to parents in education by giving them real parent
power

   Pol.   we have to some extent – by doing assisted places – and they're
very important

B. Responses which challenge the illocutionary force of a question.
    Examples:

1 *I.*   and what proportion of them [the unemployed] supposing they
all did [get on their bikes and look for work] – what proportion of them would find work

   Pol.   I cannot tell you – and you know that in asking the question

2 *I.*   would you be willing to accept a position in Mr Kinnock's
Front Bench team – whatever position that might be

   Pol.   Peter – that's a very typical question – you see you're not a bit
interested in what what – you know – the Labour Party can do
to save the British people

3 *I.*   why not put it to the test by calling a meeting of the Executive –
Mr Scargill

   TUL.   with respect – why should I listen to you Miss Chalmers – tell
me as the President of this Union what to do – it seems that the
BBC and ITV and the press are awfully concerned about what
this Union should be doing with democracy – why don't you
have a ballot to elect the Director General of the BBC

4 *I.*   when you say it's the legitimate point of view – is it also your
own point of view

   Pol.   well whether it is my point of view or not is not material

5 *I.*   but would you deny – would you – Neil – that on a personal
level you haven't had too happy a time with Mrs Thatcher in
the House of Commons – you know – and you you haven't
really stamped your ⌈self

   Pol.   ⌊who says that

Application of coding procedure How can we judge whether a politician (or
trade union leader) has answered a question? Figure 5.1 represents the
relationship of the above classification to a scale of directness–evasion in
providing answers.

    However, the relationship between a question and an answer is not always a
straightforward one, especially when the majority of answers contain a high
degree of elaboration. It may be useful at this point to discuss some of the
problems involved in assessing whether what follows a question does in fact
provide an answer.

Figure 5.1

Answer   *Direct answer* containing explicitly expressed 'yes' or 'no', 'of course' 'right', etc. *or* 'copy' type answer involving deletion *or* the selection of a disjunct.

Direct answer which supplies value for a missing variable in response to a 'wh' question.

Indirect answer which involves inference (either selection of some intermediate position between 'yes' and 'no' *or* either 'yes' or 'no' can be inferred from the answer), *or* a value for a missing variable can be inferred.

Indirect answer from which neither 'yes' nor 'no' can be inferred *or* a value for a missing variable but which maintains cohesion, topic coherence, presuppositional framework and illocutionary coherence.

Challenges of one or more of the presuppositions of a question.

Evasion   *Challenges* of the illocutionary force of a question.

Intuitively, it would seem that to provide an explicit 'yes' or 'no' (or the equivalent) response is the most direct way of answering a question. Indeed, interviewers seem to sense this and most often employ polar questions when they are attempting to force a politician to commit him/herself on a particular issue, as the following extracts illustrate:

[1] PJ: Peter Jay (interviewer); Bernie Grant (interviewee).

PJ.   may I – may I just press you about that cause i – it's become so important – these words – and I think it's important that you should have the opportunity to clear up the record – are you saying that it is not your judgement that they (the police) were given a good ⌈hiding

BG.   ⌊I'm saying

PG.   is that not a phrase that you would use

BG.   I'm saying that I was putting forward the point of view – the legitimate point of view of the young people on Broadwater Farm

PJ.   when you say it's the legitimate point of view – is it also your point of view

BG.   well whether it is my point of view or not is not material – what is material is that they have a point of view that must be put – that hasn't previously been put and that needs to be taken account of in the whole debate about what happens uh as a result of these riots

PJ.   I think there are a lot of people Mr Grant – and I apologise for pressing you on this – from the Home Secretary downwards who do think it is material whether it is your view as the elected leader of your ward – elected councillor and as the elected leader of Haringey Council – so I must ask you again – is it or is it not your view that the police got a bloody good hiding

BG.   it is my view that the young people of Tottenham acted in self-defence against a police provocation that had been going on for a number of weeks – the people of Tottenham understand my point of view – I've been their local councillor for seven years … now my position on this is that the police were the people who instigated the situation on Broadwater Farm by stopping and searching black occupants of cars only … I think now that is the – that is the issue that we need to address ourselves to

PJ.   am I right Mr Grant as hearing you saying that the reaction of those young people was legitimate and therefore right and that you endorse it – including their violent action in conflict with the police

BG.   I am opposed to violence and I'm opposed to rioting and petrol bombing –

but what I will support – I will support the right of young people – black people – old people – women – or any other section of our community in Haringey defending themselves against police attacks

[2]   *JT*: John Tusa (interviewer); *MT*: Margaret Thatcher (interviewee).

JT.   when you use that phrase [the enemy within] – you didn't specifically connect – you didn't make the connection between Mr Scargill and General Galtieri – other members of your Government did – was that a connection that you were deliberately making and do you make it

MT.   no – I said violence and intimidation must never be seen to pay – never

JT.   so you were not making a direct comparison between Mr Scargill and President Galtieri

MT.   I did not mention either

JT.   but a member of your Government did

MT.   uh I believe one of my junior ministers did – what I said is that it is always easier to defeat the enemy without because they can be seen and identified and everyone is absolutely united in defeating the enemy without – when you get violence and int – intimidation and extremism and militancy within – it is very much more difficult to defeat but violence and intimidation within are the enemy of the ballot – they are the enemy of democracy and anyone or any union that gives in to them has very little ⌈future

JT.   ⌊if I can just get this perfectly

⌈ clear (   )

MT.   ⌊(   ) liberty doesn't have any future if you give in to that – moderate trade unions have no future if we give in to ⌈that

JT.   ⌊but you – you were – you were accused of making this comparison – if I can just get it clear – that you yourself have not compared Mr Scargill with General Galtieri

MT.   no most certainly not

In both extracts, the interviewer elects to utilize highly restrictive forms of 'yes/no' questions so that the failure of the politician to produce an explicit 'yes' or 'no' (or the equivalent) response will create a 'noticeable absence'. This noticeable absence of a 'yes' or 'no' in Extract [1] illustrates the dangers of indirection and attempted agenda shifting for politicians. Bernie Grant's responses serve to heighten the audience perception of evasiveness and create the kind of unfavourable reaction in the media which Mrs Thatcher, also in response to questions on a politically sensitive and potentially contentious subject, is anxious to avoid. Both politicians attempt unsuccessfully to agenda shift by means of elaboration in the face of an interviewer who is, in each case, determined to press his point.

It is much more difficult to employ 'wh' questions in quite this way, since the failure of a politician to 'select' an answer from what may be quite a broad semantic set is much less noticeable and makes it harder for the interviewer to call the politician to account for his/her failure to answer the question. In the following extract, Jimmy Young uses a technique very similar to Peter Jay (Extract 1) and John Tusa (Extract 2) in an interview with Neil Kinnock, making clear in his reference to a 'direct question' that he wants a 'yes/no' response and calling Mr Kinnock to account when he fails to provide one.

JY: Jimmy Young (interviewer); NK: Neil Kinnock (interviewee).

JY.   well now – let me ask you a direct question then – Neil – I mean 'cause this can't have been an easy decision for Mrs Thatcher to take – I mean to allow these uh uh F-111 bombers to fly from British bases – are you saying that even if faced with the incontrovertible evidence that Libya was involved in terrorism and so on – had you been Prime Minister that you would not have permitted them to have flown

NK.   first thing on the incontrovertible evidence – that as Mr – Sir Geoffrey Howe would not admit on the radio this morning – if he had actually seen and heard the evidence uh and he was talking to the European foreign ministers yesterday and he knew that a strike was being prepared from British-based F-111s why didn't he tell them and why the – why wasn't the whole nature of those discussions changed by giving that information – the second question – I'm glad to come to your question

JY.   hmmm

NK.   that that incontrovertible evidence has existed many times before – I mentioned the killing of Policewoman Fletcher – that was incontrovertible evidence but it isn't a question of whether you respond but how you respond on the basis of that evidence – and the fact that there is evidence of Gadafi's involvement in terrorism is not new – really what we should be after is the stopping his involvement – isolating ⌜him

JY.   ⌞hmmm

NK.   and reducing his strength and influence – not adding to it – which is what this bombing strike has done

JY.   fair enough – but you didn't actually answer the question – which is had you been Prime Minister at the time would you or would you not have permitted those airplanes to take off ⌜from British bases

NK.   ⌞oh I wouldn't ⌜permit it

JY.   ⌞you wouldn't

NK.   I wouldn't and I'll tell you the two reasons...

Neil Kinnock's attempt in his initial utterance, to challenge one of the presuppositions of the question is regarded as 'evasive' and resisted by the interviewer. However, the presence of an explicit 'yes' or 'no' in a response to a question does not in itself invariably signal a direct answer, and there are some interesting borderline cases. For example, in the following extract Brian Walden is persistent in attempting to get Mrs Thatcher (then Prime Minister) to accept his reformulation of her position.

BW: Brian Walden (interviewer); MT: Margaret Thatcher (interviewee)

BW.   but – but it isn't a soft and weak caring and you are not prepared to do things that you think are wrong in the long term just to solve short-term problems – that your view of this is that we've all got to try harder and bite on the bullet because eventually long term – the problem will res – be resolved in your way – which is the only right way – that's it isn't it

MT.   you build a strong nation by governments being strong to do the things which only governments can do and by people making the response –
⌜yes – I think you have got the right way⌜
⌞but   ⌞but of course at certain short-term

BW.   costs which you sympathise with but have to be borne if you want the long-term resul⌜ts

MT.   ⌞oh yes – but we're coming through that short term – we're coming through – that's why I've had to take the flak all of these years – we're beginning to come through ⌜and that's what my opponents don't

BW.   ⌞but

> MT.   like and can't stand
> BW.   but you do agree that there are these short-term costs for these people
> MT.   do you know if we had gone the way – the short-term way – we would have
>   far worse unemployment problems now

Though Mrs Thatcher's first two 'answers' both contain an emphatic 'yes', her prior and subsequent elaboration seems to shift the reference of those explicit 'yes' tokens from an endorsement of the interviewer's proposition to the endorsement of a related proposition of her own.

Nor does an explicit 'yes' always signal agreement with a proposition put forward by an interviewer.

> JY.   in the most instant – most recent instance it was that that you didn't handle
>   yourself too well over Westland – for instance
> NK.   yes but if you look at Mrs Thatcher's speech and it was subjected to the same
>   kind of examination as mine – I think you'd come up with a different view

Here again Neil Kinnock's 'yes' does not mean that he accepts the proposition of the interviewer (that he 'didn't handle himself too well over Westland') but is rather a rhetorical preface to a quite 'different view'.

It is also possible to use a direct 'no' to answer only a part of a complex question:

> I.   so you are accepting responsibility and endorsing the mass picketing are
>   you not
> TUL.   no I'm not – uh endorsing mass picketing – I'm endorsing the request of
>   trade union members to demonstrate their support for six members in
>   Stockport

Or to qualify the agreement signalled by a 'yes' answer:

> I.   but by the same token there are thousands – tens of thousands of young
>   people who have no prospects – not because they're lazy – not because
>   they're not intelligent – not because they don't have their own aspira-
>   tions – but because there are no jobs
> Pol.   yes – I am bound to accept there are large groups but there are still many
>   who are not going to the Youth Opportunities Board

It is even possible for a politician to produce both an explicit 'yes' and 'no' in response to the same question:

> I.   but think of the implications of what you're saying – are you telling me that
>   you can train people who aren't very bright and have a fairly low IQ to have
>   a much greater IQ – that you can train people who have no competence in
>   business at all to found successful busine ⌈ sses
> Pol.   ⌊ no – I didn't say that
> I.   well then ⌈ what about them
> Pol.   ⌊ but you see – you don't – you don't need an immensely high IQ
>   to do many of the jobs that have to be done and – yes – we can train them –
>   yes we do train them – we've had astonishing success in some of the what
>   we call Information Technology Centres where we've taken young people
>   who didn't do well at all at school

Here again because the question contains several propositions, both 'no' and 'yes' can be produced in succession as direct answers to the same question without apparent contradiction.

One of the features most noticeable in political interviews is that many of the questions of interviewers, as here, contain a frame (such as 'are you saying', 'are you arguing', 'do you accept', 'is it your view', etc.) followed by an embedded proposition. In the above example, there is no apparent contradiction, because Mrs Thatcher's 'no' refers to the frame (what she is saying) and her 'yes' to the embedded proposition (that people can be trained). An example from the same interview with Mrs Thatcher provides a further illustration:

I.   so you're saying – Prime Minister – in effect he [an unemployed person] should go out and look for it [work]
Pol.   no – I'm saying we try to mobilise all efforts

Embedding a proposition within a frame provides the politician with the choice of responding to the frame ('yes I am' or 'no I'm not' saying that) rather than to the proposition directly ('yes he should' or 'no he shouldn't go out and look for work') while still providing a direct answer to the question.

Direct Answers have been discussed at some length for several reasons. First, as the highest point on the scale of directness–evasion, they are clearly important. How a politician manages his/her responses to 'yes/no' questions may conceivably play a part in constructing a political style, and in projecting the public perception of that politician as more or less 'evasive'.

The likelihood of this is strengthened by the very high proportion of interviewer questions which request, in broad terms, a 'yes/no' response. Secondly, the problems associated with coding Direct Answers demonstrate the complexity of any notion of 'directness' and the difficulties inherent in devising any scale which does justice to a complex phenomenon. What we have in the analysis that follows is thus perhaps best regarded as an approximation. Nevertheless, it does reflect some interesting features concerning the 'evasive actions' of politicians in response to questions in political interviews and, in addition, some discrepancies between the performance of certain prominent British politicians.

Implications of the analysis

The interview data is presented in 4 tables (Appendix 1). The first classifies all politicians' answers in the data sample (Appendix 2) on a scale of directness-evasion. The second extracts from the sample of the responses of Margaret Thatcher and Neil Kinnock, while the third examines the responses of all other politicians in the sample. The responses of politicians are then inserted, by way of comparison, in Table 5.4 which analyses responses in other institutional contexts. The most obvious conclusion from the analysis of the data is that Direct Answers feature in only a minority of responses to questions for all politicians, just under 40%. Indeed, though some 73% of all questions are polar questions which request a 'yes/no' response, explicit 'yes' and 'no' tokens (or their equivalent) occur relatively infrequently, in fewer than 20% of responses. This in itself is significant and may in part account for the widespread public perception of politicians as evasive. To put it the other way around, just over

60% of politicians' responses in the data involved some type of indirection.

That politicians appear to be evasive becomes more apparent when they are compared as a generic group with other respondents in institutional contexts.

Analysis of interview data

Comparing the results of this research, which involved question/answer sequences in court discourse, police/suspect interrogation, medical discourse and police/member of the public interaction, makes clear a number of interesting differences. First, politicians do appear to be evasive and to make use of a much higher degree of indirection in their answers to questions than do other respondents in comparable institutional contexts. The figure of just over 39% for Direct Answers is considerably lower than that of any other group of respondents, suggesting that the widespread public perception is not merely fanciful but can be linked to some kind of empirical evidence. Their rate of indirection (at just over 37%) is correspondingly high, more than twice the percentage of any other respondent group.

Secondly, the nature of questions asked in political interviews would appear to lead not only to elaboration but to indirection. The high proportion of Direct Answers from respondent groups such as defendants and members of the public in police stations undoubtedly reflects the large number of restrictive and mainly factual questions which occur frequently in those contexts but which are largely absent from political interviews. However, even given this fact, the amount of indirection shown by politicians is exceptionally high and the proportion of Direct Answers very low in a comparative as well as in a real sense.

Equally interesting are the substantial differences which the analysis reveals between Margaret Thatcher and Neil Kinnock, especially in relationship to Direct Answers. Mrs Thatcher appears to give a substantially higher proportion of Direct Answers in response to 'yes/no' questions than does Mr Kinnock, whose total is approximately equal to that of other politicians (see Table 5.3). It is interesting to note that this discrepancy applies only to polar questions, and that their respective Direct Answers in response to 'wh' questions are remarkably similar. What is also clear from the analysis of data is the tendency of all politicians to elaborate, even when Direct Answers are provided. Robin Day's contention that politicians attempt to shift the agenda, to put forward their own propositions, has some validity.

The high proportion of Indirect Answers (37.88% for all politicians) reflects this tendency quite clearly, and most Indirect Answers tend to be highly elaborated. Here again, there is an interesting difference between Mrs Thatcher and Mr Kinnock. While Mrs Thatcher has quite a high proportion of Indirect Answers (40.16% of her total responses), Mr Kinnock is less prone to indirection (28.6% as opposed to 42.4% for other politicians). However, Mr Kinnock is much more likely to challenge the presuppositions of a question (29.6% as opposed to 3.28% for Mrs Thatcher and 12.4% for other politicians).

However, any comparative account of the political style of major politicians must inevitably be qualified by several factors. First, and probably most important, all interactional strategies are embedded in a complex hierarchy of social and political structures, in a set of contextual givens, which not only constrain what can happen but also set clear limits on how what happens can be interpreted. Looking again at the Thatcher–Kinnock comparison, some of the interactional differences which appear quite clearcut may contain a high degree of contextual motivation which must qualify their apparent significance. During the period in which the interviews for the data base were recorded (1984–7), Neil Kinnock's views were known to conflict with a substantial body of opinion in a Party which was often deeply divided. He was frequently invited to express views about Party policy that he could not answer directly without damaging consequences for his own agenda for his Party. As Leader of the Opposition, it is conceivable that he was subject to a higher degree of 'hostile' questioning (Jucker, 1986; Heritage, 1985) than was Mrs Thatcher, who during that period had reset the agenda of British politics and was, broadly speaking, at her most dominant.

Evasiveness is most likely to emerge in response to questions which seek to expose contradictions in a position, draw attention to intra-party conflicts or the deficiencies of unpopular policies. A data base consisting of political interviews recorded during 1990 might possibly yield different results, as interviewers were presented with unexpected opportunities for hostile questioning, especially of Mrs Thatcher and other leading Conservatives, in the face of the considerable changes in the British political context to which major politicians were forced to respond (and which ultimately led to the resignation of Mrs Thatcher as Prime Minister). And even if there are genuine and consistently definable differences between the way major politicians respond to questions, how we *interpret* those strategies may also be affected by a particular set of historical circumstances and ideological norms which tend to elude definition in empirical terms.

Secondly, empirical work which makes use of what real politicians say and do with language has only begun to define the nature of 'political style' (Beattie, 1983; Atkinson, 1984; Carroll et al., 1986; Maitland and Wilson, 1987; Clayman and Whalen, 1989; Wilson, 1991) from a sociolinguistic perspective. What such work has in common is ultimately the recognition both of the importance of 'context' and that 'style' itself consists not of any single linguistic feature but of sets of features, which interact with each other in complex ways. There is no simple means of defining a political or any other generic style conclusively. Isolating a single feature, how politicians respond to questions, is only a first step towards a more complex stylistic analysis which has of yet scarcely begun.

Conclusions

First, there does seem to be empirical evidence for the widespread public perception that politicians are evasive, at least in political interviews. Especially when compared with other respondents, they demonstrate a disproportionately high degree of indirection and a disproportionately low percentage of Direct Answers. Moreover, it is possible to construct at least an approximate scale of 'evasiveness' and to define it in linguistic terms fairly explicitly by identifying certain linguistic features. This is not to imply that only the match between questions and responses contributes towards a politician being regarded as either 'evasive' or 'direct', but responses to questions may well contribute significantly to the construction of a particular political style.

Secondly, politicians are constrained by the syntactic and semantic properties of questions to a large degree. They are not free to ignore interviewer questions with impunity, and they can be and are called to account for not answering a question. On the other hand, this lack of freedom is only a relative one. Highly elaborated responses have become the norm in political interviews, and attempts at agenda shifting by politicians are extremely frequent and often successful.

Thirdly, there are some apparently meaningful differences in the ways major British politicians respond to questions, especially Margaret Thatcher and Neil Kinnock. However, these must be qualified and interpreted in the light of the particular set of historical and political circumstances during the period of the recorded political interviews which form the data base. Yet despite an inherent degree of contextual motivation, analyses based on real language data are an essential step in working towards a more explicit definition of what we mean by 'political style' and the nature of political discourse.

Appendix 1

Table 5.1 *Classification of politicians' responses according to a scale of directness–evasion*

I. Direct answers	No. of responses	% of total
A. Responses containing explicit 'yes' or 'no', 'of course', 'right', etc. *or* 'copy' type answer involving deletion in response to question requesting polarity choice *or* the selection of one disjunct	107	29.81
B. Responses which supply a value for a missing variable in response to a 'wh' question	34	9.47
Direct answers	141	39.28
II. Indirect answers		
A. Responses which involve inference (either selection of an intermediate position between 'yes' and 'no' *or* either 'yes' or 'no' can be inferred from the answer *or* a value for a missing variable can be inferred in response to a 'wh' question)	83	23.12
B. Responses from which neither 'yes' nor 'no' (nor a value for a missing variable) can be inferred but which maintain cohesion, presuppositional framework and illocutionary coherence	53	14.76
Indirect answers	136	37.88
III. Challenges		
A. Responses which challenge one or more of the presuppositions of a question	51	14.21
B. Responses which challenge the illocutionary force of a question	31	8.63
Challenges	82	22.84
Total number of responses:	359	

Table 5.2 *Comparison of responses of Margaret Thatcher and Neil Kinnock according to scale of directness–evasion*

I. Direct answers	No. of responses		% of total	
	NK	MT	NK	MT
A. Responses containing explicit 'yes' or 'no', 'of course', 'right', etc. *or* 'copy' type answer involving deletion in response to question requesting polarity choice *or* the selection of one disjunct	23	50	23.4	41
B. Responses which supply a value for a missing variable in response to a 'wh' question	9	11	9.2	9
Total	32	61	32.6	50
II. Indirect answers				
A. Responses which involve inference (either selection of an intermediate position between 'yes' and 'no' *or* either 'yes' or 'no' can be inferred from the answer *or* a value for a missing variable can be inferred in response to a 'wh' question)	14	36	14.3	29.51
B. Responses from which neither 'yes' nor 'no' (nor a value for a missing variable) can be inferred but which maintain cohesion, topic coherence, presuppositional framework and illocutionary coherence	14	13	14.3	10.65
Total	28	49	28.6	40.16
III. Challenges				
A. Responses which challenge one or more of the presuppositions of a question	29	4	29.6	3.28
B. Responses which challenge the illocutionary force of a question	9	8	9.2	6.56
Total	38	12	38.8	9.84

Percentages in each case of respective total number of responses, 122 in the case of Margaret Thatcher and 98 for Neil Kinnock.

Table 5.3 *Analysis of responses excluding Margaret Thatcher and Neil Kinnock*

I. Direct answers	No. of responses	% of total
A. Responses containing explicit 'yes' or 'no', 'of course', 'right', etc. *or* 'copy' type answer involving deletion in response to question requesting polarity choice *or* the selection of one disjunct	34	24.5
B. Responses which supply a value for a missing variable in response to a 'wh' question	14	10.07
Total	48	34.57
II. Indirect answers		
A. Responses which involve inference (either selection of an intermediate position between 'yes' and 'no' or either 'yes' *or* 'no' can be inferred from the answer *or* a value for a missing variable can be inferred in response to a 'wh' question)	33	23.7
B. Responses from which neither 'yes' nor 'no' (nor a value for a missing variable) can be inferred but which maintain cohesion, topic coherence, presuppositional framework and illocutionary coherence	26	18.7
Total	59	42.4

continued over

Table 5.3 *continued*

	No. of responses	% of total
III. Challenges		
A. Responses which challenge one or more of the presuppositions of a question	18	12.94
B. Responses which challenge the illocutionary force of a question	14	10.07
Total	32	23.01

Table 5.4 *Response types which occur following questions in other institutional contexts*

Respondent	Response type					
	Direct answer		Indirect answer		Other	
magistrate	61.7%	(37)	15.0%	(9)	23.3%	(14)
police (in interrogation of suspects)	57.9%	(33)	5.3%	(3)	36.8%	(21)
nurse	62.6%	(47)	13.3%	(10)	24.0%	(18)
police (with member of public)	60.8%	(93)	9.8%	(15)	29.4%	(45)
politicians	*39.28%*	*(141)*	*37.88%*	*(136)*	*22.84%*	*(82)*
defendant	77.7%	(725)	8.1%	(76)	14.2%	(132)
suspect	69.7%	(211)	11.6%	(35)	18.8%	(57)
patient	65.6%	(162)	4.4%	(11)	29.9%	(74)
member of public (police station)	80.3%	(298)	8.1%	(30)	11.6%	(43)

Percentages are calculated in relationship to the total number of questions asked of a participant group. The numbers in brackets represent the numbers of responses given in the data.

Appendix 2

Data base of recorded political interviews:

1. *The World this Weekend.* BBC Radio 4 (6 October 1985). Triona Holden/ Jeffrey Archer.
2. *A Week in Politics.* Channel 4 (7 October 1984). Peter Jay/Bernie Grant.
3. *Weekend World.* ITV (17 November 1985). Brian Walden/Margaret Thatcher.
4. *A Plus 4.* Channel 4 (15 October 1985). Gillian Neville/Margaret Thatcher.
5. *Newsnight.* BBC2 (14 July 1984). John Tusa/Margaret Thatcher.
6. *Diverse Reports.* Channel 4 (17 July 1985). Christine Chapman/Margaret Thatcher.
7. *Newsnight.* BBC2 (17 July 1985). Donald McCormick/Neil Kinnock.
8. *Newsnight.* BBC2 (30 July 1985). Donald McCormick/Margaret Thatcher.
9. *Newsnight.* BBC2 (23 July 1985). Donald McCormick/David Steel and David Owen.
10. *Tuesday Call.* BBC Radio 4 (20 March 1984). Sandra Chalmers/Arthur Scargill.
11. *World at One.* BBC Radio 4 (11 February 1987). Robin Day/Brian Gould.
12. *A Week in Politics.* Channel 4 (10 January 1984). Peter Jay/Tony Benn.

13. *World at One.* BBC Radio 4 (3 November 1984). Robin Day/Lord Marsh.
14. *World at One.* BBC Radio 4 (3 November 1984). Robin Day/Joe Wade.
15. *Panorama.* BBC1 (13 January 1986). Fred Emery/John Biffen and Michael Heseltine.
16. *Interview.* BBC Radio 3 (15 April 1986). Michael Charlton/Neil Kinnock.
17. *Jimmy Young Show.* BBC Radio 2 (29 April 1986). Jimmy Young/Neil Kinnock.

Notes

1. BBC2 series *Yes, Minister* (1983).
2. Cohen (1987) compares the television news interview as it is practised in the US, Israel, West Germany (as it was then) and the UK, highlighting both similarities and significant differences. He presents some interesting data, though the emphasis is very much on the 'practical' and, hence, probably by design, the material examined is very general and under-theorized. Nevertheless, Cohen puts forward some useful comparative conclusions, though the book contains no analyses of recorded language.
3. Patrick Hannan speaking in *I'm Very Glad You Asked Me That.* BBC Radio 4 programme (12 March 1986).
4. Robin Day, speaking on political interviews in *I'm Very Glad You Asked Me That* (BBC Radio 4, 12 March 1986). From the perspective of a politician, Tony Benn has suggested that some interviewers 'bully and cross-examine as if they were prosecuting lawyers in a murder trial' and that 'others I think ignore the point that's being made and try and switch the subject – particularly in politics – to personalities' (BBC Radio 4, 6 March 1988). He has also suggested that the BBC has established its own norm of political opinion and that 'anyone who varies from it is outside the pale'.
5. Some interesting recent work has been done on the strategies interviewers use to maintain 'neutrality' in political interviews (Harris, 1986; Clayman, 1988). This work focuses mainly on types of questions and questioning strategies.
6. Heritage (1985: 112) uses the terms 'cooperative' and 'uncooperative' to characterize question and answer sequences, though he insists that these terms neither 'assess interviewer conduct not characterise the global import of particular utterances'. Clayman (1990) explores the nature of newspaper accounts of interviews in an interesting way. He argues that quoted questions can function to make statements recognizable as 'answers'. Furthermore, newswriters often tactically preserve the sequential context of questions and answers in order to show 'evasiveness', to characterize a public figure's interactional conduct (p. 97). While such writers are hesitant to describe public figures explicitly as reluctant, evasive, misleading etc. the sequencing of their talk implies this. What politicians say is assessed and evaluated in the light of how they say it.
7. The majority of non-interrogative questions take the form of declarative propositions which are put to the interviewee for agreement or disagreement. The number of moodless items is negligible.
8. The same problem occurs in the analysis of court discourse. Magistrates and lawyers frequently make use of questions in declarative form which are put as propositions in order to solicit agreement or disagreement from defendants and witnesses (see Harris, 1984). In this context, as in political interviews, such propositions clearly serve the function of pragmatic questions.
9. *Britain and the World,* No. 3 *Callaghan,* Channel 4 (24 April 1987). Discussed on Channel 4's *Right to Reply,* where a number of viewers wrote in expressing indignation at Brian Walden's interviewing style. Clayman and Whalen (1989) describe a similar, and indeed even more widely publicized, encounter between Dan Rather and George Bush in the run-up to the 1988 American election. Clayman and Whalen argue that both parties to the interview move the action away from the question/answer framework so that that framework is weakened and eventually transformed into a conversational mode which is argumentative in tone. As in the Walden/Healey interview, most of the public criticism which followed was directed at the interviewer (Rather).

10. Once again, accusations in question form are common in court discourse (see Harris, 1984, with defendants and witnesses clearly demonstrating their understanding of the intended accusation in their responses. Such questions are less common in political interviews but frequent enough to be a source of interest.

11. I am indebted to the research of Ruth Riley (1986) for this analysis of responses in selected institutional contexts. Her analysis of responses is slightly different from mine but close enough to be comparable. Her category of 'Other' includes not only what I have called 'Challenges' but also certain other types of responses which are less likely to occur in political interviews.

References

Atkinson, J.M. (1984) *Our Masters' Voices: the Language and Body Language of Politics.* London: Methuen.

Beattie, Geoffrey (1983) *Talk: an Analysis of Speech and Non-verbal Behaviour in Conversation.* Milton Keynes: Open University Press.

Blum-Kulka, Shoshana (1983) 'The Dynamics of Political Interviews', *Text*, 3(2): 131–53.

Burns, T. (1977) *The BBC: Public Institution and Private World.* London: Macmillan.

Burton, Deirdre (1980) *Dialogue and Discourse.* London: Routledge Kegan Paul.

Carroll, D., A.M. Simon-Vandenbergen and S. Vandepitte (1986) 'Mood and Modality in Political Interviews'. Mimeograph.

Clayman, Steven (1988) 'Displaying Neutrality in Television News Interviews', *Social Problems*, 35(4): 474–92.

Clayman, Steven (1989) 'The Production of Punctuality: Social Interaction, Temporal Organisation, and Social Structure', *American Journal of Sociology*, 95: 659–91.

Clayman, Steven (1990) 'From Talk to Text: Newspaper Accounts of Reporter–Source Interactions', *Media, Culture and Society*, 12(1): 79–103.

Clayman, Steven and Jack Whalen (1989) 'When the Medium Becomes the Message: The Case of the Rather–Bush Encounter', *Research in Language in Social Action*, 22: 241–72.

Cohen, Akiba (1987) *The Television News Interview.* London: Sage.

Day, Robin (1961) *Television: a Personal Report.* London: Hutchinson.

Day, Robin (1975) *Day by Day.* London: William Kimber.

Day, Robin (1991) *Grand Inquisitor.* London: Pan.

Dimbleby, Jonathan (1975) *Richard Dimbleby: a Biography.* London: Hodder and Stoughton.

Greatbatch, David (1986) 'Aspects of Topical Organisation in News Interviews: the Use of Agenda-Shifting Procedures by Interviewers', *Media, Culture and Society*, 8(4): 441–55.

Greatbatch, David (1987) 'A Turn-taking System for British News Interviews', *Warwick Working Papers in Sociology*, University of Warwick.

Harris, Sandra (1984) 'Questions as a Mode of Control in Magistrates' Courts', *International Journal of the Sociology of Language*, 49: 5–28.

Harris, Sandra (1986) 'Interviewees' Questions in Broadcast Interviews', *Belfast Working Papers in Language and Linguistics* 8: 86–123. Belfast: University of Ulster.

Heritage, John (1985) 'Analysing News Interviews: Aspects of the Production of Talk for an Overhearing Audience', pp. 95–117 in T. van Dijk (eds.) *Handbook of Discourse Analysis* Vol. 3: 'Discourse and Dialogue'. New York: Academic Press.

Heritage, John, Steven Clayman and Don Zimmerman (1988) 'Discourse and Message Analysis: the Mind-structuring of Mass Media Messages', pp. 77–109, in R. Hawkins, S. Pingree and J. Wiemann (eds), *Advancing Communication Science: Merging Mass and Interpersonal Processes* (Vol. 16 in *Sage Annual Review of Communication Research*). Newbury Park: Sage.

Jucker, Andreas (1986) *News Interviews: A Pragmalinguistic Analysis.* Amsterdam: John Benjamin.

Kumar, Krishnan (1975) 'Holding the Middle Ground: the BBC, the Public and the Professional Broadcaster', *Sociology*, 9 (1): 57–68.

Levinson, Stephen (1983) *Pragmatics.* Cambridge: Cambridge University Press.

Maitland, K. and J. Wilson (1987) 'Pronominal Selection and Ideological Conflict', *Journal of Pragmatics*, 11: 495–512.

Philips, Susan (1984) 'The Social Organisation of Questions and Answers in Court Discourse', *Text*, 4(1/3): 225–48.

Riley, Ruth (1986) 'An Investigation of the Formal and Functional Properties of Utterances which can be Identified as Questions in Certain Asymmetrical Contexts'. Unpublished PhD thesis, CNAA: Trent Polytechnic.

Schegloff, E.A. (1972) 'Sequencing in Conversational Openings', pp. 346–80 in J. Gumperz and Hymes D. (eds), *Directions in Sociolinguistics*. New York: Holt, Rinehart and Winston.

Walden, Brian (1985) 'Interview: Weekend Walden', *Communication and Media*, 1: 4.

Wedell, E.G. (1968) *Broadcasting and Public Policy*. London: Michael Joseph.

Whale, John (1977) *The Politics of the Media*. London: Fontana.

Wilson, John (1991) 'The Linguistic Pragmatics of Terrorist Acts', *Discourse and Society*, 2(1): 29–46.

6

Ideology, Scripts and Metaphors in the Public Sphere of a General Election

Greg Garton, Martin Montgomery and Andrew Tolson

The 1987 General Election is the most media-conscious, computer-fed election we have enjoyed (or should that be endured?). (John Cole, Chief Political Editor, BBC [British Broadcasting Corporation])

The perception that the media play a constitutive role in British political life, especially during general elections, is now very familiar. In television studies, this has been an established view ever since Pateman's pioneering work on the General Election of 1974 (Pateman, 1974). Pateman's argument about a 'television election' was timely, in so far as it served to counter the sometimes simplistic notion of political 'coverage' which assumed that an independent political process was 'reflected' in the media. On the contrary, Pateman pointed to the growth in popularity of TV, the fact that certain television events (like interviews) were themselves newsworthy, and the phenomenon of politicians increasingly adapting their campaigning techniques to suit the requirements of the media. However, Pateman's study is limited in that it refers only to television; for though this is widely regarded as the pre-eminent mass medium, it does not exist in a vacuum.

For all the media interest in visual entertainment, spectacle, 'photo opportunities', etc. the political process in Britain retains an element of old-fashioned verbal debate and commentary which is appropriate to the notion of a 'public sphere' (Garnham, 1986; Scannell, 1989). In fact the public sphere of a British general election is a complex combination of inputs from all three major mass media (newspapers, radio, television), from public relations and advertising agencies and from the politicians themselves. What happens in this process is that talk is endlessly circulated around all these sites in practices of commentary, quotation and polemical reformulation. Statements are thus re-presented in different discursive domains, and in this re-presentation they are transformed. But in looking at the 1987 General Election what we have discovered is the persistence of basic narrative models which serve to organize the circulation of talk, and for which the media (with politicians as accomplices) are responsible. Such narrative models contain ideological presuppositions which provide popular focus to the political process.

In this process, a central mediating role is played by politicians themselves. In modern general elections the activities of key politicians (national spokespersons) are tightly organized into a routine daily schedule. This routine is a direct example of Pateman's point about campaigning techniques, in that the daily schedule is designed for the benefit of the media and to facilitate, not just 'coverage', but journalistic participation. Thus any single day in an election campaign will involve: (a) a morning press conference; (b) a daily round of canvassing activities (including 'photo opportunities'); and (c) a political rally and major speech in the evening. These activities will be correspondingly reported: (a) in lunchtime news bulletins (press conference agendas); (b) in the early evening news (press conference/canvassing); (c) in late evening news/ current affairs programmes (the events of the day plus quotations from major speeches). Through all these phases, however, the morning press conference has something of a determining status, in so far as it is where political parties seek to influence the public debate in terms of their own agendas for the day.

But of course the 'press conference' is also precisely that: i.e. a key event in the schedule where politicians are not so much answerable to the public, as to journalists themselves. The 'press' (including TV journalists) take full advantage of this privilege. For instance, it is usual for journalists not only to question a party's preferred agenda (acting as 'devil's advocates', etc.), but also to raise other matters which they consider newsworthy. Such matters may be derived from the agendas of rival political parties, but they may also be determined by the press itself (reports in the morning newspapers, etc.). Now an interesting situation arises here: for it is possible that an item of interest to the press, derived from a press report, may be relayed to a politician for comments, which are subsequently reported in the TV news. In short the politician's press conference plays a role in mediating a press report to the television screen. We will assume that television fulfils its legal and statutory function to report faithfully the politician's statement. But the substance of the statement (its field of reference and its entailed presuppositions) may have originated in the highly partisan atmosphere of a politically motivated newspaper.

The emergence of the defence debate

No single issue can be said to have dominated the 1987 General Election campaign as a whole. Rather, each political party, at its daily press conference, attempted to present its own 'issue of the day' – and it was rare to find any agreement over what constituted the daily agenda. In this situation, representatives of the press could assume a role of presenting each party's arguments to the others, airing a variety of subjects which would be subsequently reflected in more or less 'balanced' reports on the television news. Certainly this was the pattern during the first, third and fourth weeks of the campaign. However, it seems that there was some deviation from the standard routine in week 2.[1] The second week of the campaign was an exception to the general rule in that the media seemed to be all but unanimous in their agreement over what was the dominant issue. That is to say, the political parties, particularly the Labour Party, persisted with their own agendas – but as far as the media were concerned, the lead story (in almost three-quarters of all news bulletins) was defence.

Significantly this story was not, in the first instance, generated by any of the political parties; rather it was triggered by remarks made by Neil Kinnock in an interview with David Frost on the independent television Sunday morning programme *TV-AM* (24 May 1987). On that Sunday afternoon, journalists from the *Daily Telegraph* and the *Daily Express* contacted Conservative Party headquarters and prompted George Younger (Tory spokesman on defence) to respond to the statements made by Kinnock. At the same time, John Cartwright for the Social Democratic Liberal Alliance made a public comment. It was this series of statements and comments which formed the basis for newspaper headlines the following day. Subsequently, 4 days of media coverage of the campaign were dominated by what Kinnock said, or didn't say, to David Frost on television that Sunday morning.

Here is a transcription of Kinnock's statement. He was responding to Frost's invitation to speculate as to what he would do, as Prime Minister, if a non-nuclear Britain were threatened by an aggressor who possessed nuclear weapons. Kinnock replied:

> In those circumstances, the choice is again posed – and this is the classical choice – of either exterminating everything that you stand for and, I'll use the phrase 'the flower of your youth', or using resources that you've got to make any occupation totally intenable, untenable.
>
> And of course, any effort to occupy Western Europe, or certainly to occupy the United Kingdom, would be utterly untenable and any potential force knows that very well and are not going to be ready to engage in attempting to dominate conditions that they couldn't dominate.

By George Younger, Kinnock's statement was subsequently glossed as advocating a policy of 'take to the hills'. John Cartwright was even more rhetorical; to him it seemed as if 'the Mujahideen in Penge High Street were expected to deter Soviet nuclear blackmail'. These two interpretations were then taken as the basis for the following Monday morning's headline in the *Daily Telegraph* which read: 'Guerilla War a Deterrent Says Kinnock'.

From such beginnings, the second week's news coverage of the election campaign became very interesting on a number of levels. First, it is interesting to speculate why, at the outset, a series of mass-mediated quotations might take on such immense public significance. Secondly, the whole process provides an instructive case study of relations between the press, broadcasting institutions and political parties, which we have argued is crucial to the procedure of modern electioneering. Thirdly, and more specifically from our point of view, it is significant that the entire week's coverage was dominated not by actual events, nor even by published policies, but rather by talk, and talk about talk on television. As we go on to show, certain assumptions are made and presuppositions are circulated in the organization of this talk which are precisely not reducible to policy statements, but are more consistent with narrative formations in popular culture. Fourthly, however, to recognize this level of popular narrative broadcast talk is not to diminish its serious political consequences; for it can be argued that this defence 'debate', generated in the first instance by sections of the press, ultimately proved to be a decisive setback for the Labour Party.

Kinnock's 'gaffe'

By Tuesday 26 May, with references to Kinnock's remarks on the front pages of every newspaper, television news bulletins belatedly took up the story. By now, however, the issue of defence (an inevitable subject of debate in any general election) had been reformulated in the popular press as 'Kinnock's gaffe', and it was this inflection which set the TV agenda. Thus the precise content of Kinnock's original statement was soon displaced, and the utterance itself was rarely quoted in full. Rather, discussion was now directed in two ways: first, towards imaginary scenarios and hypothetical consequences associated with a foreign occupation; and secondly, speculation as to the apparent damage done to Labour's chances in the election. On television in other words, the 'gaffe' had become a *fait accompli:* it was now a matter for the Conservative and Alliance parties to exploit to the full, and for informed political commentators (like John Cole) to assess. Typical of the phrases which were variously recycled through TV news bulletins on Tuesday 26 May (all quotations from BBC's *Nine o'Clock News*) were 'guerilla resistance to an invasion of Britain', 'guerilla warfare and Dad's Army', 'a threat to use Dad's Army against the Russians'. The question was not whether Neil Kinnock actually used any of these words, but rather how would he now respond.

In fact Labour's first response was to attempt to ignore these allegations and to continue to promote its own preferred agenda. But such an approach was singularly unsuccessful. The defence issue continued to dominate the news, to preoccupy correspondents and interviewers, and Labour's alternative issues (Health, Law and Order, the Economy) barely interrupted the flow. In fact it is a noticeable feature of that week's television news bulletins that their structure, more often than not, placed the Labour Party on the defensive, obliged to respond to a lead story in terms of which the Tories and the Alliance together were making the running.[2] The fact that the Labour Party had decided to campaign and hold its press conferences that week in the regions, and not in London, may have been a contributing factor. For it allowed Norman Tebbit to develop an attack which focused on the personality of Labour's leader, as much as on the policies of his party:

> If only we could think that Mr Kinnock would show the same determination to face up to Britain's problems or our potential adversaries as he shows in his determination to run away from the press.
> But from the safety of his carefully prepared and scripted television extravaganzas he just talks.
> And he talks of a run-away victory.
> But it is Mr Kinnock who's the run-away.
> He's a run-away from the questioning Press.
> He's a run-away from the questioning voters.
> He's a run-away from the Trades Union bosses.
> He's a run-away into the arms – of his own extremists.
> And he would be a run-away from any bully, however big or small, who threatened this nation. (BBC *Nine o'Clock News*, 27 May 1987)

In this way the press (which, we must remember, initiated the story in the first place) becomes doubly recruitable to an anti-Labour position. The whole process is like a relay race in which the press hand the baton to politicians who hand it back to the press (and TV), who hand it back to the politicians, etc. – but without the Labour Party who have refused to enter the race.

And as we have suggested, there is some evidence that all this activity did the Labour Party no good at all. Throughout the first week, and for most of the second week of the campaign, the opinion polls consistently indicated a gradual increase in support for the Labour Party at the expense of both the Tories and the Alliance. However, at the end of the second week of campaigning, the polls registered the first drop in support for Labour and the first rise in support for the Conservatives. Pollsters have found that it takes approximately 3 days for events to filter through the media before they begin to register in opinion-poll surveys. So this drop in support for the Labour Party can be traced back from the Friday to the Tuesday or the Wednesday of the second week i.e. precisely the time, as we have seen, that the defence issue (as it was presented in the media) – played a key role in the outcome of the election campaign. During the period that this was running as lead story, the fortunes of the two main parties were reversed.[3]

Defence: a discursive formation

However, it is not our primary purpose in this paper to speculate on the specific reasons for Labour's 1987 defeat. Rather, we want to take a broader view of the political process, and in particular to examine the ways in which it is constructed by discursive formations. Such formations may themselves have political effects which (at least in this case) are detrimental to the Labour Party; but we would argue that these effects can only be understood on the basis of a concern for the analysis of forms of broadcast talk – such as has rarely, if ever, been attempted in previous work on the media and politics.[4] Our concern then, having traced the institutional development of 'Kinnock's gaffe', is now to give particular attention to its discursive construction. In this section and the next we examine, first, the apparent 'logics' of interpretation and presupposition which produce various glossings from Kinnock's original statement; and secondly, the way these glossings are inflected in a populist direction, particularly in their mobilization of popular cultural vocabularies. Hopefully then, in taking a systematic look at the discourse of the defence debate, we will be able not only to identify certain formal characteristics of its structure, but also to return to the general discussion of forms of talk on television, particularly in relation to their impact on the political scene.

Let us then begin our formal analysis with the basic point that what Kinnock said to Frost in his *TV-AM* interview is indeed open to interpretation; or more precisely, that different kinds of inferencing will lead to different interpretations of this remarks. We would imagine, for instance, that 'using all the resources you've got to make any occupation totally untenable' might refer to the use of conventional weapons as a deterrent to the threat of a possible occupation. However, sections of the press and spokespersons for the other political parties, inflected Kinnock's remarks in a quite different way.

Another statement from Younger, quoted in the *Daily Telegraph* (25 May 1987), claims that 'it is a policy of surrender'. Michael Heseltine, quoted in the *Daily Express*, claims that 'what Kinnock is proposing is positively inviting people to attack'. Whilst this is manifestly not the only possible reading of Kinnock's utterance (note for example, that he was not immediately challenged by Frost in these terms), there is nonetheless a certain consistency about the kinds of readings that achieve discursive prominence over the next few days. The process by which this is achieved is interesting in a number of ways:

A   It is manifestly a discursive process, involving considerable exegesis of the original utterance, which is referred to but rarely quoted in the act of interpretation. Thus spokespersons often include disclaimers in the glossing activity: 'This appears to me to be . . .' (George Younger); 'That is what it seems to me they are talking about . . .' (Margaret Thatcher); '. . . a Soviet occupation, I presume . . .' (Margaret Thatcher).[5]

B   The subsequent glossing aims to fix the range of possible interpretations in a particular direction, by attempting to control its potential ambiguities. The interpretations suggested by the glossings are also intended to reflect badly on the speaker of the original utterance.

C   The patterns of inference required to move from Kinnock's remarks to their subsequent glossings are not automatic, but elaborative and evaluative. (See Brown and Yule [1983: 257], who suggest that the notion of inferencing should be reserved for supplying connections of a non-automatic kind. Indeed, 'they might be based on such diverse beliefs, that on the one hand, all Americans in China are CIA agents, or alternatively that the Chinese continually harass foreigners for no reason'.)

D   Precisely because the inferencing involved is evaluative, it depends upon assumptions which are ideological in character; and specifying such assumptions helps to display the implicit ideologies at work upon the original remarks. At the same time, however, their non-automatic character makes it difficult to formalize them in a demonstrably exact fashion. Nonetheless there is sufficient consistency in the range of glossings to suggest broad patterns for the inferencing.

For example, to claim that:

using all the resources you've got to make any occupation totally untenable (Neil Kinnock, *TV-AM*, 24 May 1987)

is equivalent to:

a policy of surrender (George Younger, *Daily Telegraph*, 25 May 1987); an invitation to attack (Michael Heseltine, *Daily Express*, 25 May 1987)

entails core bridging assumptions of the following kind, which we state initially in their most general terms:

1   A nation has enemies.
2   Enemies are potential aggressors.
3   Potential aggressors are prepared to attack.
4   Some weapons deter a potential aggressor.

From these general assumptions some fairly obvious implicatures can be derived. Thus, from:

4   Some weapons deter a potential aggressor.

can be derived:

5   Some weapons do not deter a potential aggressor.

At the same time, however, these core assumptions have a particular socio-historical provenance. Thus, by a process of common-sense reasoning, those weapons which deter are seen as nuclear, whereas those weapons which do not deter are seen as conventional. Hence,

4.1   Nuclear weapons deter a potential aggressor.

and

5.1   Conventional weapons do not deter a potential aggressor.

Again by a process of common-sense reasoning, the generalized noun phrase 'a nation' is filled with the proper noun 'Britain', and 'a potential aggressor' is filled (in 1987) by 'the Soviet Union'. Hence:

1.1   Britain has enemies.
4.1.1   Nuclear weapons deter the Soviet Union from aggression.
5.1.1   Conventional weapons do not deter the Soviet Union from aggression.

In this connection we would add that such common-sense reasoning also frequently involves the importation of anthropomorphic assumptions as to the characteristics of nation-states. That is to say, not only is the existence of such entities assumed, but also they are implicitly invested with cultural habits and psychological traits – i.e. precisely *characterized*. It is this attribution of 'personality' to nation-states which explains (in common-sense reasoning) why only certain identities will appear in the 'potential aggressor' position.

Ideological inferences and narrative scripts[6]

Now it will be observed that inferential processes 1–5 are basically logical (we might say ideo-logical) in character. That is to say that the inferential reasoning outlined above takes the form of an argument, based on certain assumptions. But once this basic argument is in place, it seems that a further set of speculative inferences can be made, which are not so much a series of propositions, as possible narrative scenarios. The basic common-sense reasoning now becomes infected through narrative scripts – i.e. stereotypical event sequences. One such script is 'The Nuclear Blackmail Script':

6.1   Britain relinquishes nuclear weapons.
6.2   (By doing so) Britain loses its deterrent.
6.3   (Thus) Britain cannot deter the Soviet Union (see 4 and 5 above).
6.4   The Soviet Union threatens nuclear strikes against Britain.
6.5   Britain surrenders to threat.

6.6 The Soviet Union occupies Britain.

The crucial point about these assumptions is that they interlock as a chain of actions and consequences, in which hypothetical consequences are derived from possible actions in a speculative narrative of cause and effect. It is not a script for which we have historical precedents. There is, however, an associated script, loosely based on historical precedents, which may be described as 'The Origins of World War Two Script'. Basic constituents of this script are as follows:

7.1 In the search for peace European nations disarm.
7.2 Germany covertly re-arms.
7.3 (By this means) Germany gains a military ascendancy over other European nations.
7.4 Germany uses its superior power to threaten weaker nations.
7.5 The weaker nations are unable to resist Germany.
7.6 Germany occupies the territory of weaker nations by force.

Note that the end point of this latter script has some resemblance to the end of 'The Nuclear Blackmail Script'. The last constituent of each may be seen as triggering what may be referred to as 'The Occupation Script', whereby:

8.1 A strong nation occupies the territory of a weaker nation by force.
8.2 The strong nation crushes overt resistance by the weaker nation.
8.3 The government of the weaker nation surrenders.
8.4 But the population engages in heroic if piecemeal resistance.

This script has in fact two key subvariants, the first of which is 'The World War Two Occupation Script':

9.1.1 German forces occupy the territory of a weaker nation.
9.1.2 Germany crushes overt resistance.
9.1.3 The government of the weaker nation surrenders.
9.1.4 But the population engages in heroic if piecemeal resistance.
9.1.5 Allied forces liberate the territory.

The second variant is 'The Post World War Two (Cold War) Occupation Script':

9.2.1 Russian forces occupy the territory of the weaker nation.
9.2.2 The population engages in heroic if piecemeal resistance.
9.2.3 Russian forces quell overt resistance.
9.2.4 Russian forces install a puppet government.
9.2.5 Russian forces withdraw.

It appears that significant portions of these scripts and their core assumptions can be assimilated to a single master script – 'The Bully Script':

10.1 If you have the strength to stand up to a bully he leaves you in peace.
10.2 But if you are too weak to stand up to a bully he persecutes you.

For instance, it is this master script that underlies the opening lines of a Ministry of Defence leaflet:

> How To Deal With a Bully – Many of us have had to stand up to a bully at some stage of our lives. The only answer is to say: 'Let me alone – or you'll be sorry.' And to have the strength to back up your words...[7]

Clearly in 'The Bully Script', the anthropomorphic identities attributed to particular nation-states are recruited to a more general form of common-sense psychology. In the British context we would suggest that this script works on two related levels, for it is both highly specific and yet it is taken to be universal. Specifically 'standing up to a bully' involves images of a masculine ritual, a rite of early manhood, associated with single-sex institutions like the army or public school. But it is very interesting (and says much about the culture) that such specific incidents can be taken as exemplary situations which teach universal 'truths'. Not that these bear any necessary correspondence to actual historical situations (for instance, the real post-war foreign policy of the USSR). It must be stressed that these narrative scripts are stereotypical event sequences. In fact they amount to sedimented forms of 'common sense'.

Speculative scenarios

However, it is these assumptions and these narrative scripts that underlie the glossings that develop over the days following Kinnock's remarks. Younger's gloss that 'it is a policy of surrender' is derived from 4.1.1 and 5.1.1, but it also draws upon 6.1–6.5 of 'The Nuclear Blackmail Script'. Heseltine's claim that 'what Mr Kinnock is proposing is positively inviting people to attack' is similarly derived, but it also implicates 'The Bully Script', 10.2. As the week proceeds, however, the use of these speculative narrative scenarios becomes more and more explicit. The trajectory can be made clear simply by focusing on quotations in the *Daily Telegraph* from Mrs Thatcher. On Tuesday 26 May 1987, she is reported as saying:

> It seems to me like a policy of surrender, because you can't have guerillas until you have been occupied.

This way of glossing Kinnock's utterances begins to make explicit some of the inferencing that underlies making 'any occupation totally untenable' equivalent to 'guerilla warfare'. In effect, it begins to spell out components of 'The Occupation Script', particularly steps 8.3–8.4:

8.3 The government of the weaker nation surrenders.
8.4 But the population engages in heroic if piecemeal resistance.

This same narrative script is elaborated by Thatcher in Wednesday's *Telegraph:*

> It is a policy for defeat, surrender, occupation, and finally prolonged guerilla fighting.

And in Friday's *Telegraph*, it is emphatically re-stated, so that the major components of the script have finally surfaced:

> He seemed to accept defeat, invasion and occupation. The British people under a Labour government would then have to rely on guerilla resistance to the enemy army of occupation.

Which again precisely corresponds to steps 8.1–8.4 of the script:

8.1   A strong nation occupies the territory of a weaker nation by force.
8.2   The strong nation crushes overt resistance by the weaker nation.
8.3   The government of the weaker nation surrenders to the invaders.
8.4   But the inhabitants engage in heroic if piecemeal resistance.

These are instances of the generalized 'Occupation Script' at work.

This same script can, however, be given more particular historical reference, as in the following, where it is actualized in terms of Afghanistan:

> Are we to face the sort of casualties and violence that Afghanistan has suffered? (Younger, *Daily Telegraph*, 25 May 1987)

And a similar reference lies behind Cartwright's comments reported in the same paper:

> It seems as if 'the Mujahideen in Penge High Street' were expected to deter Soviet nuclear blackmail. (*Daily Telegraph*, 25 May 1987)

Kinnock's denial is carried briefly the following day on the BBC's *Nine o'Clock News:*

> There is no question of guerilla warfare or Dad's Army. (BBC1, 26 May 1987)

But the next day the same sentence is quoted in the *Daily Telegraph* with an interesting extension to it:

> But he said the example of Afghan guerillas demonstrated the point that massive military power could not subdue even primitively armed people intent on maintaining their independence. (*Daily Telegraph*, 27 May 1987)

This is the first sign that the narrative scripts are potentially unstable when given historical realizations. The *Daily Telegraph* on Friday features a relatively extended quotation from a Thatcher speech, which may be understood as activating and blending selected historical realizations across a range of scripts in order to preserve the most favourable narrative outcome:

> She said it was absurd to argue, as Mr Kinnock had done, that the Afghan resistance had shown that military power could not subdue a people devoted to their liberty.
> Five million Afghans have fled; more than a million have been killed; the country has been ravaged; and Afghanistan is still occupied. So is Hungary; so is Czechoslovakia; so is Poland. (*Daily Telegraph*, 29 May 1987)

The Afghan example is thus reassimilated to 'The Cold-War Occupation Script'. However, the speech then continues by activating 'The World War Two Occupation Script', again with specific historical realizations:

> Europe was liberated from Nazi occupation not by its resistance movements, brave

though they were, but by the Allied armies using most modern weapons. (*Daily Telegraph*, 29 May 1987)

Thus several components of scripts become salient – for instance, almost the whole of 'The World War Two Occupation Script' surfaces in the last sentence:

9.1.1   German forces occupy the territory of a weaker nation (Nazi occupation).

9.1.4   But the population engages in heroic if piecemeal resistance (Resistance movements).

9.1.5   Allied forces liberate the territory (Europe was liberated... by the Allied armies using most modern weapons).

Thus, the way in which glosses develop from Kinnock's original comments on *TV-AM* may be summarized as follows. Initially, the glosses invoke individual scripts in a partial and elliptical fashion. The presence of scripts, however, is presupposed in the path that the glossings take. It is at least necessary to posit some such organization of knowledge and background assumptions, in order to take account of how 'using all the resources you have got to make any occupation totally untenable' can come to be heard as, for example, 'a policy of surrender'. As the glosses develop, more of the scripts are made explicit. Although separable in principle, in practice they become interwoven so that their separate components not only interrelate within discrete scripts but also overlap between one script and another. In this way, they apparently reinforce each other, and also reinforce the crucial background assumptions – in particular that 'the Soviet Union is a potential aggressor' (derived from 1 and 2) and that 'conventional weapons do not deter the Soviet Union' (see 5.1 above, derived from 4 and 5).

Two important additional points need to be made about this process. First, throughout the debate these key background assumptions never become the focus for discussion. They remain taken for granted in the structure of the debate without being reflected in it. Secondly, however, once they have been initially activated, the scripts themselves become productive of developing glosses. And these not only structure the discourse within the political sphere; they also seem to provide frameworks for selection from the political process for its representation in the media. For example, many of Thatcher's comments quoted here from the *Daily Telegraph* also figure in the TV news bulletins. To this extent the media's coverage of politics is also implicated in the kinds of assumptions and narrative models which we have discussed here. It is to this discursive interpenetration of different sites, around common assumptions and forms of talk, that we now turn our attention.

Key signifiers and the use of metaphors

The particular wording adopted in the glossings is of course significant. For instance, a key expression used throughout the week is 'guerilla warfare'. Its first occurrence in the media may be traced to the *Daily Telegraph* and the

Daily Express on Monday 25 May. Thus we find Cartwright for the SDP (Social Democrat Party) observing:

> The idea of guerilla warfare in the streets of London is ludicrous. (*Daily Express*, 25 May 1987)

and Heseltine for the Conservatives declaring:

> The idea of guerilla warfare in the streets of London is ludicrous. (*Daily Express*, 25 May 1987)

The productive potential of such terms consists in the fact that they work as key signifiers which organize the developing discourse on at least two interrelated levels. Thus, firstly they invoke the specific scripts we have discussed: in this case 'The Occupation Script' is applied to Britain, and at the same time background assumption 5.1.1 is reinforced – i.e. 'conventional weapons do not deter Soviet aggression'. In fact it is by reproducing such imaginary scenarios, with their background assumptions, that certain newspaper headlines make their impact: 'Guerilla War a Deterrent says Kinnock' (*Daily Telegraph*, 25 May 1987).

As long as the background assumption 5.1.1 is retained, then Kinnock appears to have made a ludicrous claim. And conversely, as long as the claim attributed to Kinnock seems ludicrous, then the background assumption is preserved. In effect, the headlined attribution trades off the background assumption at the same time as it confirms and consolidates it.

However, at the same time as these scripts and assumptions are drawn upon to render Labour's defence policy 'ludicrous', 'absurd', 'utter nonsense', etc. some components of the scripts become transferable to other fields. This slippage occurs where key signifiers (like 'guerilla warfare') seem to trigger off an associated lexicon whose fields of reference are extremely diverse. We have already seen that historical references for guerilla warfare (e.g. Afghan resistance) may be invoked. But a more general extension of the idea of 'guerilla warfare in the streets of London' is apparent in the following remarks from David Owen:

> He wants Dad's Army back and Captain Mainwaring's return to colours. Or does his confidence stem from his own extensive experience of fifth columnists in the Labour Party? (*Independent, Daily Telegraph*, BBC1, 26 May 1987)

In fact, *The Independent* prefaced this quotation in the following way:

> The SDP leader ridiculed Mr Kinnock's question in a weekend interview that there was little point in the Soviet Union invading a non-nuclear Britain because an occupation would be totally untenable.

In this way, the Owen quotation is located within 'The Post World War Two (Cold War) Occupation Script', but it extends that script from the defence issue to Labour's internal politics.

We have previously quoted from Norman Tebbit's speech on 26 March 1987 in which he invokes 'The Bully Script' to identify Kinnock as a 'runaway' (see above, p. 103). In this case a script which is initially associated with the field of defence (where its prime role is to justify a certain level of deterrence) is subsequently transferred to the personality of an opponent. Tebbit in fact runs the negative form of 'The Bully Script' (10.2) with Kinnock as its point of reference. However, through his stylistic use of parallel structures, this single script is again extended to cover a range of issues. Thus Kinnock's alleged inability to stand up to the trade unions, becomes one with his alleged inability to stand up to extremists, becomes one with his alleged inability to stand up to the Russians. The point then is not merely to call defence proposals into question by inscribing Kinnock in a clearly negative position in the script; but also to use the script in such a way that his personality is simultaneously called into question across a wide range of issues.

The main point we would make about the key signifiers contained in these glossings (e.g. 'guerillas'/'Dad's Army'/'fifth columnists'/'bully'/'run-away') is that they function as metaphors. Specifically, basic assumptions and scripts are invoked, but through a highly condensed lexicon which can be transferred to various referential fields. It is also frequently the case that such key signifiers inhabit basic scripts and narrative scenarios with characters drawn from popular culture – in so far as the rhetorical strategy is to invoke common cultural knowledge. So fictional television characters (like Captain Mainwaring) are introduced to the discourse of politics; but also Tebbit's speech makes liberal use of characters alluded to in the popular press (Trades Union 'bosses', Labour Party 'extremists', etc.). In this way the syntagmatic structures we have identified in the defence debate are invested, through metaphorical condensation, with the paradigms of populist rhetoric.

We presume that such rhetorical strategies have a hegemonic purpose. That is to say, they are addressed to 'the voting public'/'the people', and are oriented to mobilizing and winning consent by operating on the terrain of common sense, reaffirming or reworking its contours. At the same time, however, they are reactive within the discursive domains where they become established. They become regulative or productive mechanisms in the composition of discourse, inasmuch as ensuing discourses are framed in ways that extend the presuppositions of an established script, until they seem to be played out. (There does, for example, seem to be an institutional life cycle for scripts on issues of public policy of between 3 and 5 days). But during its period of dominance, a script and its associated vocabulary will be metaphorically extended to assimilate various kinds of new material, and will exclude other material that cannot be so assimilated.

Which metaphors/scripts prevail and win a wide dispersal across domains and genres? The vitality of a script/metaphor seems to be related to the following factors:

1 It should be consonant with a given field of reference – e.g. military/ pugilistic metaphors for the defence issue.
2 At the same time it should be productive of a metaphorical chain – being reworked in slightly different terms in extended scripts.
3 It should trade off and crystallize established and common-sense perceptions.

4 It should recruit its recipient to a clear position.
5 It should have a clear actantial role for one or other of the key public participants. (4 and 5 are closely related – perhaps 4 is achieved by virtue of 5)
6 While remaining consonant with the issue debated, it should nonetheless be capable of maximally organizing diverse aspects of the issue and be transferable from one aspect to another.

Metaphorical transfer in TV news narration

In this connection a very interesting form of metaphorical transfer seems to occur on a regular basis in the discourse of television news. In examining the transcripts of TV news bulletins during the second week of the election, we have been struck by the way glossings which develop in the political sphere become incorporated into the discourse of news stories themselves. More specifically, the kinds of metaphors we have identified in the speeches of politicians are not, in TV news, simply confined to quotations – rather they spill over into the narration spoken (or read) by the newscaster.

We are not sure why this happens. To some extent there seems to be a curious tendency, as we have mentioned, towards the production of metaphorical chains, in extended scripts, which are consonant with the material represented. For example, recent coverage of the plight of the National Health Service has frequently employed metaphors drawn from the medical sphere (transfusions of cash, applying sticking plasters to sores, services which have been cut to the bone, policies which are leeching the health services etc.). Similarly in the second week of the election, the defence issue was frequently discussed using military, or more generally pugilistic frames of reference. For instance, the following phrases were all used in the course of the narration of the *Nine o'Clock News* (BBC1, 26 May 1987):

> the big guns were out
> the Thatcher counter-attack began
> Norman Tebbit launched his own broadside
> As the first missile of the campaign landed, missing its target [shots of a squashed tomato, thrown at Mrs Thatcher].

And the headlines for *Newsnight* (BBC2, 26 May 1987) were:

> Mrs Thatcher's all out assault on Labour. What will Labour's tactics be in reply?

There may be other general reasons for the tendency to employ militaristic metaphors in the narration of an election campaign. In part, the very notion of a 'campaign' is perhaps conducive to the employment of metaphors of strategy and combat (offence, retreat; attack, counter-attack, etc.). In British general elections this tendency seems to be reinforced by the limited, 4-week duration of the campaigning period, which lends itself to a certain kind of narrative representation. Thus, there is the predetermined denouement of election day, to which all strategies can be seen to converge; but there is also the sense in which each new week of the campaign adds a further level of intensity to the struggle. For instance:

> The election campaign sharpened up today as both the Conservatives and the
> Alliance tried to land punches on Labour...
>   Conservatives and Alliance both rounded on Labour today, trying to halt
> Labour's rise in the polls in the first week of the campaign. Both went for what they
> believed to be Labour's weakest points. (BBC1, *Nine o'Clock News*, 26 May 1987)

At times, the narrative bears some resemblance to a sporting contest (e.g.
boxing); and the fact that Labour has apparently had a successful first week
almost seems to demand that the second week should be characterized in
terms of a Tory counter-attack.

We must be careful in the next stage of our argument, for we certainly do
not wish to appear to be accusing television journalists of conscious political
bias. As we have previously stated, for the most part the 'balance' of election
coverage was scrupulously fair. But as soon as we move from its quantitative
measurement to a more precise discursive analysis of the news, it does become
apparent that, to say the least, there is a certain consonance between the
scripts and metaphors used by some politicians and those used in news
narration. Thus there is a level of script reinforcement if, whilst Kinnock is
being described by Tebbit as a 'run-away', that quote is framed by a narration
which describes both Conservatives and Alliance as trying to 'land punches'
on Labour, going for Labour's 'weakest points', etc. To this extent, the script
of the TV news is consonant with 'The Bully Script' and certain all-pervasive
forms of common-sense reasoning.

That this is not simply a conspiracy, however, is apparent in John Cole's
commentary (BBC1, *Nine o'Clock News*, 26 May 1987). Certainly the pugilistic script is in place (he talks about parties 'fighting the election on their own
strengths and their opponents' weaknesses'). But this is a script whose terms
can be directed against Mrs Thatcher as well as Neil Kinnock: 'she's vulnerable
if only they can find the right punch'. So the reduction of politics to pugilistic
confrontation is not in any simple sense a form of pro-Tory propaganda. The
real point is slightly more complex and more subtle. It is that these scripts and
metaphors for the political process make Labour's task of presenting a non-
nuclear defence policy to the public doubly difficult. For, in the first place,
Labour must meet the critical objections of its opponents; but in the second
place Labour must present its policy in terms of a script which reduces
complex political processes to dramatic confrontations, and through a metaphorical rhetoric which is built around binary oppositions: friends vs enemies;
strength vs weakness; deterrence vs appeasement; 'taking a stand' vs 'running
away', etc. Our point is that it is difficult to make a differentiated defence
policy credible in these terms. In particular, the notion of allied cooperation in
the use of conventional forces flies in the face of all the basic assumptions we
have outlined – especially the all-pervasive 'Bully Script', reproduced by
politicians and by journalists alike, where 'shows of strength' are taken to be
fundamental to the maintenance of political credibility.

There are in fact occasional moments when the TV news narration directly
and explicitly reproduces common-sense reasoning on defence:

> 'There's no question of guerilla warfare and Dad's Army' he said, rejecting

suggestions that that was all Labour would rely on to repel a Soviet invasion. (BBC1, *Nine o'Clock News*, 26 May 1987)

But our argument does not rely on such overt instances of ideo-logic (cf. basic assumptions 4.1.1.–5.1.1 above). Rather, we are more concerned here with the narrative scripts which reproduce such ideologies as their implicit pre-suppositions, which construct chains of imaginary consequences, and which make metaphorical connections which are historically vague and yet universal, in common-sense terms. The narrative scripts associated with defence seem to be a particularly fertile ground for such metaphorical productivity, which is applied without much difficulty to the political process, and more extensively, through 'The Bully Script', to certain lessons about 'life' in general. Such lessons (e.g. standing up to a bully) are entirely appropriate to the anecdotal form of story-telling favoured by television news (cf. Tolson, 1985), and to the frameworks of popular narrative construction reproduced generally by television (cf. Hall, 1984). It is not surprising, therefore, that they appear not only in the rhetoric of politicians, but also in the discourse of the 'television election'.

It is also apparent that these discursive processes make life very difficult for any political party which wishes to introduce policies which question or contradict common-sense narrative frameworks. It is in these terms that we would explain the hesitances and the ultimate failure of the Labour Party in presenting its 1987 defence policy.

The 'public sphere' of broadcasting: towards a reassessment

During the 1980s much discussion of broadcast television in Britain has been haunted by the prospect of a 'technological revolution', supported by the present government's commitment to a free market economy. We have become familiar with the argument that a greater diversity of channels, organized on a commercial basis, poses a specific threat to the BBC, to the tradition of public service broadcasting, and more generally, to the idea of a 'public sphere' of democratic debate which that tradition represents (Garnham, 1986). In some versions of this discussion two equally monolithic principles ('public service' vs 'the market') seem to be engaged in inevitable confrontation. In these arguments it would appear that any expansion of the commercial principle can only be to the detriment of the 'public sphere' ideal. It becomes necessary then to propose a concerted defence of the principle of the public sphere:

> When the public sphere is invaded by commercialization, as Habermas makes clear, the difference between commodity circulation and social intercourse is erased. It seems to us important to justify and defend a public forum above and beyond commodity and exchange relations. (Robins and Webster, 1986: 44)

In this connection, we would argue that a study of formations of broadcast talk is directly relevant to the question of a 'public forum'. That is to say, we do not simply see the study of broadcast talk as an area of interest to linguists who may be turning their attention to forms of institutional discourse. Rather, we would suggest that our focus on the reproduction of scripts and metaphors in broadcast political debates begins to make some specific observations as to how the public forum is presently constructed. It indicates, as we have tried to show, that particular ideological assumptions and narrative scenarios occupy a place of dominance within this forum, to the extent that their pervasive solidity as forms of common sense is very difficult to challenge. Moreover, such forms of discourse are not simply restricted to the fields or topics (such as defence) which they represent, but are also mobilized, metaphorically, in the way public debate is reported (e.g. in TV news narration). So the study of broadcast talk illuminates the specific forms of communication which permeate the contemporary public sphere – building on the suggestion of Stuart Hall (1984) to which we have previously referred. We also think that there is scope for further investigation into the institutions which comprise this public sphere – for example, looking at specific instances of the circulation of news stories around and between the press, broadcasting institutions and political debates.

So this, for us, is the principal focus of our interest in broadcast talk: specifically those forms of discourse which institute a 'public forum' in contemporary Britain. But finally, we would also argue that what this entails is some reconsideration of the concept of 'public sphere' itself, both in its original form (as developed by Habermas, 1989) and in the recent debate in the UK about public service broadcasting. We do not have the space here for a full discussion, but we will just indicate the site of a problem, where the term 'public sphere' is mobilized *both* to describe an historical formation of public institutions, *and* to provide a principle of critique – a standard of rationality and democracy by which those institutions may be judged (cf. Tolson, pp. 195–6, this volume). Here we will note that many discussions of the 'public sphere' tell a story of compromise and decline from its classical eighteenth-century foundations. In this context, the concept of the public sphere remains an idealization to be set against the history of its 'structural transformation'; and this is the form in which it has reappeared in debate about the history of broadcasting. To quote Robins and Webster once again:

> [A] social democratic (Keynesian) public space existed pre-eminently through the media of radio and television; it was the BBC that created the public space of citizenship. The space that was established, however, was in reality a pseudo-public sphere. Participation was vicarious and remote, with the citizen as spectator consuming images of the political process. (Robins and Webster, 1986: 33)

Perhaps the 1987 General Election, with its increasing hype of public relations, glossy party politicals and photo opportunities, represented a culmination of this notion of the citizen as spectator. But without further audience research we would be loath to generalize about viewers' responses to the political debates we have described. In the meantime we would suggest that it is too simple to posit some general tendency towards the disintegration of the public sphere in the face of commercial pressures, particularly in Britain. On the contrary, what our research seems to indicate is the long-term continuity of certain common-sense discourses, imaginary scenarios and popular metaphors, which are deeply rooted in the political process. Some of these discourses (e.g. 'The Bully Script') have been in circulation for over a century. In this respect television continues to reproduce a type of 'public forum', in which politicians and the press also participate, and which has a very long history of decidedly detrimental effects for the articulation of progressive political positions.

Notes

The ideas developed in this paper owe much to discussions within the Strathclyde Linguistics and Politics Group; membership of which included the following: Christine Ali, Chris Carne, Andrew Goodman, Sara Mills, Alison Tait, Shan Wareing and others. They are not, of course, responsible for any errors of fact or argument. Earlier versions of the material developed here formed the basis of presentations to a national Linguistics and Politics conference in Liverpool, the Poetics and Linguistics Association conference in Birmingham, and a John Logie Baird seminar in Glasgow. Financial support for the work discussed here was provided by the research committee of Queen Margaret College, Edinburgh.

1. For example, one indicator of an overall 'balance' in news reporting might be the extent to which the agenda of each party was reflected in the structure of news bulletins, by being placed as the 'lead story' in coverage of events of the day. In these terms, during the first, third and fourth weeks of the campaign, bulletins did not significantly and systematically favour the Conservative Party over the combined opposition.

In weeks 1 and 4: the Conservative Party's agenda was reflected in the lead stories of 50% of news bulletins; whereas Labour was given the lead in 40%, and the SDP/Liberal Alliance in 10% of bulletins.

In week 3: the Conservatives were given the lead in 45% of bulletins, whereas the Labour Party's agenda was reflected in the lead stories of 55% of news bulletins.

However, the second week of the campaign saw a departure from this relatively even-handed approach, giving the lead story to the Conservative Party in 66% of news bulletins. Labour was allotted only 25%, and the Alliance only 9% of lead stories.

2. It could be argued that if a political party is regularly given the lead story in TV news bulletins, then this would give the impression that the argument/events associated with that party are more important than those associated with its opponents. Furthermore, if television's representation of the election is persistently structured in this way, opposition parties will appear systematically to occupy a secondary, responsive position.

3. We are not arguing here that the opinion polls were accurate in their predictions; the methodology of the polling organizations is not at issue here. What must be recognized, however, is the fact that all media organizations habitually give prominence to opinion-poll surveys – especially during by-election and general election campaigns. The opinion polls have thus attained the status of general currency within the media and political spheres. It need hardly be mentioned that the polls can trigger a 'bandwagon/coat-tails' effect, whereby a slight rise in the fortunes of a party or candidate, as measured by the polls, leads to a prediction which becomes self-fulfilling. The notion of 'electoral momentum' is thus crucial to the public perception of any political party's fortunes. It would seem that at the end of the second week of the election, the Labour Party began to lose the momentum it had built up in the first 10 days of campaigning – a setback which proved to be decisive.

4. There is, of course, a substantial literature relating to the coverage of politics in the media, and more particularly to the coverage of general elections. However, many studies – such as those compiled by researchers at Oxford University (Prof. David Butler) and at Essex University (Prof. Ivor Crewe) have a psephological emphasis: that is, they focus upon apparent shifts in voting behaviour which they attempt to explain with reference to underlying demographic developments. In more recent years, Butler has also been concerned with the effects of party campaigns, and his last three studies have devoted separate chapters to the role of broadcasting and the press. Here, however, the focus is again statistical (air-time and column inches) rather than an investigation of the discursive paradigms which have dominated election coverage.

5. All quotations from the *Daily Express*, 25 May 1987.

6. The concept of script is drawn from the work of Lehnert (1980).

7. The quotation is taken from an undated (1980s) Ministry of Defence Leaflet, 'How to Deal With A Bully: Peace Through Deterrence – The Only Answer To A Bully's Threat'. This leaflet is also discussed by Paul Chilton (1988).

References

Brown, G. and G. Yule (1983) *Discourse Analysis*. Cambridge: Cambridge University Press.

Chilton, P. (1988) *Orwellian Language and the Media*. London: Pluto.

Garnham, N. (1986) 'The Media and the Public Sphere', pp. 37–53 in P. Golding et al. (eds), *Communicating Politics: Mass Communications and the Political Process*. Leicester: Leicester University Press.

Habermas, J. (1989) *The Structural Transformation of the Public Sphere*. Oxford: Polity Press.

Hall, S. (1984) 'The Narrative Construction of Reality', *Southern Review*, 17.

Lehnert, W.G. (1980) 'The Role of Scripts in Understanding', in D. Metzing, *Frame Conceptions and Text Understanding*. Berlin: Walter de Gruyter.

Pateman, T. (1974) *Television and the February 1974 General Election*. London: British Film Institute.

Robins, K. and F. Webster (1986) 'Broadcasting Politics: Communications and Consumption', *Screen*, 27 (3–4): 30–44.

Scannell, P. (1989) 'Public Service Broadcasting and Modern Public Life', *Media, Culture and Society*, 11(2): 135–66.

Tolson, A. (1985) 'Anecdotal Television', *Screen*, (2).

7

The Organization of Talk on Talk Radio

Ian Hutchby

In this chapter I consider some of the interactionally accomplished organizational features of the talk produced by hosts and public participants in current affairs radio phone-in broadcasts.[1] The analysis of the communicative relations on display here can yield interesting results in two respects. First, the analysis may be seen as bearing upon discussions within the sociology of media and mass communications about the interfacing of the 'private' and the 'public' (Horton and Wohl, 1956; Avery and Ellis, 1979; Gumpert and Cathcart, 1986; Montgomery, 1986; Scannell, 1986, 1988, 1989). And secondly, the research reported on here may be thought of as complementing recent conversation analytic work on the *in situ* production and development of news or 'sense' in interactive broadcasting formats (Heritage, 1985; Greatbatch, 1986; Crow, 1986).

The talk produced on talk radio[2] exhibits a variety of features which formally liken it to everyday or 'mundane' conversation, on the one hand, and more 'institutional' forms of verbal interaction (e.g. broadcast news interviews, courtroom or classroom exchanges), on the other. Sacks et al. (1974) have formulated an extensive series of observable rules for the turn-taking organization of mundane talk, while Heritage (1985), Drew (1985) and Greatbatch (1986) have undertaken comparative analyses, from the same conversation analytic perspective, of broadcast news interviews and courtroom interaction. Heritage (1985) outlines some characteristics of the verbal negotiation of 'sense' in mundane and institutional conversational settings, seeking to elucidate the formal distinctions observably operative there. For instance, the work of 'news receipt' displays a far more 'negotiative' character in mundane talk – with frequent use of responsive utterances such as 'newsmarks' (Jefferson, 1981), 'continuers' (Schegloff, 1982), or '*oh* receipts' (Heritage, 1984b, 1985) – than in institutional talk, where virtually no use of such response strategies occurs (cf. Greatbatch, 1986). In general we can say that mundane talk is designed, interactively, *explicitly for co-participants* and is differentiated from institutional talk by the fact that the latter is designed, and displays itself as being designed, *explicitly for overhearers*. However, as Heritage (1985: 100, Note 3) points out: 'An intermediate case between talk that is produced as private and talk whose design exhibits its production for overhearers is perhaps to be found in radio shows incorporating a phone-in format.' Hence talk radio talk, which might in these terms be dubbed 'intermediate' talk, can be seen as of significance and of interest in so far as it is designedly an approximation of *mundane* talk, projected somehow into a *public* domain, and thus exhibiting features of institutional talk.

Openings

A central job of interactional work performed in the opening sequences of mundanely occurring telephone conversations is that of identification/recognition (Schegloff, 1979). Identification is an important task for social animals, and of significance for social analysts, since frequently 'social behaviour is differentiated by reference to its recipient or target' (Schegloff, 1979: 25). This phenomenon, termed 'recipient design', by Sacks and Schegloff (1979) is pervasive in conversation; it manifests itself in identification or other-party-referencing sequences initially as a preference for 'recognitionals' (e.g. names). Such recognitionals themselves are in turn preferredly 'minimized', for example 'Joe', 'she', or 'that guy', as against dispreferreds like 'my friend Mary who lives in that small house with her sister'. In the opening sequences of conversations occurring on talk radio, minimized recipient-designed co-participant identification is preferredly, and overwhelmingly, achieved within the span of the first two turns, as in [1] (for transcription conventions, see p. vi):

[1]   *H.* 23 January 1989

1.   *H.*   John is calling from Ilford good morning
2.   *J.*   .h good morning Brian

Here, the host (H) offers the caller (J) a *vocal signature* (i.e. a purportedly recognizable lexical-intonational sample) in the first turn (T1), which serves as a projected 'recognition source' (Schegloff, 1979: 63) to which the 'recognition solution' is provided by J in a minimized recipient-designed recognitional greetings utterance at T2. Thus the optimal three-turn identification/recognition sequence discerned in mundane telephone conversation openings by Schegloff (1972, 1979) is here compacted into two turns. Clearly this is because, the caller having already identified him or herself for the radio station's switchboard and been lodged on a call-stacking mechanism prior to receiving the host's vocal signature, there is no requirement for self-identification on the caller's part: the host, in accessing each caller in turn to the air, incorporates their name and geographical location (in [1], 'John' and 'Ilford') into his opening utterance.

J's T2 opening utterance in [1] clearly manifests his understanding that the host's first turn has been produced as an *invitation to speak*, as what Crow (1986), analysing phone-in talk in a televisual context, identifies as a caller-selecting, channel-opening utterance, rather than as strictly a 'greeting'. As such, the caller's first turn takes the form, in this initial citation, of, itself, a greeting, acknowledging that the T1 'vocal signature' has been adequately processed. However, if we observe the *continuation* of J's first turn in [1], we find evident his routine negotiation of what I suggest is a second 'factor of reciprocation' formally constraining callers' first turns; that requiring that hosts' first turns be received as *invitations to produce 'news'*, this being putatively the purpose for which access to the air has been granted:

[1]   23 January 1989

1. *H.*   John is calling from Ilford good morning
2. *J.*   .h good morning Brian (0.4) .hh what I'm phoning up is about the cricket

The reciprocation constraints emanating from this *tacit* 'news requesting' are, clearly, effects of the *context*, the specific situation in and by means of which this interaction is constituted. In the course of any current affairs phone-in broadcast the caller necessarily occupies, at least initially, the conversational locus of 'news-producer' while the host occupies the locus of 'news-elicitor'. Such constraints are overwhelmingly shown to be negotiated routinely by callers and hosts throughout the data corpus. In the vast majority of cases, following an opening sequence in which identification/recognition work is done successfully within the span of the first two turns, it is the caller who goes on, via a second 'section' in his/her opening utterance, to produce some further data (or 'news'). Another example of what might thus be called the 'requisite opening' is given in [2]:

[2]   *H.*   30 November 1988: 10

1. *H.*   Mill Hill:: i:s where Gloria calls from: good morning
2. *G.*   good morning Brian .hh erm re the Sunday opening I'm just phoning
   from the point of vie:w .hh as a:n assistant who actually does do this.

Again, the first section of G's opening utterance at T2 here consists of a 'formal' greetings unit while the second section, heralded by a short inbreath and subsequent section-transitional unit, or buffer ('erm'), consists of a *direct and unprompted* launch into a treatment of the caller's 'reason for calling': this marks the onset of what I label the 'call validation'. Call validations are ordinarily treated as being characterized essentially by substantive production of 'news', and as being the *necessary* and *autonomous* work of the caller alone. That such practices are oriented to by hosts, and necessarily, over-whelmingly, by callers also, as 'institutional realities', that is, as requisite forms of conduct within the bounds of this interactional situation, is demon-strable by means of consideration of some 'deviant cases' – i.e. non-requisite openings.

News delay

There are generally speaking two means by which the transition from opening to call validation can be delayed: one effects an extension of the opening sequence, the other is an effect of a disintegration of the normative structuring of the transition itself. In the former cases, opening sequences are extended usually through the agency of the caller. In such 'affiliative openings' what is observable is an attempt on the caller's part to enter into 'pre-news-giving' interaction: that is, to establish and request the host to acquiesce in the establishment of recognizably *interpersonal* relations which breach, even if only momentarily, the formal constraints which I am suggesting are an intrinsic element of the situation of the interaction, given by the caller's contextually necessary initial occupation of the locus of 'news-producer'. Affiliative openings occur only rarely within the present data corpus, but on their occurrence can run to some length, as in [3]:

[3] *H.* 26 January 1989: 10

```
 1. H.   Frances good morning
 2. F.   .h hello:: .h when you said .h Francesca³ is your next I thought I was
         really getting somewhere
         (.)
 3. H.   oh I seehh yes you: uthought
         th⌈at you'd been ele⌉vated
 4. F.     ⌊o::h (.) yes    ⌋
         I said .h o::H Brian .h however you didn't hear me I hope so that was
         all hhri ⌈gheh heh heh
 5. H.            ⌊no and anyway I didn't mean you did I
 6. F.   no you didn't⌈hh
 7. H.                ⌊how deflating .h
         (0.4)
 8. F.   yes terribly (.) ⌈desperate I was
 9. H.                    ⌊never mind
         never mind pu ⌈ll yourself up and er
10. F.                 ⌊bu- yes .hh
         well in any case you see last night
         was quite something wasn't it
```

Here, caller F gets to delay offering her news-producing call validation until T10. What we witness prior to that point is an elaborate sequence in which F (who seems to present herself as a regular participant, although she appears nowhere else in the data corpus) attempts to bring into play what might be thought of as some subjectively perceived 'intersubjectivity rights', the derivation of which can perhaps be traced to what Scannell (1986: 391) refers to as 'the approximation of relations of presence' characteristic of the communicative ethos of contemporary broadcasting (see Scannell, 1988). Horton and Wohl (1956) have argued that the 'personae' developed by broadcasting hosts tend across time to lodge in the everyday practical routines of their audience members and there take on qualities of realistic density; hence the public participants in current affairs phone-in broadcasts exist in a world in which *the host already has presence*, whereas for hosts callers appear at random and exist prior to their occurrence as verbal interactants only as listed name and location categories.

Attempted affiliative openings, therefore, may perhaps be seen as problematical largely from the perspective of the host. Callers having instigated such an opening format, hosts are presented with two alternatives: either (a) to *adopt* the offered communicative mode, thus both legitimating to some degree the caller's breaching of the convention recommending that he/she should move, on completion of a two-turn opening sequence, directly into the substantive production of 'news', and simultaneously committing the call to a sequence of 'affiliation' talk of indefinite length; or (b) to *shun* the caller's affiliation attempt, thereby sanctioning the breaching and requesting the caller to mobilize his/her assumed *tacit knowledge* of the turn organization of the requisite opening sequence. In [3], for instance, the host might have made something approximating the following utterance at T3:

[3a]   (Invented)

3.   *H.*   y<u>es</u>: well wha'd'you have to s<u>a</u>y

Instead, following the caller's somewhat cryptic remark at T2, H, at T3, makes a display of his *comprehension* of F's reference, thereby adopting the caller's affiliative mode:[4] the exchange then becomes problematical, since it is necessary that at some point 'soon' the talk must move out of the affiliative and on to the call-validational terrain. In this instance this transposition is achieved by means of H adopting 'dominant' speaker locus at T5 and conducting F towards a 'news-producing denouement' at T10, thereby managing: (a) to *preserve* in some degree the *form* of interpersonal relations which the caller has manifested an interest in developing; and (b) simultaneously to *require* the caller to observe the *routines* of call-structurational practices (at H's T9 invitational utterance, 'never mind pull yourself up and er').

A second means by which these routines are breached involves 'normative disintegration', and is exemplified in [4]:

[4]   *H.* 2 February 1989: 6

1.   *H.*   .hh it's Ge<u>o</u>ffrey next in Woodford Gr<u>ee</u>n
             (.)
2.   *G.*   good m<u>o</u>rning Brian
             (1.0)
3.   *H.*   y<u>es</u>
4.   *G.*   er I'm c<u>a</u>lling about the: rep<u>o</u>rt

This 'collapsed opening' exhibits a marked breakdown in relations between caller and host. The significant feature is the one-second pause lodged between T2 and T3. G, at T2, has produced the requisite minimized recipient-designed greetings utterance, but has failed to move, or to display his understanding of any requirement that he move, *autonomously* from this point into his call validation. H allows him 1 second – in this context a relatively lengthy pause – for 'repair' before drawing him into the call-validation with a terse *'yes'* at T3. In so far as this can be heard as a request for 'missing' information (i.e. the call validation), it alone does the task of situating the caller on the terrain of 'beginning news production': a task which, as we have seen, within the systematics of the 'requisite' opening sequence, the caller is wholly successful in achieving him/herself.

Another 'collapsed' opening, this time founded more clearly upon caller-manifested *context-misapprehension*, is the following:

[5]   *H.* 2 February 1989: 7

1.   *H.*   Jo:<u>h</u>n next
             (.)
2.   *J.*   he-hell<u>o</u>/
3.   *H.*   hell<u>o</u> John in: M<u>a</u>rylebone

4. *J.* er- hello er your- your people didn't give me any wa:rning er (.)
         okay ⌈.h
5. *H.*   ⌊well I said hello: you're John: now that was the warning now what
         d'you have to say
6. *J.* right erm (.) i:t's about the dogs

Although H's T1 vocal signature here is skeletal, offering J only *minimal*
opportunity for recognition, the root basis of the trouble lies in J's 'mis-
apprehension' of the context, his incorrect *event-sequence expectation*. This is
made explicit at T4, where, following upon H's T3 expansion of his vocal
signature, J indicates that he had been *expecting* some 'warning' from the
host's 'people' (presumably the switchboard staff) that his air-access was
imminent. J later in this turn displays willingness to make the opening-call
validation transition himself (with 'okay'), but H interrupts him at T5 with an
utterance that we can see as a remarkably explicit verbalized illustration of the
strength of hosts' orientation to the structural feature which I am emphasizing,
whereby callers are requested, indeed *constrained* to produce their first news
directly upon completion of an optimal two-turn opening sequence, *regardless*
of whether or not they receive any further prompt or 'continuation marker'.

Topical structure

Once the transition so described is achieved with any occurrent troubles
having been repaired, the caller enters into the task of 'beginning news
production'. I have termed this the 'call validation', since overwhelmingly it
appears to be treated by callers as, at least initially, a place for explicating their
reason for calling. Call validations tend strongly to be opened with comment-
prefacing units like: 'I want to talk about', or 'what I'm calling about' or 'yeah
it's about the'; or else with topic-introducing units like: 'I watched a programme last night', or 'I heard an item', or 'there was a report published'. In
short, the work of *topic introduction*, in each call, is done by the caller, and
each call's initiated topic can be either new to this broadcast or ongoing within
this broadcast.

The maintenance and development or organization of 'topic' in everyday
conversation has proved highly problematical, even recalcitrant, as a
phenomenon for conversation analytic research. Work that has been done in
this domain (e.g. Jefferson, 1984) has highlighted, among other things, the
immense complexity of members' topic-structuring work and the wide range
of procedures utilized by co-conversationalists in the management of topic
flow or *shift*. In describing/analysing the organization of talk on talk radio
these complexities of practical reasoning are to some extent mitigated,
since the topic to be managed in the course of any given 'unit call' remains more
or less singular: the situational contingencies of talk radio as a broadcasting
phenomenon effectively disallow the overt introduction of more than one
topic in the course of any call.[5] The same contingencies effect within any given
exchange some degree of 'solidification' of the local roles of news-elicitor and
news-producer; although, as I illustrate below, within the problematics of this

phase of the unit call (which for the sake of convenience I am referring to as the 'interrogation'[6]), these particular local roles and the footing implied in them may, momentarily but significantly, shift.

An at-this-stage problem for co-participants in any given call consists in the practical definition of the point at which the caller's 'first news production' either: (a) ends; (b) hits a 'snag' requiring, in the host's interpretation, interruptive repair of some sort; or (c) reaches a point of 'sufficient elaboration' to allow the 'interrogation' section to be otherwise interruptively instituted. In other words, such an at-this-stage problem is, essentially, a *host's* problem, since it is at this stage that the host needs to discern the point in the caller's production of 'first news' at which his re-entry into the talk is relevant and necessary. It is the case that, in some instances, this problem, which might be seen as a problem of 'transition-relevance' (cf. Sacks et al., 1974), is varyingly alleviated by means of the caller offering some explicit *invitation* to the host, thus *requesting* him/her to take a turn at talk. For instance, the caller may elicit information as to the host's 'stock of knowledge' in so far as their proposed topic is concerned, as in [6]:

[6] *H:* 30 November 1988: 4

2. S. .hh e:rm: (.) uh I: know it's impossible for you to:: get in touch with every
         programme=I was wondrin' if you saw the Oprah Winfrey show yesterday
3. H. no I didn't n ⌈ o
4. S.   ⌊ a::h well that's a great shame

Or, more equivocally:

[7] *H:* 26 January 1989: 8

2. M. good morning e:rm (.) you had a man on earlier about putting the guards
         back on the trains/
         (2.0)
3. H. yes?
4. M. well (.) I always thought the guard ((...))

In these instances the caller, in forming his/her first turn into an adjacency pair first part, creates a 'transition-relevance space' which the host is 'compelled' to fill. H's recognition of and willingness to comply with such a caller strategy clearly varies across these two fragments. In [7], it is possible that the *ambiguousness* of M's question (it has the lexical structure of a statement, and achieves its status as a question only by virtue of its slightly upward-inflected intonational pattern) and, perhaps more significantly, its *obviousness* (since H was a participant in the call referred to, he may deem it unnecessary for him to verbally acknowledge the 'truth' of the statement-question) combine to allow H to interpret this as a preamble to M's own comments rather than as an adjacency pair first part (hence, perhaps, the lengthy 2-second pause preceding his rather terse, 'forced' response at T3 – though compare this with the similarly long pause in [4] above). In [6], on the other hand, the caller's 'question' is made more readily recognizable by the prefatory 'I was wondrin' if . . .'. To this the host correspondingly readily provides a requisite (in this case negative) second pair part response.

It is, however, far more frequently the case that the host *interruptively* institutes the 'interrogation'. In general (we may say, again, overwhelmingly), hosts' first interrogative turns take the form of either: (a) *requests for* or *productions of* clarifications of some description relating to points raised in callers' first news-producing turns; or (b) overt, but varyingly explicit, *challenges* to the gist of, or one or more of the points raised in, callers' first news-producing turns. In [8] and [9], the host, in different ways, requests the caller to produce, or more strictly to acquiesce in the host's own production of, a *clarification* of some description:

[8] *H:* 26 January 1989: 14

2. *S.*   er I'm basically ca:lli:ng referring to: er the Royal Family going to the
          Japanese Funeral the:
          Japa⌈nese ( )
3. *H.*   ⌊the Royal Family by: (.) that you mean the Duke of Edinburgh
4. *S.*   (th) Duke of (.) the Duke of Edinburgh yes=I don't think we should go
          under any circumstances

[9] *H:* 30 November 1988: 5

5. *R.*   .h anyway I w's appalled when I saw it (.) absolutely dis-
          gust⌈ing programme
6. *H.*   ⌊(n-d-) this is the: the Channel Four programm:e (.).h
          e::r which is essentially about erm (.) black
          affairs ri⌈ght/
7. *R.*   ⌊yes=
8. *H.*   =°ys°

In both these examples, the host, H, *interruptively* produces a clarification unit which, evidently, the respective callers understand as some form of *routine request for acquiescence*, or *search for grounds of agreement*. In [8], it seems, H has in mind, at T3, a minor feature of 'detail' ('the Royal Family by: (.) that you mean the Duke of Edinburgh'); but although clearly this offering is seeking to correct *factually* S's prior utterance, S's response at T4, is merely to acquiesce summarily in its 'correctness' before proceeding with his comments on the issue in question. In [9], by contrast, H's T6 interruptive utterance offers for the caller's acceptance explicitly *additional data* putatively appending (again factually) R's own identification of his to-be-commented-upon topic (R had, in a previous turn, merely *named* the TV programme in question). Initially R, in similar fashion to S in [8], briefly acknowledges the accuracy of H's comment; yet, as consideration of the continuation of this call demonstrates, after a short pause R decides that these 'additional data' in fact require *comment* from him:

[9] *H:*   30 November 1988: 5 ("continuation")

          (0.4)
9. *R.*   ( ) e-erm a- well that's fair enough I mean that's a format if they want
          to uh e- y'know give some ti:me
          to⌈that kind⌉of thing that's fair enough
10. *H.*   ⌊oh yes: ⌋

So that the caller, in this instance, can be seen to be interpreting the host as momentarily adopting the local role of *news-producer* in order to issue surplus information which, on reflection, is judged to be of such significance as to necessitate some response. Fragment [9] thus constitutes the first example presented here of a shift in 'footing' (Goffman, 1981). In judging that R's call validation has hit a 'snag' requiring 'repair', H commences on the production of data specifically *excluded* from R's topic-introducing utterance. These data are intended, to some extent at least, as 'news' for reception by the broadcast's overhearing audience, as well as operating as a 'clarification' and thus seeking acceptance from the caller. Hence displayed here is a simultaneous orientation on the host's part to both the 'private' and the 'public' aspects of talk radio talk.

An alternative device via which hosts negotiate the problem of instituting the interrogation section involves the far more overtly 'interrogative' strategy of offering an explicit *challenge* to the validity, morality, sensibleness, meaningfulness or whatever, of the caller's call validation. Such a strategy is evident in [10]:

[10] *H:* 21 November 1988: 11

2. *M.* ((...)) y'know if you try to get a child into a nursery (it's) very difficult in this country .hh and in fact it's getting wo:rse
3. *H.* what's that got to do with it
4. *M.* .hh well I think w- wha- (that's) gotta d-do with it is that there is a sort of e:r (.).h a: ethos produced by these erm: e:rm e:rm telethons that in fact this country is very caring towards children ((...))

M is attempting to argue that a recent 'telethon' produced to raise money for children's charities throws up a contradiction in the politics of childcare in the UK, in so far as the need for such charities arises from the inability of the welfare agencies to deal with their designated problems, whereas the rhetoric of the telethon posits a society that 'is very caring towards children'. H, at T3, abruptly and explicitly challenges M's treatment of this topic on grounds of *relevance* ('what's that got to do with it'); and at T4, M clearly demonstrates his understanding of this utterance *as* a substantive challenge by producing (somewhat hesitantly, or nervously) an *explanation* or 'secondary validation' of his position. It is the case that, in this instance, H's relevance-challenge prefaces a series of overtly disputatious turns which, together with M's response, constitute the call as a largely antagonistic exchange; however, although the data corpus presents a number of examples of such early-stage challenges being followed by disputatious turn-series, this is by no means consistently so. Any combination of disputatious or challenge-bearing turns with non-disputatious elicitations or further-news-producing utterances may be employed by hosts in the complex ongoing process of 'managing' the 'sense' of callers' calls. For example, in [11], caller R is arguing that a reported visit by the Princess of Wales to the USA is tainted by a hypocritical stance as regards homelessness:

[11] *H:* 2 February 1989: 3

8. *R.* er th- her stay in a thousand pounds a night hotel plus VA**T::** and on her schedule she's visiting a home- p- place for the ho̲meless .hh a:nd there's going to be a ba:ll: .hh where the (.) the Americans are clamouring for

tickets at a thousand pounds a ni-<u>e</u>r th- a thousand pounds
each⌈<u>I</u> th⌉ink it's obsc<u>e</u>ne
9. *H.*   ⌊mm⌋<u>h</u>m
10. *H.*   whi<u>c</u>h (.) part is obsc<u>e</u>ne
(0.3)
11. *R.*   (d-th-) b<u>o</u>th th-the fact that sh<u>e</u>'s staying in a thousand pounds a night
hotel plus VA<u>T</u>: and the: .hh the price of the tickets for the b<u>a:ll</u> an- e-
(a- w-) added (.) al<u>o</u>ngside all that she's visiting a place for the h<u>o</u>meless
12. *H.*   w<u>e</u>ll (.) we: would h<u>a</u>v:e to understand what that money for the b<u>a</u>ll: would
be g<u>o</u>ing to: and I'm pr<u>e</u>tty sure that it's going to ch<u>a</u>rity

Here, although the host produces a 'challenge' at T10 (although one
admittedly less severe than that encountered in fragment [10]) to which R
responds, after a slight pause (perhaps indicating momentary bafflement) at
T11, his next utterance at T12 itself *responds to* and *seeks to develop* R's T11
reiteration of her argument by producing further news suggesting that the
'money for the b<u>a</u>ll: [is] going to ch<u>a</u>rity'. Later in the same call, further
complexities of interrelationality in topic-structuring work are revealed:

[12]*H:*   2 February 1989: 3

28. *R.*   ((...)) I still think a thousand pounds a night at a hot<u>e</u>:l: .hhh a:nd the f<u>a</u>ct
that she's going on to visit p- h<u>o</u>meless p<u>eo</u>ple⌈ i- ( )
29. *H.*   ⌊where should sh- where
should she be st<u>a</u>ying in New <u>York</u>
(0.4)
30. *R.*   w<u>e</u>:ll ( ) at a ch<u>ea</u>per place I don't think the money .h w<u>e're</u> paying that
money for her to st<u>a</u>y there and <u>I</u> think it's °obscene°
31. *H.*   well we're n<u>o</u>t actually paying the:⌈tho- m- money
32. *R.*   ⌊well wh<u>o</u>'s paying for it
33. *H.*   well th<u>e</u>: erm I im<u>a</u>gine the the the m<u>o</u>ney that the Royal F<u>a</u>mily has .hh
er is paying f<u>o</u>r it .h or ind<u>ee</u>d it m<u>a</u>y be paid for by somebody <u>e</u>lse .hh
erm but .h y'know <u>if</u> the: Princess of Wales l<u>i</u>ves in: (.) a p<u>a</u>lace in th<u>is</u>
country w-w-wh<u>y</u> do you think she should not l<u>i</u>ve in something which is
(.) c<u>o</u>mparable .hh when she's visiting New Y<u>o</u>rk/
34. *R.*   well <u>I</u> should think she c<u>o</u>uld find something comparable that- that- (or-)
e- it could be f<u>ou</u>:nd for her that doesn't c<u>o</u>st that m<u>o</u>ney

In this complicated exchange the caller makes a further restatement at T28
of her initial, general argument (reported in [11]), while at T29 H again
challenges her to deal with specifics ('where should she be staying in New
York'). It is evident that R's T30 *response* to this challenge succeeds in
effecting a minor *shift* in the topic (or, perhaps more accurately, the focus of
the topic) being dealt with in this call. From the general question of what R
thinks of as the hypocrisy of the born rich showing sympathy for the born
poor, her sudden observation at T30, 'we're paying that money for her to stay
there' (i.e. in the 'thousand pounds a night hotel'), redirects attention towards
the more powerful question of the ultimate liability of the taxpayer for what R
sees as the excessive luxury of the Princess of Wales' trip. That such a shift in
topic-focus is recognized and oriented to as such by the host is clear from his
response at T31, which in effect challenges the *accuracy* of R's claim. But the
most significant feature of this exchange for present purposes, R's challenge-
bearing utterance at T32, itself plainly derives from, is provided with its

conditions of production in, this same worked shift in topic-focus. R's T32 interruptive response to H's T31 accuracy-challenge is itself an *interrogative turn:* a challenge, produced by the caller, requesting the host to *clarify* his claim that 'we're not actually paying the: tho- m- money'. So that what is visible here is a footing shift which succeeds in locating the caller as news-elicitor and the host, therefore, as news-producer: in other words, a reversal of local role-adoptions which the host does not find the opportunity to 'rectify' until midway through his utterance at T33, with his re-adoption of the local role of news-elicitor. He thereby clearly re-establishes the 'original' agenda of the call, shifting the focus of the topic away from 'taxpayer liability' and back towards 'hypocrisy of the philanthropic rich'; and (b) re-locates the caller as the respondent to the host's 'interrogative' initiatives rather than as herself the initiator to whom the host is asked to respond. Thus, within the body of the unit call, significant shifts in footing occur and are 'worked out' as the host seeks to re-establish the institutionally given, or situationally *allocative*, footings for himself and callers.

Formulations

Conversation analysis has proceeded on the premiss that conversational interaction is a *self-explicating phenomenon:* 'A member may treat some part of the conversation as an occasion to describe that conversation, to explain it, or characterize it, or explicate, or translate, or summarize, or furnish the gist of it, or take note of its accordance with rules, or remark on its departure from rules. That is to say, a member may use some part of the conversation as an occasion to *formulate* the conversation'. (Garfinkel and Sacks, 1970: 350). Such formulations, of course, occur in a wide variety of mundane talk; and some of their properties have been investigated empirically by Heritage and Watson (1979). However, Heritage (1985) has isolated some specific classes of formulations occurring with marked frequency in the particular *institutional* context of the news interview. Institutions are themselves 'self-explicating phenomena' (see Pollner, 1979; Sharrock and Anderson, 1987); that is to say, in their observable organization are *displayed* the requirements of given bureaucratic practices: and one such radically observable locus of organization lies in the common bureaucratic requirement for 'successful' *processing* of lay members passing through the institutional machinery ('cases', 'patients', 'interviewees', 'defendants', 'callers'). In this respect talk radio broadcasts are no different to any other institutional phenomenon: callers must be 'processed' – that is, have their topic, once introduced, dealt with, assimilated (or rejected) in so far as it makes (or fails to make) 'some sense' of an issue-in-question, and their call terminated in order to make way for another caller. And this processing must be directed, in a necessarily ad hoc, rule-of-thumb manner, by the individual who is the 'visible' organizational hub of the entire institution, and who operates *at the interface* of lay member and institution, namely the host.

Formulations produced by news-elicitors in an institutional setting like the talk radio broadcast can be seen to 'work' on a number of levels. In an immediate sense, formulations of gist or upshot work to focus or 'pare down' the 'meaning' of the news offered prior to their production. At the same time they recognize the 'public' and the 'private', the 'institutional' and the 'interpersonal' dimensions of talk radio. As summaries of callers' calls-so-far, they are directed both towards 'assisting' the caller in developing the 'sense' of his/her call and towards 'clarifying' that 'sense' in an overarching manner *for the overhearing audience.*

Fragment [13] displays adequately the focusing/refocusing qualities of the formulation:

[13]*H:* 21 November 1988: 11

```
10.  M.    ((...) I think we should be working at breaking do:wn that separateness
           I ⌐think⌐these (.) telethons actually increase it
11.  H.    ⌊how/⌋
12.  H.    well (.) what you're saying is that charity does
13.  M.    .hh charity do::es ye:s⌐ I think it's-
14.  H.                           ⌊ok so you're .h so you're going back to that
           original argument we shouldn't have charity
15.  M.    well (.) no I um I wouldn't go that far= what I would like
           to⌐see is-
16.  H.      ⌊well how far are you going then
17.  M.    well I would- what I would like to see ((...))
```

Here, two formulations are evident: one involving *gist* at T12 and one involving *upshot* at T14. At T12, in formulating the gist of M's prior news-producing utterance(s), H clearly not only *focuses* M's 'point' concerning the contradictory effects of 'telethons' (which, while rhetorically encouraging wider concern with problematic features of our social structure, in fact, M claims, promote a passive altruism and exacerbate the 'separateness' between donor and donee), but *refocuses* it, expanding its field of reference from telethons alone – the restrictive topic of M's call – to charity in general. It is the case that, throughout the course of the call so far, M had made no attempt to generalize his point in this way; hence it might be said that H's T12 formulation of gist presents an example of what Heritage (1985: 108) labels the 'inferentially elaborative probe'. H here infers, and verbally proposes, that M's restricted critique is in fact, and in this specific way, generalizable and, as is visible at T13, M acquiesces in the proposal by restating the inferred elaboration, somewhat emphatically, himself (we might call this an *inference reinforcement*).

H's second formulation, at T14, links itself to, and builds upon, this acquiescing utterance at T13, attempting to relate the inferred 'underlying sense' of M's contribution, formulated by H at T12, to another call, aired earlier in the broadcast, whose contribution (centring around the argument that, as H states it, 'we shouldn't have charity') had instigated an ongoing debate within this broadcast on the question of the overall validity of organized charities. M, at T15, responds negatively to this attempted extension with 'no I um I wouldn't go that far', which utterance, shaped as it is as a 'weak' declination (as opposed, for instance, to an outright rejection of H's formulation of upshot), provides, in the first instance, for a further, clarifying utterance from the caller; or, in the absence of such a clarification, a requesting of it by the host in next turn. In fact, as is visible at T15 and T16, both these provisions are realized, with M moving directly from his declinational unit into a proposed clarification; and H, at T16, having 'anticipated' the sequential relevance of this clarification, producing his request for it even though M has, pre-emptively, entered into the task of accomplishing it.

In this sequence, therefore, are visible what Heritage (1985) identifies as 'cooperative' and 'uncooperative' features of formulations as conversational phenomena in institutionalized news-generating settings. Formulations project for the caller the alternative responsive strategies of *acceptance* (in which case the formulation and its response may be characterized as 'cooperative') or *rejection* (in which case the formulation and its response may be characterized as 'uncooperative', and further talk pertinent to the declination may be judged relevant and requested). Thus the formulation, while in an obvious sense serving the overhearing audience by 'parcelling' the overall gist, or some particular aspect, of the news produced within the call, may also serve the caller by allowing him/her either to accept the pared down version of their reporting and so take up in further talk the direction proposed by the formulation, or to reject this version and so take up in further talk their account of the grounds for this rejection. In either case, the formulation serves simultaneously as 'newsmark' and 'further-news-elicitation', and so intrinsically operates as a mechanism facilitating the interactive management and collaborative production of news or 'sense' in talk radio talk.

Closings

As Schegloff and Sacks (1973: 289) observe: 'the unit "a single conversation" does not simply end, but is brought to a close'. The 'closing' of a conversation in everyday life is not something which occurs randomly due to an unaccountable decision by one party to cease conversing and engage in other activities, but something which is, like every other feature of conversational activity, a negotiated, interactively produced, accountable, accomplished, *self-explicating* practice. Members' work in closing conversations has been analysed at length in, for instance, Schegloff and Sacks (1973) and Button (1987): the specific issue being that, 'while conversational openings regularly employ a common starting point – with greetings etc. – and then diverge over a range of particular conversations, conversational closings converge from a diverse range of conversations-in-their-course to a regular common closure with "bye bye" or its variants' (Schegloff and Sacks, 1973: 291, Note 3). Clearly, the same circumstance holds for talk in the setting of the talk radio broadcast; notably, however, the technical problematics of the accomplishment of a call's 'closing' exhibit a radical dissimilarity from those observable in mundane talk: a dissimilarity emanating, once again, from the talk's 'institutional' colouring, and gravitating around one pervasive characteristic, namely that conversational closings in talk radio talk are not required to be, and overwhelmingly are not in practice, *negotiated* in any overt respect between host and caller. Given the host's institutional siting as organizational 'hub' of the broadcast, as processing agent both accessing callers to the air and removing them from the air, it is in a very basic sense the host's task not only to 'open' calls (as we have already seen) but also to 'close' them.

Note that it is not being claimed by this that hosts may or must, consistently, unilaterally and *arbitrarily* close off callers' air-access, but that it is consistently the *host's task* to discern 'some' point in the organization of turns structuring a given call at which a relevant and/or necessary *bid for closing* might be made. As I show below, such a bid for closing may be accepted or rejected by the caller in question; but the point remains that ordinarily no exchange of 'ritual' closing utterances (e.g. 'goodbye' or 'see you') is required or offered in talk radio talk, and that, by virtue of both bureaucratic and technological siting, the host is not 'compelled' to pay regard to the caller's response to any closing bid, as might be the case, for example, for an accountable participant in everyday conversation.

In facilitating closing a mechanism sometimes employed is the summarizing formulation.

[14] *G:* 26 November 1988: 2

28. *M.*   ((...)) I mean (0.3) .h it- it is it's really it is the poor: the poorer pensions
           that've had it taken away from them (0.4) because of this: er money that's
           been e:r the means uh th- the needs allo:wance money
29. *H.*   so you don't think the government's being all that marvellous and
           generous ab⌐out this
30. *M.*   ⌊I think they're
           dis:gusting (.)⌐I really do
31. *H.*   ⌊thank- thank you Margaret

H's T29 formulation here pares down M's critique of the government's restructuring of the state pensions system into a simple, parcelled statement of opposition to the legislation, allowing M, at T30, to reinforce this negative summarization, after which H, having thus fashioned an appropriate possibility for withdrawing the caller from the air, closes the call with a peremptory (and commonly occurring) 'acknowledgement token' ('thank you Margaret') at T31. An alternative strategy involves the projection of some *isolated aspect* of the call, as in [15]:

[15] *H:* 30 November 1988: 8

22. *E.*   but all we saw was a woman's
           grief⌐(.) and an ordinary⌐young man who⌉ =
23. *H.*   ⌊ok well erm   ⌊y-y-yeh   ⌋
22a. *E.* = was in the⌐boy scouts and who: was °whatever°
24. *H.*   ⌊right I understand (.) I understand Eva and er understand
           m- the point you're making particularly fr- from the your starting point
           which was that .hh you will see .hh controversial programmes from .hh a
           particular (.) point of view .hhh and we've had two of those particular
           points of views .h er yours and earlier Richard's thank you very much
           indeed for calling us

Here, H's closing formulation at T24 involves an explicit *selection* of a *certain* point made by the caller ('particularly... your starting point') which the host cites here as the newsworthy content to be preserved (for the overhearing audience) from this call. Noteworthy in this fragment are two features distinguishing it from fragment [14]: first, that the host, on his first attempt at instigating the closing – with 'ok well erm' at T23 – retracts the attempt when it becomes clear that the caller's turn is not yet completed, and tries again a moment later ('right I understand' at T24), whereupon E, finishing her utterance rapidly, withdraws; and second, that once the closing formulation is entered, there is no further response from E, and indeed H, unlike the host in [14], fashions no space *for* a response by the caller. Thus the closing summary in [15] exhibits greater *selectivity* and *finality* than that offered in [14].

A closing of a different type, but illustrating another *retraction* of a closing bid by the host, is exemplified in [16]:

[16]*H:* 30 November 1988: 2

```
28b.K.  = it gives people the choice as to whether they want to shop on a Sunday
31. H.   t okay .h┌thank-
32. K.            └I mean those who want to keep Sunday special by all means let
         them I'm not against that┌(.) ┐those that do =
33. H.                            └yes┘
32a.K.  = but I mean we must move wi- with the times I think (.) in my opinion=
34. H.   =mm hm=
35. K.   ┌anyway I (   ) okay °Brian°┐
36. H.  =└ok thank you very much uh  ┘   (.) thank you very much Keith
```

Here, no formulation is involved: H appears to opt, at T31, for what might be called a 'simplest' closing bid, namely one constituted solely by an acknowledgement, thanking the caller for his/her call. K, however, interrupts this attempt with a further elaboration of his point concerning Sunday trading at T32, with the result that H, as in example [15], withdraws his attempt. Subsequently, however, at T35, K himself acknowledges belatedly the closing attempt made by H, allowing, with 'anyway' (a unit identified in Button (1987), as, thus sequentially located, a *first or second close component* – i.e. a component indicating that the speaker is seeking to move, or is acknowledging another's attempt to move, into a closing sequence), a space for H to reinstigate his closing; although, as is clear, at T36 H has pre-emptively reinstigated closing himself, in an overlapping utterance.

A final closing strategy considered here, and perhaps the most radical, is the 'explicit dissension', wherein, quite simply, the host appears to override the caller *in the course of their speaking* in order to produce, as the closing turn of the call, a summarization of his own, usually dissenting, view as regards the topic addressed in the call. An example is given in [17]:

[17]*H:* 21 November 1988: 11

```
36. M.   well no I what I think is that these telethons are educating people but
         they're educating them in a certain wa:y they're educating them to give
         money what they should be doing is educating them to take an interest in
         their community .hh instead of just giving money which can in fa:ct .h
```

37. *H.*

stop them being interested⌐because –
⌊well I don't think the job of the telethon is
to educate people to do anything .hh er it gives them an opportunity .h er
throu:gh a kind of entertainment if you like .hh er to give money now
you may not like that and so therefore you don't have to watch it .hh I
don't find it (.) terribly entertaining or interesting to wa:tch .hh but I
certainly wouldn't prevent people who do enjoy it .hh er from seeing it .h
being enterta:ined and at the same time giving money .h whether it salves
consciousnes- consciences or not .hh thank you Martin

Plainly, in this fragment, H's lengthy utterance at T37, interrupting R's T36
summarization of his 'point', itself produced in response to an earlier
elicitation from H (data not shown), both: (a) *explicitly dissents* from the
viewpoint elaborated by R in the body of the call; and (b) in itself *closes* the
call, allowing no space for any responsive utterance from the caller. Notably,
H's dissension here addresses itself not merely to the point raised in R's
immediately prior turn (i.e. the *educative significance* of telethons), but also to
two major points broached earlier in the call: that involving the possible
'prevention' or 'banning' of telethons (see text to example [10] above), and
that concerning the suggestion that televised charity events operate in some
way to 'salve consciences'. So that, in this example at least, the explicit
dissension of the host operates on a quite comprehensive level: at T37, H
systematically articulates the three major points raised by this caller to his own
critical point, namely that 'I certainly wouldn't prevent people who do enjoy
it, .hh er from seeing it .h being enterta:ined and at the same time giving
money'.

In sum, then, whether the closing is effected by means of a summary
formulation, a selective summarization, a 'simplest' acknowledgement, or an
explicit dissension, we see that the 'leading party', the occupant of what might
be termed 'dominant speaker locus' within the bounds of the sequence, is the
host. Although hosts may frequently *defer* to callers, at least momentarily,
withdrawing closing bids in face of offerings of further news by their interactants, the bureaucratic processual imperatives implicit in the structuring of
the talk radio broadcast *as a broadcast*, as 'that kind of phenomenon', and the
interactional constraints generated by the context in which talk radio talk *sui
generis* is brought into being, endow the host ultimately with the task of
'organizing' the passing of the caller through the machinery of the broadcast,
of 'directing' the processing of each individual call. And I want to suggest that
it is, therefore, in the routinely self-explicating work of the *closing* of conversations on talk radio that the operation of the broadcast as a *bureaucratic
phenomenon*, and of the host as the *organizing agent at the interface of the
'public' and the 'private' in talk radio talk itself*, is at its most immediately
visible.

Conclusion

In this report I have treated the current affairs radio phone-in broadcast as an
accountable formal structure talked into being by its member-participants.

What I have illustrated is the practical researchability of the ethnomethodo-logical proposal that 'the details of little, local sequences which at first [seem] narrow, insignificant and contextually uninteresting, turn out to be the crucial resources by which larger institutionalised activity frameworks are evoked' (Heritage, 1984a: 290).

It is by developing and working out finegrained, detailed analyses of the actual operation, in and through talk, of news-generating broadcasting institutions that we can more adequately conceptualize their *practical* 'effects' as bearers of some part of the 'common sense' of our culture. Talk radio represents a unique case in these terms, since its news-generating activity involves the input, in an absolutely essential way, of lay members of society whose substantive moral, political, intellectual convictions are treated, by professional broadcasters, as the bases for discussions, in the 'presence' of overhearers, of 'issues' defined as signifi-cant by callers themselves. In this way, the descriptive analysis of the organization of talk on talk radio enables us to gain some purchase on the communicative mechanics of the interfacing, within broadcasting as a news-generating institution, of the 'public' and the 'private', the 'institutional' and the 'interpersonal'; and, too, of the *situated work* of the production and development of 'news' within such (apparently increasingly popular) inter-active broadcasting formats.

Notes

1. The broadcast from which most of these data were drawn is *The Brian Hayes Programme*, broadcast daily on LBC Radio (London) between 10 a.m. and noon. Ordinarily, the open-line phone-in component of the programme occupies the first hour; the second hour frequently consists of interview matter usually incorporating a much more restricted phone-in component. Not every broadcast is hosted by Brian Hayes himself. *The Brian Hayes Programme* was chosen as the major data source principally because of Hayes' evident desire to discuss with his callers with some degree of *seriousness* and *purposefulness* issues of some interest to callers or of some 'consensually agreed' *general* relevance.

2. We might distinguish between the terms 'radio talk' and 'talk radio' in the following way. 'Radio talk' may be taken as referring to all forms of talk encounterable on radio, from DJ talk through interview to phone-in talk. 'Talk radio', on the other hand, may be taken as referring more restrictively to the phenomena of radio interview and radio phone-in broadcasts. Specifically, 'talk radio' in what follows implies the 'open line' current affairs phone-in broadcast: these terms are treated as more or less interchangeable.

3. F is referring here to the host's introduction of a caller appearing in the broadcast some three calls previously. Among other things, this is significant for demonstrating something of the length of time potential callers can remain lodged on the call-stacking mechanism after passing through the switchboard, awaiting their opportunity to address the host.

4. Crow (1986) has noted, in another phone-in context, that hosts appear ordinarily not to opt for the shunning alternative when offered the phenomenon he encounters in his data corpus – the 'compliment sequence' – but consistently to *adopt* the proffered mode; moreover, should compliment sequences break their optimal boundaries (because of caller nervousness or whatever), hosts will not 'downgrade' compliments (Pomerantz, 1978) but rather *upgrade* their response for one exchange and then (by means of silence or peremptory elicitation) terminate the compliment sequence should the caller 'go too far'. Note, however, that affiliative openings are not themselves examples of 'compliment sequences'. The latter are intrinsically restricted in length and also constrained in terms of their possible formal manifestations. Affiliation sequences, while they clearly express some complimentary intent on the part of the caller, are not characterized by either of these conditions.

5. This is not to say that multi-topic calls do not happen: on occasion, they do, and indeed the present data corpus offers a small number of examples of that phenomenon.

6. The noun 'interrogation' connotes some degree of authoritarian communicative relationship in its common usage within our culture. It should be noted that in employing it in the present context I do not mean to imply any such relationship between host and caller (although of course some kind of relationship of authority may well exist, and be perceived as existing by particular callers and hosts). I merely want to indicate that the section of the unit call with which I am now dealing is that in which (among other things) the host *questions* the caller as to the 'sense' or otherwise, the 'validity' or otherwise, the 'morality' or otherwise and so on and so forth, of his/her comments.

References

Atkinson, J.M. and P. Drew (1979) *Order in Court: The Organisation of Verbal Interaction in Judicial Settings*. London.

Avery, R. and D. Ellis (1979) 'Talk Radio as an Interpersonal Phenomenon', in G. Gumpert and C. Cathcart (eds), *Inter/Media: Interpersonal Communication in a Media World*. New York.

Button, G. (1987) 'Moving out of Closings', in G. Button and J. Lee (eds), *Talk and Social Organisation*. Clevedon.

Crow, B. (1986) 'Conversational Pragmatics in Television Talk: The Discourse of *Good Sex', Media, Culture and Society*, 8(4).

Drew, P. (1985) 'Analysing the Use of Language in Courtroom Interaction', in T. van Dijk (ed.), *Handbook of Discourse Analysis*, Vol. 3. London.

Garfinkel, H. and H. Sacks (1970) 'On Formal Structures of Practical Actions', in J.C. McKinney and E.A. Tiryakian (eds), *Theoretical Sociology*. New York.

Greatbatch, D. (1986) 'Aspects of Topical Organisation in News Interviews: The Use of Agenda-Shifting Procedures by Interviewees', *Media, Culture and Society*, 8(4).

Gumpert, G. and C. Cathcart (eds) (1986) *Inter/Media: Interpersonal Communication in a Media World*. New York: (third edition).

Heritage, J. (1984a) *Garfinkel and Ethnomethodology*. Oxford.

Heritage, J. (1984b) 'A Change of State Token and Aspects of Its Sequential Placement', in J.M. Atkinson and J. Heritage (eds), *Structures of Social Action*. Cambridge.

Heritage, J. (1985) 'Analysing News Interviews: Aspects of the Production of Talk for an Overhearing Audience', in T. van Dijk (ed.), *Handbook of Discourse Analysis*, Vol. 3. London.

Heritage, J. and D.R. Watson (1979) 'Formulations as Conversational Objects', in G. Psathas (ed.), *Everyday Language*. New York.

Horton, D. and R. Wohl (1956) 'Mass Communication and Para-Social Interaction: Observations on Intimacy at a Distance', *Psychiatry*, 19(3).

Jefferson, G. (1981) 'The Abominable "ne?": A Working Paper Exploring the Phenomenon of Post-Response Pursuit of Response'. Occasional paper no. 6. University of Manchester, Dept. of Sociology.

Jefferson, G. (1984) 'On Stepwise Transition from Talk about a Trouble to Inappropriately Next-Positioned Matters', in J.M. Atkinson and J. Heritage (eds), *Structures of Social Action*. Cambridge.

Montgomery, M. (1986) 'DJ talk', *Media, Culture and Society*, 8(4).

Pollner, M. (1979) 'Explicative Transactions: Making and Managing Meaning in Traffic Court', in G. Psathas (ed.), *Everyday Language*. New York.

Pomerantz, A. (1978) 'Compliment Responses: Notes on the Co-operation of Multiple Constraints', in J. Schenkein (ed.), *Studies in the Organisation of Conversational Interaction*. New York.

Sacks, H. and E. Schegloff (1979) 'Two Preferences in the Organisation of Reference to Persons in Conversation and Their Interaction', in G. Psathas, (ed.), *Everyday Language*. New York.

Sacks, H., E. Schegloff and G. Jefferson (1974) 'A Simplest Systematics for the Organisation of Turn-Taking for Conversation', *Language*, 50(4).

Scannell, P. (1986) 'Editorial', *Media, Culture and Society*, 8(4).

Scannell, P. (1988) 'The Communicative Ethos of Broadcasting'. Paper presented at The International Television Studies Conference, London (BFI).

Scannell, P. (1989) 'Public Service Broadcasting and Modern Public Life', *Media, Culture and Society*, 11(2).

Schegloff, E. (1972) 'Sequencing in Conversational Openings', in J. Laver and S. Hutcheson (eds), *Communication in Face to Face Interaction*. Harmondsworth: Penguin.

Schegloff, E. (1979) 'Identification and Recognition in Telephone Conversation Openings', in G. Psathas (ed.), *Everyday Language*. New York.

Schegloff, E. (1982) 'Discourse as an Interactional Achievement: Some Uses of "uh-huh" and Other Things that Come Between Sentences', in D. Tannen (ed.), *Georgetown University Roundtable on Language and Linguistics 1981*. Washington, DC.

Schegloff, E. and H. Sacks (1973) 'Opening Up Closings', *Semiotica*, 8(4).

Sharrock, W. and R. Anderson (1987) 'Work Flow in a Paediatric Clinic', in G. Button and J. Lee (eds), *Talk and Social Organisation*. Clevedon.

8

Our Tune: A Study of a Discourse Genre

Martin Montgomery

> Each genre has the capacity to deal with only certain aspects of reality; to each
> belong certain principles of selection, certain manners of envisioning and con-
> ceptualising reality; each operates within a certain scale of depth and range of
> treatment. (I.R. Titunik)

> It is in the narratives of everyday life . . . that . . . the ideological features of discourse
> may be discerned. (J.B. Thompson)

> There is no such thing as society. There are only individuals and their families.
> (M. Thatcher)

A few minutes after 11.00 a.m. most weekday mornings the normal cycle of
music and chat on BBC Radio 1 is interrupted for several minutes while the
resident DJ – Simon Bates – summarizes a listener's letter, using it as an
extended dedication to a record which the letter requests. The letters are of a
particular type. They recount personal dilemmas and emotional traumas –
divorce, psychiatric breakdown, family bereavements – and Bates extem-
porizes from them against a background of muted orchestral music from
Zeferelli's *Romeo and Juliet*. Although unlisted in the schedules, the event has
acquired a name and a definable slot in the morning's programme. It has also
acquired a large following. It is supposed to generate 500 letters a week and
attract an audience of over 10 million; and whilst there may be some doubts
about the latter figure (since official BBC figures suggest a reach of 2 million)
it does coincide with the peak in daily audience figures for Radio 1.

As a speech performance it is interesting in a variety of ways. For one thing
the discourse is doubly authored: it is delivered by Bates but as an extempore
adaptation of a letter from a listener. It is therefore projected as rooted in the
real-life experience of an actual member of the audience. As such it deals most
often with private dilemmas, but here broadcast in the public domain to a
mass audience by one of Radio 1's best-known disc jockeys. There are various
kinds of tension present in this performance: a tension between the private
world of individual experience and the public world of the broadcast event; a
tension between the anonymity of the letter-writer and the familiar persona of
Bates; a tension between the implied narration of the letter (first person;
written) and the actual narration at the moment of broadcasting itself (third
person; spoken); and finally a tension between the family both as community
and as the site of personal dislocation.

In this chapter I examine how these tensions are negotiated in the discourse
of Our Tune. More broadly, however, I am concerned with how the event

constitutes a particular genre within broadcasting, adopting a recognizable discursive structure with associated lexicogrammatical forms, which in turn realize particular kinds of meanings. And, since Our Tune as a genre is heavily dependent upon the rehearsal of past events, the notion of 'narrative' constitutes an important part of the approach. As narrative, Our Tune can be considered (following Culler, 1975; Chatman, 1978; Rimmon-Kenan, 1983) from two complementary directions. From one perspective Our Tune is seen as a set of texts which display a range of particular kinds of discursive practice, inasmuch as it variously reports narrative events, situates them, moralizes about them etc., these practices being for the most part configured in a particular sequence (for example, the playing of the record typically takes place only after the narration of core events has been completed). From this perspective, it is possible to address and comment upon surface features of the texts themselves, inasmuch as certain kinds of discursive practice have associated with them particular patterns of lexicogrammatical selection.

From another perspective, however, Our Tune is considered in terms of its basic story materials – the typical event-line and the recurring types of actor – that comprise the substance of the narrative. The emphasis in this latter approach is less upon the 'surface' of the text, and more upon its underlying components. The shift from one perspective to the other thus corresponds loosely to a shift from a concern with how Our Tune negotiates a particular set of conditions of utterance associated with the broadcast event to a larger concern with a characteristic kind of 'content' or 'ideology' which this event mobilizes.

Our Tune as discourse

Despite the now extensive literature on spoken narration (see, for example, Tolson, 1989; Chafe, 1980; Polanyi, 1985) Labov's (1972) paper on 'The Transformation of Experience in Narrative Syntax' remains an important starting-point, which has informed much subsequent research (see, for example, Martin and Rothery, 1980/1; van Dijk, 1985). Labov's discussion of spoken story-telling rests upon a crucial distinction between *narrative clauses* and *free clauses*. The former carry the basic structure of the narrative and reflect the logico-temporal order of the events depicted. The sequencing of such clauses is accordingly part of their narrative meaning and any attempt to displace or reorder them is likely to disturb the overall trajectory of the story. If narrative clauses establish the basic logico-temporal sequence of the story, 'free clauses', on the other hand, perform important contextual and evaluative work around this basic structure: and they are 'free', inasmuch as there do not seem to be the same positional constraints on their placement.

In addition, Labov proposed that the oral narratives tend to display a determinate shape dependent upon the ordering of different types of discursive strategy. These he enumerates as follows:

1 Abstract
2 Orientation

3 Complicating Action
4 Evaluation
5 Result or Resolution
6 Coda

Thus, the discourse of the narrative does different things at different points in its narration. An *Abstract* may occur at the beginning of the narrative in the form of one or two clauses briefly summarizing the whole story. An *Orientation* will follow an abstract (if the latter occurs) and will set the scene for the story in terms of time, persons and circumstances. The *Complicating Action* and the *Resolution* must be realized by narrative clauses and provide the crucial components of the narrative inasmuch as they spell out its event-line. *Codas* occur at the end of the narrative and 'have the property of bridging the gap between the moment of time at the end of the narrative proper and the present. They bring the narrator and the listener back to the point at which they entered the narrative.' (Labov, 1972: 365) *Codas* also set up no predictions for further narrative events and so do not prompt the question 'and then what happened?' *Evaluations* are more difficult to define. Labov describes them as places 'in which the action is suspended while elaborate arguments are developed' (p. 369). In Labov's examples these not untypically take the form of reported speech; and, more generally, he emphasizes that they are crucial components of narratives of personal experience.

Complication and Resolution, according to this account, are obligatory elements of the discursive structure of the narrative. The remaining elements are optional. Amongst these the Abstract and the Coda have positional constraints upon them, such that the former tends to occupy initial position in the narrative text, whereas the latter occupies final position. Orientations and Evaluations, however, are less positionally constrained. Nonetheless, it is possible to suggest that, inasmuch as Orientations are prospective in their purpose, they are likely to precede the first narrative event, even though successive Reorientations may take place as the narrative unfolds, especially as new Complicating Actions are introduced. And it is also possible to suggest that inasmuch as Evaluations operate retrospectively on narrative events they are likely to occur after Complicating Actions and Resolutions. Generally, it would seem to be the case that the discourse of spoken narration can switch into and out of Orientations and Evaluations as the narrative unfolds.

Some of the core elements of Labov's scheme provide an immediately relevant starting-point for the specification of some of the generic properties of Our Tune. I adopt them as an initial framework and modify or develop them in the discussion of specific examples.

Tense marking and narration in Our Tune

In Our Tune the basic event-line of the narrative is provided by main clauses in the simple past tense where, typically, the verb encodes a material rather than a relational process – what Halliday (1985) terms 'a process of doing' rather than of 'being' or 'having'. In addition to the use of the simple past tense, the encoded event should exhibit a clear temporally bounded character. Exceptionally, clauses where the main verb encodes a mental or verbal process may also carry the event-line. Examples of the event-line being realized in this way are thus as follows:

> her parents split up
>
> she discovered that the woman who was in bed with her husband was the mother of one of his children
>
> she found a lump
>
> she was told she would have to have a mastectomy

All of these are treated as instances of a narrative clause. Also included in this category would be verb constructions of the inceptive type ('started to ...', 'began to ... ') Thus, examples such as

> things started to go wrong
>
> divorce proceedings started

both count as narrative clauses.

Other kinds of tenses clearly play a pervasive role in the discourse of Our Tune: e.g.

present:	the sister is now expecting the first child
past continuous:	they were living together
past perfect:	the divorce hadn't gone through
past perfect continuous:	they had been struggling to make ends meet

These, however, are prototypically associated with free clauses rather than strict narrative clauses. As such they tend to provide an explanatory framework for narrative clauses that develop the core event-line of the narrative.

Narrative clauses and the event-line of the story

For any particular instance of Our Tune, it is possible to display the basic skeleton of the story in terms of its event-line, by isolating out the narrative clauses in the order in which they occur. Thus Maxine's story in one Our Tune is carried by the following narrative clauses:

> (a happy family initially)
> 1. and then things started to go wrong
> 2. and almost inevitably her parents split up
> 3. one day Mum just got up and walked out
> 4. after a while... (Dad)... met someone else
> 5. and brought the lady home for them to meet
> 6. and after a while they settled down
> 7. and then out of the bushes and out of the blue... Mum reappeared back on the scene
> 8. and so she (Joan/the lady) left
> 9. so Mum came back
> 10. and to be honest it didn't work out
> 11. divorce proceedings started
> 12. and... (Joan/the lady)... reappeared

13. and picked up the pieces
14. and so ... they got married
     (and although the family's been hurt
     by sticking together
     they've won out)

Significantly, this simple series of fourteen narrative clauses from different points in the narration of Our Tune seems clearly ordered in terms of Complicating Actions and Resolutions. Thus:

Complication 1
  1. and then things started to go wrong
  2. and almost inevitably her parents split up
  3. one day Mum just got up and walked out

Resolution 1
  4. after a while ... (Dad) ... met someone else
  5. and brought the lady home for them to meet
  6. and after a while they settled down

Complication 2
  7. and then out of the bushes and out of the blue ... Mum reappeared back on the scene

Resolution 2
  8. and so she (Joan/the lady) left
  9. so Mum came back

Complication 3
  10. and to be honest it didn't work out
  11. divorce proceedings started

Resolution 3
  12. and ... (Joan/the lady) ... reappeared
  13. and picked up the pieces
  14. and so ... they (Dad + Joan) got married

The specific nature of the Complications and the Resolutions in Our Tune is clearly of great interest, not the least because they tend to be drawn from a rather narrow range of possibilities, as we see below ('Events', p. 165-70). We may note in passing, however, that in this particular instance the relationship of the first Complication to the last Resolution fits neatly into the kind of structural homology proposed by Greimas (1966), whereby:

| *The initial situation:* | *The final situation::* | *The complication:* | *The resolution* |
| 'A happy family': | 'A happy family':: | Mum leaves home: | Dad re-marries |

But, if extracting the narrative clauses enables the Complication + Resolution structure of the narrative to be displayed, it does clearly pose a problem concerning the relation of the narrative clauses to the total text of any Our Tune. Although the event-line is the most central constituting feature of the genre, it accounts for only a relatively small proportion of any individual text produced within that genre. In effect, the discourse of Our Tune is concerned with much more than laying down the basic event-line.

The free clauses of Our Tune are concerned with two broad types of activity: (a) organizing the structure of the discursive event itself, and (b) managing its reception by the audience. More particularly, it is possible to distinguish (in addition to Complication + Resolution) the following components of Our Tune as a total discursive event.

The discourse structure of Our Tune

Framing Although Our Tune is not mentioned in published notices of 'what's on' Radio 1, it does occupy a recognizable slot in Simon Bates' morning show. It commonly occurs around 11.00 a.m., which is almost exactly half-way through Bates' programme; and during the course of the first part of Bates' show references are made to it as an upcoming item. As a discursive event various techniques are used to separate it from the rest of the medley of music and chat. Narration takes place against a background of orchestral 'theme' music, so that the onset of this music is itself a signal that Our Tune is about to begin. And continuation of the theme music is an enduring signal of the switch from desultory patter to sustained narrative monologue. In addition there are verbal markers of the onset and termination of Our Tune. Onset is marked by utterances of the following type:

this one is from the Midlands
it's from Staffordshire
which is all anybody needs to know

this letter... comes from the South of England
it is from a lady called Marianne

this one comes from North of the border
and that's all I need to say
but I will say it comes from a lady called Lynn

and this one which is from Brian who lives in Kent
er actually started the letter off...

Prototypical *framing* utterances display the following format

proximate demonstrative+	'one'/ text reference item	+copula/	'comes'+	'from'+	location/ person
this	one	is		from	the Midlands
this	letter		comes	from	the South of England
this	one		comes	from	North of the border
this	one	is		from	Brian

Apart from the obvious role of marking the onset of Our Tune as a discursive event, framing serves important additional purposes. It helps to bracket the ensuing discourse as in some way originating from a source outside the broadcasting institution itself; so that attributing a source for the material by name and region is partly a way of authenticating it as the real-life story of a real person from a nationally dispersed audience. At the same time with-holding the full name and address of the source distinguishes it from any simple record dedication and further marks the material as potentially transgressing a boundary between private experience and the public domain ('there are some things you just don't talk about in public'), thus the full identity of the source is kept secret. Finally, it also makes possible partial disclaimers of responsibility for any offence which the material might generate.

Framing to mark the end of Our Tune depends upon more ritualized utterances, involving simple formulas such as:

and that's Our Tune today

it's Our Tune
Stand By Me
Ben E. King

drop us a line
Simon Bates
BBC Radio One
London W1A 4WW

it's Our Tune
Simon Bates
BBC Radio One
London W1A 4WW

will you drop me a line please
that's Nilsson
Simon Bates
BBC Radio One

The production of these final framings coincides with marked prosodic shifts by Bates. There is some increase in voice amplitude and a marked acceleration of tempo. It is also noticeable that the retrospective boundary marking performed by these framings is supported by the kind of demonstrative reference adopted, which tends to be distal rather than proximate ('that' rather than 'this'), consonant with its use anaphorically as a text reference item. And the use by the DJ of his own name, coupled with a reference to the station, seems to return the discourse unambiguously to its institutional site leaving behind the doubly authored discourse of the narrative section. Final framings also tend to coincide with musical shifts in which the orchestral background 'theme' is replaced by a fade-in lead to the next record. Generally, final framings reverse the priority of onset framings; station name rather than audience names; London rather than the regions; distal demonstratives rather than proximate; and acceleration rather than slowing of tempo.

Focusing   Rather than use Labov's term, Abstract, I have adopted the term *focusing* from Sinclair and Coulthard (1975). Although focusing usually occurs immediately after the initial framing it does not strictly provide a prospective summary of the narrative. Instead, focusing provides an oblique and very general indication of what the narrative will be about. In this sense its role seems to be to suggest what kind of interpretative set needs to be adopted by the audience in finding 'the point' of the story. Focusing may be exemplified as follows:

and it's a story that's very simple
and I guess also it's a story about the way people survive things
because you have preconceptions about divorce
and you have preconceptions also about the way it affects kids
and sometimes you forget about how it affects the adults as well in a family

the letter really is about her growing up
and going through all the traumas that most people avoid
I guess she's avoided a few herself
but on the other hand there there's some pretty bad times in there
and in the end coming out with a realisation that is much the same as the Mike
the Mechanic's record
you'll understand why when we get through it

er it's about basically the way people survive from things
and the way people come through from the other side.
and you'll understand it.

Thus it can be seen that focusing most usually takes the following form:

text reference item	+copula	+ text reference item	+copula	+ 'about'	+ topic
it	's	a story		about	
		it	's	about	
		the letter (really)	is	about	

There are several significant aspects to focusing. Firstly, despite the particularities of the narrative which they preface, the proposed topics are extraordinarily similar:

it's... about the way people survive things

the letter... is about... her going through all the traumas
and in the end coming out

it's about... the way people survive from things
and the way people come through

They are about 'going through', 'coming through' and 'out' and hence 'surviving'. At the same time, however, they are formulated at such a level of generality that they do not give much clue as to the particularities of the forthcoming narrative. To some extent then they paradoxically defeat their own apparent purpose, since they do not give the sense of the story in advance. Instead, they depend upon completion of the story for sense to be made of them. ('You'll understand it'; 'You'll understand why when we get through it'.) In this way, they come close to being 'fake' focuses which project forward enigmatically over the course of the narrative, providing a kind of bait for the audience. Finally, they are commonly offered with a hedge against being taken as a definitive statement of the story's meaning:

I guess also it's a story about
er it's about *basically*
the letter *really* is about

An extreme variant of the faked and hedged focus is the negative focus:

this one is the kind of letter that's going to get everybody ringing in
the phones are going to ri light up like Christmas trees basically with ladies
er ringing in to complain that I shouldn't do it
an(d) I can probably understand how they feel about it
mainly because I can't grasp the import of what the lady has to say
...
but she's honest

and that's the reason for using this Our Tune
it's something that I can't comprehend at all
no bloke could
er whatever you hear people say on the radio
the kind of people who reckon they're experts about things can't understand
something that is exclusively female
I don't believe it to be honest
any more than ladies can understand things that are exclusively male either

This kind of focus avoids projecting the topic of Our Tune, on the grounds that the material in question resists comprehension or interpretation. It is even possible to run one kind of focus into the other, as in the following:

when I first read it I thought oh here's a lady who's been through helluva lot
and I can't quite see what she's getting at
and then I suddenly realised
er because *the letter really is about her growing up*
and going through all the traumas that most people avoid
I guess she's avoided a few herself
but on the other hand there there's some pretty bad times in there
and in the end coming out with a realisation that is much the same as the Mike
the Mechanic's record
you'll understand why when we get through it

Situating refers to the way in which parts of the narration are devoted to defining the time and circumstances of the narrative, corresponding loosely to what Labov described as *Orientation*. This latter term, however, will be reserved for a rather different type of discursive activity in Our Tune, which Labov had little need to take account of in his own data (see *'Orientation'*, pp. 148–50). Situating takes place after the initial framing and focusing and introduces characters in a situation.

starts in nineteen seventy-two with a lady called Maxine
er Mum and Dad four kids
two boys and two girls of which Maxine was the youngest
a happy family initially

it goes back a few years
and take maybe ten years ago
and she was going through a tough time because her father had died
and she was a teenager
and he'd died suddenly and tragically
and as a result of that she'd got a little bit maybe loose and a bit wild
Dad had been very protective
she hadn't gotten on as well maybe as she should with her Mum
but that's two ladies living together
and she had a brother
and the focus of the Mum went on to the brother
so I guess Maxine went a little haywire
she had a few pennies which her father had left her

her name is Marie
she lives in Burnley in Lancashire
she is twenty-seven years old
she is divorced
she has a three four-year-old little boy

and she hasn't been the luckiest person in the world
but she's honest
now this lady is an honest person
she's also a person who's been through a great deal
an(d) as she says some of it is her own fault

after splitting with her husband she lived with her parents for ten months
and she finally managed to get a little house, for her son
and she, and she's the kind of person who is fiercely protective
and the kind of person also who's determined to do things on her own
now it looked pretty good 'cos when she got the little house she had a job an(d)
she had a roof over her head an(d) it was her own and it looked like she could
relax a little bit and get on with life
now what is also true reading between the lines is that this lady is fairly lonely
she hasn't got a fella around
she hasn't time
and she cares about her kid enough to be in every night
and that means it's the black'n white television and not a great deal of money
I would think reading between the lines that means that sometimes in the winter
the heating isn't always on
an(d) all she cares about is making sure that her three four-year-old kid has
got the clothes and got the right things in his life
but it was independence

Situating occurs necessarily after the initial framing and focusing, even though it is distinguished by free rather than narrative clauses. When free clauses are situating they tend to figure relational processes rather than material and mental processes and tend to select present tense or past continuous, past perfect or past perfect continuous rather than simple past tense. Thus:

she lives in Burnley in Lancashire

she is twenty-seven years old

and she was going through a tough time because her father had died
and she was a teenager

A distinctive feature of situating is the way in which this is used to introduce the basic actants of the narrative, as in the following:

er Mum and Dad four kids
two boys and two girls of which Maxine was the youngest
a happy family initially

or:

she is twenty-seven years old
she is divorced
she has a three four-year-old little boy

It is precisely this tendency that motivates the choice of the term since situating does effectively delineate the baseline situation out of which the event-line of complication and resolution will spring. The subsequent evolution of the event-line in narrative clauses, however, does force changes in the initial situation to such an extent that subsequent portions of the narrative become devoted to re-situating the action. Re-situating, amongst other things, is used to fill in background on new characters or to update on actions involving other established characters, and leads to the following kinds of utterance:

> er the sister
> the elder sister
> became the person who looked after everybody
> doing as much cooking and cleaning as she could as well as going to school
> but it was Dad who brought home the bacon
> and Dad who was always there
> and Dad who sorted out problems
> and Dad who was up till all hours making darn certain that everything was okay
> in the house and making certain that there was a baby-sitter there if he was out
> working or whatever.

> by this time really her daughter had become her mother's daughter
> if you understand what I mean
> the mother was looking after her constantly
> and the daughter looked to her grandmother
> not to her real Mum
> for everything

> er this fella was Chris
> he was a friendly guy
> and he wasn't a whirlwind romance
> he wasn't a torrid affair
> they didn't jump into bed at the first sight of each other
> he was just going through a separation which was leading towards a divorce

Re-situating, therefore, is a constant concern of the discourse and its presence certainly outweighs that of the event-line in Our Tune. One striking aspect of the examples given above is the emphasis they accord to relationships between actants within the narrative. These seem invariably to be characterized in familial terms, especially if we take this to include entry to the family through birth, romance or marriage; or exit from the family via death, separation or divorce. The event-line is important, of course, because it is this precisely that provides the catalyst for change of state from one situation to another. But a major interest of Our Tune is in the quality of relationships of a familial type around the central protagonist – usually the Epistolary Narrator.

Orientation   Although the term is used by Labov to refer to the kinds of narrative work handled above under the notion of situating, I have preferred to reserve its use for cases where free clauses are used to orient the audience behind the experience of a character, or where they are used to anticipate some likely or possible audience reaction. Indeed, it seems possible to distinguish in this way between two contrasting types of orientation.

Empathetic orientation. This involves projections by the Broadcast Narrator, apparently on behalf of the audience, about what a particular experience must have been like for one of the actants in the narrative. Thus:

> you know how an atmosphere can go out of a room and up the stairs and right
> round a house
> and you know there's something dreadfully wrong

you can imagine the poor little four-year-old kid
didn't know whether he was coming or going
he couldn't work out why Mum was in hospital
and why everybody was panicking and rushing around
it was very hard

so you can imagine
not only has she tried to top herself and got herself taken to hospital
but now as she's recovering from that she's had the biggest blow
or one of the biggest blows you can have

Empathetic orientation may thus be seen as resting upon two kinds of discursive features. Typically they involve direct address to the audience via the second person pronoun (see Montgomery, 1988). And they also involve a cognitive verb such as 'know' or 'imagine' to project the audience into a particular emotional state attributed to one of the actants in the story. Alternatively, they may be realized through the use of a model verb, thus:

now that must have been nerve-wracking for him in the first place
because hhh I mean taking a lady home for kids to meet is pretty tough

and everybody does automatically think about the kids
how terrible it must be for them
a::nd, I suppose it is and was

the person who suffered the greatest must have been her Dad

must have been the most difficult decision of her life
she'd totally committed herself to the family

it must be a really bitter pill to swallow

Sometimes this appeal to the audience works in a negative way, where the kind of emotional experience identified in the orientation is characterized as defying projection by the audience into the situation suffered by the actant. Thus:

now unless you've been in that situation of gradually having the panic rise
inside you you probably can't imagine how she felt

. . .

and no one can prepare for the shock that Marie had
because when she went in she was sat down
and she was told that she had a cancerous growth on her breast
and she was told that she would have to have a mastectomy

I don't know what you do under those circumstances
presumably you scream and shout and yell
and that's certainly what Marianne did

now she's just twenty-seven years old
and so it's a double shock
an(d) a double horror
and that's what I meant by trying to say at the beginning of this that
no fella can possibly understand what it feels like

This kind of negative empathetic orientation is build upon a paradox. At the same moment as it denies the possibilities of projecting into the position of a narrative actant, it simultaneously operates as an injunction to do precisely that. It is not, therefore, a precise and literal denial or refusal of empathy; rather it is a way of marking an event or situation as extreme and as lying outside the normal order of experience. To appreciate fully the quality of the experience undergone by an actant in such a situation requires a special effort of empathy.

Orientation to audience.   If one kind of orientation seemingly recruits the audience to a position occupied by an actant, another kind of orientation projects outwards from the narrative to the position of the audience. Again it involves varieties of direct address.

> and one night
> you guessed it
> she took half a bottle of pills
>
> now it's easy to look at the radio and say
> you're saying it's third time lucky
> and I am saying it's third time lucky
>
> and believe it or not
> as you look at the radio
> and maybe you're a little bit cynical about it
> nothing happened
>
> an(d) you're looking straight at the radio now and saying
> ah she met somebody
> no
> one evening at the end of May last year she was in the bath
> and she found a lump

In all of these cases the Broadcast Narrator re-orients the discourse away from the direct process of narration itself and realigns the discourse with the process of reception. It projects into the position, not of a narrative actant, but into the position of its hypothetical audience. Significantly, many cases of orienting the narration alongside the audience involve anticipating what the likely next event will be and either confirming the event-line or signalling a departure from it.

A different kind of audience orientation involves anticipating the likely evaluative framework that the audience may bring to bear upon narrative events, as in the following:

> because you have preconceptions about divorce
> and you have preconceptions also about the way it affects kids
> and sometimes you forget about how it affects the adults as well in a family
>
> a::nd ehyou can't make any . accusations . about whose fault it was because those things do happen in relationships
>
> this one is the kind of letter that's going to get everybody ringing in
> the phones are going to ri light up like Christmas trees basically with ladies
> er ringing in to complain that I shouldn't do it
> an(d) I can probably understand how they feel about it

Evaluation: generic maxims   These provide a pseudo-explanatory framework within which the specific events or situations of the narrative can be understood by reference to some proposed class of actions. It is difficult to specify precise realizational features for this component of the discourse of the narrative but they seem instantly recognizable in practice. I have referred to them as *generic maxims* because they tend to be built around classes of situation, action or person ('people grow away...', 'those things do happen...'; 'that's something that you need at those times'; etc.) In the course of Our Tune they rarely extend over several clauses as is the case with situating and with orienting. Instead, they protypically operate as a single 'free' clause. Nonetheless, they are significant as segments of assumed common-sense wisdom which intrude into the narrative particularly at moments where it might attract adverse judgement from the audience.

> a::nd ehyou can't make any . accusations . about whose fault it was
> because those things do happen in relationships

> over three years people grow away from each other
> when they don't see each other

> she'd hadn't gotten on as well maybe as she should with her Mum
> but that's two ladies living together

> nothing happened
> it is possible to have a boyfriend without having a physical relationship
> and that's what they had

> they just provided shoulders
> and that's something that you need usually at those times

> the kind of people who reckon they're experts about things can't understand
> something that is exclusively female
> I don't believe it to be honest
> any more than ladies can understand things that are exclusively male either

Instances of generic maxims are not dissimilar from what Barthes (1975) singled out as realizations of 'the cultural code' in his analysis of Balzac's novella *Sarrasine*. For Barthes, the cultural code consists of references to taken-for-granted cultural knowledge drawn from common sense, popular science, lay psychology, literary history, etc. Thus, a sentence such as

> 'Be still,' she said, with that forceful and mocking air all women so easily assume when they want to be in the right.

displays, for Barthes, the operation of a taken-for-granted assumption or stereotype about female psychology. And he notes how such 'didactic material' is

> mobilized in the text ... often ... as a basis for reasoning or to lend its ... authority to emotions. (Barthes, 1975: 205)

He further notes that:

> these codes by a swivel characteristic of bourgeois ideology, which turns culture into nature, appear to establish reality, 'Life'. 'Life' then, in the classic text, becomes a nauseating mixture of common opinions, a smothering layer of received ideas. (Barthes, 1975: 206)

They are, however, particularly resistant to critique, as he rather gnomically observes (almost in a parody of the cultural code itself):

> a critique of the references (the cultural codes) has never been tenable except through trickery... In fact, the cultural code occupies the same position as stupidity: how can stupidity be pinned down without declaring oneself intelligent? (Barthes, 1975: 206)

These observations seem not inappropriate to the generic maxims of Our Tune, which are, it must be noted, inherently unstable. Either they are tautological, and hence 'go without saying':

> nothing happened
> it is possible to have a boyfriend without having a physical relationship
> and that's what they had

Or, they are easily susceptible to contradiction by some other piece of popular wisdom. A generic maxim, such as

> over three years people grow away from each other
> when they don't see each other

would be easy to contradict by some other piece of common-sense wisdom such as 'absence makes the heart grow fonder'.

The 'patronizing' or 'condescending' tone that some listeners attribute to Our Tune may be traced, in part at least, to the operation of generic maxims. Certainly, they are difficult to take at their face value, and may best be understood either as a way of accounting for actions or events that are not precisely predictable within the terms of the narrative or as a way of countering a potentially negative evaluative framework within which the action might be judged. This latter type of function, for instance, may underlie the following instance:

> she'd hadn't gotten on as well maybe as she should with her Mum
> but that's two ladies living together

The negative assessment implicit in 'she'd hadn't gotten on as well maybe as she should with her Mum' (despite the modal expression, *maybe*) is here countered by the generic maxim which follows it. Indeed, it seems reasonable to suppose that generic maxims reflect points at which the evaluative structure of first person epistolary narration comes into conflict with the requirements of third-person broadcast narration. Basically, self-assessment carries different evaluative overtones than other-assessment (see below, pp. 159–60).

Codas   The narrative discourse of Our Tune is typically rounded off in some way either before the playing of the record itself, or immediately after it. The culmination of the complicating actions in a final resolution is not sufficient in itself to bring this about, and there is frequently some attempt to bring the narrative up-to-date. In this respect, they correspond closely to Labov's definition in which *codas* 'have the property of bridging the gap between the moment of time at the end of the narrative proper and the present' (Labov, 1972: 365). A prototypical example of a coda from Our Tune is the following:

and from then on
and this is why it's an ideal Our Tune in many ways
everything's got better
all of them
the family
agree that no one could have better parents
Joan isn't a step-mum
she's Mum
simple as that
er the sister and one of the brothers has got married
the sister is now expecting the first child
and although the family's been hurt
by sticking together they've won out
and that's mainly because of a lady by the name of Joan...

One of the markers of the coda is the switch from simple past into forms of
the present tense ('she's Mum') and the past perfect ('one of the brothers has
got married').

Occasionally, the narrative can set up a train of complicating actions that
have no resolution at the moment of broadcasting. Significantly the narration
not only registers this as a notable absence but then upgrades the coda as a
substitute for the completion of the event-line, as in the following:

now there's no end to this story
because it's still going on
she's now on chemotherapy
she's also been on special treatment
radium treatment
which is pretty tough
and the reason for telling you the story is that er
when I first came across it last weekend I had a good look and thought
well someone's going to complain and say
a man shouldn't do this
and so I actually rang Marie this morning and said
how are you
because all this took place six months ago
and she was really cheerful on the phone
an(d) she said
erm I'm fine I'm fine
an(d) I'm coping
I said
how fine are you
an(d) she said
to be honest I don't know
I'm still having the treatment
I'm under doctors' orders and it's still pretty tough to come to terms with
but she didn't sound downhearted at all
she sounded extremely bright

The record   The completion of the narrative sets the scene for the record,
which then comes to embody some aspect of the story. Indeed, it is presented
as if selected by the Epistolary Narrator in order to crystallize some moment
of the memories or situation that the letter recounts. In some ways, therefore,
Our Tune works like an extended dedication slot. But the detailed way in
which the narrative sets an experiential framework for the music to operate

within tends radically to revalue it. Normally, the lyrics of popular music – if they are attended to at all – are available for appropriation by the listener, to some extent on the listener's own terms. In Our Tune, however, the lyrics are *pre*-appropriated, as it were, by the narrative context. When the first bars of *I Can't Live if Living Is Without You* come through on Our Tune they are no longer simply available for appropriation by the listener in the position of the '*I*' or the '*You*' (see Durant, 1984; Montgomery 1988). The deictic spaces of the lyric have been filled by (in this case) 'Dad' and 'Joan'. And if we identify with the words of the song at all it is in terms of the represented experience of protagonists in the story. If anything, therefore, the record functions in the total context of Our Tune as an amplification or intensification of the processes of empathetic orientation noted above. It thus provides a particularly striking example of a tendency noted by Barnard (following Coward, 1984), of the way in which Radio 1 roots musical meaning 'in memory or evocative value' (Barnard, 1989: 146) rather than in musical appreciation on its own terms. We may also note, however, that the placement of the record within the total discursive context of Our Tune actually reverses the normal priorities of DJ talk versus music on Radio 1, inasmuch as the patter is normally only an incidental support to the music. Here, instead, the music becomes an expressive support to the discourse.

Closing   The closing section spans from the Our Tune record until the next record and includes: (a) a *reprise* summarizing the final events and situation of the narrative (sometimes replaced by the coda); (b) a *moral* giving the final point of the story; and (c) the final *frame*.

Reprise.   A reprise only recapitulates events which have already been narrated. It does not re-open the narration although it may add some details to already-narrated events. In the following reprise, events that have been narrated just prior to the record are here repeated with some amplificatory detail:

> well that's the song
> it's the song that Mum liked the theme from Champions it's Elaine Page
> and Marianne who swallowed a few bitter pills in her life really had a kick in
> the teeth
> because two weeks before she had the second child the son on October the sixth
> Mum died
> and it was Mum who had been helping her to go to Mothercare
> and get everything ready
> and it was Mum who put the seal if you like on the relationship that Marianne's
> now there's no end to this story because it's still going on
> the only good thing about it I guess is that as far as Mum is concerned she did
> see her daughter happy
> what she didn't get round to seeing is her daughter with a grandchild

The moral.   The moral is partly an expression of the point or 'message' of the story, but it is frequently expressed in the form of an injunction to those who may be going through similar experiences, as in the following:

if there's a message
and it's Marianne's it's don't give up on life
it is too hard to come by
and don't give up on yourself
because if you look round you'll notice that there's somebody who will actually
give you a boost
all you have to do is recognise that they're waiting to help
it was Marianne's Mum on this occasion

Occasionally the moral may actually preface the record, as in the following:

don't give up
what you have to do is what Marie did
and I just act as a conduit on it
just look inside yourself
if you look to your family and to your friends they will rally round
and they will look after you
but the hardest part is to look deep inside yourself
an(d) if you do
if you really do
then you'll find the strength to carry on

A notable discursive twist in drawing the moral consists of displacing responsibility for it away from the Broadcast Narrator to the Epistolary Narrator. The moral, therefore is usually clearly attributed to the Epistolary Narrator in ways such as the following:

but the one thing that's pretty apparent from that Our Tune
from Maxine's story anyway
is the way the family stuck together

if there's a message
and it's Marianne's
it's don't give up on life
it is too hard to come by

an(d) I do want to say what Marie says in her letter
just a just as a codicil to the whole thing
some people have coped better than others through this

what you have to do is what Marie did
and I just act as a conduit on it
just look inside yourself

Nonetheless, even though the moral is ascribed to the Epistolary Narrator, its exact status remains ambiguous. This is fundamentally because, whatever the particularities of experience represented in the narrative, this component of the discourse is invariably realized (as the examples demonstrate) in terms of a unitary, all-purpose moral of endurance and solidarity in adversity. Thus, it would seem that there are strong generic constraints on the kind of moral Our Tune as a discursive event is designed to support. Even if the epistolary materials themselves display the moral ascribed to them, this is the negotiated outcome of a process of selection in which, of course, the broadcast institution in the persons of the production team and the Broadcast Narrator play a crucial role.

Summary discourse structure of Our Tune

Following work by Hasan (1980) on discourse analytic approaches to genre
we may summarize the foregoing account of the discursive components of a
prototypical Our Tune in the following way:

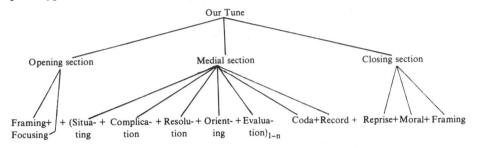

There are, of course, a number of difficulties with this mode of representing
the basic structure which need to be noted. For one thing it is difficult to
capture economically the way in which orientations and evaluations (in the
form of generic maxims) may surface at any point in the medial section. And
codas, as we have seen, may well migrate from the medial section to the final
section. Furthermore, it cannot claim to be a completely exhaustive account
of the structure of Our Tune, since there do remain some residual elements
that have resisted inclusion in this model.

This summary does, however, suggest the main structural outlines of the
genre. This is not to claim that every instance of Our Tune corresponds rigidly
to this format in all particulars (though many do). A particular Our Tune, for
instance, may lack a satisfactory *resolution*. In such cases, however, it is
significant that the discourse itself explicitly treats the lack of a resolution as a
notable absence: it is discursively noted in formulations such as

> now there's no end to this story because it's still going on

In this way the main outlines of the structure are confirmed even at moments
of departure from it.

The model does also highlight the way in which developing the event line of
the narrative in terms of *complication* and *resolution* comprises only a
relatively small proportion of the total discourse. The event-line itself may
well be the constitutive feature of the genre, but its narration depends
significantly upon a variety of other discursive mechanisms relating to the
management of the discursive event as a bounded whole, and – perhaps even
more crucially – relating to its reception by the audience.

At one level, of course, Our Tune is not in this respect significantly different
from other forms of extended extempore monologue. Extempore lectures, for
instance (see Montgomery, 1977) display a like division between discourse
that develops the topic and discourse that handles its reception, so that
speakers of monologue in general can be seen to operate reflexively in the
production of this type of talk, shifting their stance to digress from, or gloss,
what they have just been saying by way of clarification, qualification,

comment and so on. In this way they display an interactive dimension to the discourse even within and while holding to an extended turn. For the shifts from one strand of discourse to another (from main to subsidiary, as I called it) can best be understood in terms of speakers' adjustments designed to take account of hypothetical or actual audience reaction. As Goffman remarks:

> It is as if the speaker here functioned as the broker of his own statements, a mediator between text and audience. (Goffman, 1981: 177)

And in this respect, at least, the broadcast narration of Our Tune displays some similarity with other forms of extempore monologue.

Some distinctiveness, however, may be found in the precise form of the different components that manage the construction of the discursive event and its reception by the audience. Narrative, in any case, would be an untypical (though not inconceivable) generic mode for a lecture; and more particularly it would be unusual for lecture discourse to be littered with evaluations of the generic maxim type. Most fundamentally, of course, the Broadcast Narrator has a distinctive mediating role in this type of discourse. He mediates between a text supplied by a member of the audience and the audience as a whole. He may, in part, be a 'broker of his own statements' (to use Goffman's phrase); but he also, and even more significantly, constructs himself as a broker of statements by the audience to itself – 'I just act as a conduit on it', as Bates says at one point. But in this role of honest broker, the practices of situating, orienting, evaluating and moralizing on the narrative all play a pervasive role. In the last analysis we can see that the broadcast institution retains a very active mediating role at the very moment it effaces itself as the source of the material. It is to further details of this mediating role that we now turn.

Narration in Our Tune and the generic contract

It has been clear throughout the foregoing section on discourse structure that the materials are doubly authored and hence have an ambiguous status. They are based upon readers' letters – some 500 a week according to a feature in the *Sun* newspaper cited by Barnard (1989). And the initial framing and focusing of Our Tune openly acknowledge, and indeed stress, this fact. The source of the story materials, thus, is owned up to and ascribed to an Epistolary Narrator whose existence is emphasized and presupposed in the presentation of Our Tune even though the name of the Epistolary Narrator will be routinely changed (see 'Framing', pp. 143–4). The letters are not, however, read out verbatim in the first person. Rather are they transformed in the moment of broadcasting into third-person narration. (On the rare occasions when a segment of a letter is actually read out this will be explicitly marked as direct quotation.) Accordingly, it is necessary to distinguish between Epistolary Narrator (first-person protagonist of the putative letter) and Broadcast Narrator (the 'mediator', 'broker' or 'conduit' of the Epistolary Narrator's tale). This sense of a double narration is arguably an important component of what might be called the 'generic contract' that underpins Our Tune. The notion of generic contract is useful inasmuch as it embraces more than merely the recurrence of certain kinds of formal feature and discursive mechanism in regular kinds of combination. It is broad enough to include also background assumptions about what kind of discursive event is at stake. In the case of Our Tune these very general background assumptions may be stated (in a form akin to felicity conditions on speech acts) as follows.

It is assumed for any Our Tune that:

1   there exists a letter from a nameable source (the Epistolary Narrator) (e.g. 'this letter . . . comes from the South of England . . . from a lady called Marianne'); and that
2   the events depicted in such a letter actually happened to the Epistolary Narrator (e.g. 'now this lady is an honest person'); and that
3   the Broadcast Narrator sincerely believes that the depicted events actually happened to the Epistolary Narrator (e.g. 'so I actually rang Marie this morning'); and that
4   the Broadcast Narrator will have rendered the essential events of the letter in a truthful fashion.

As noted above (see 'Framing', pp. 143–4) aspects of the opening and closing sections of Our Tune are designed to secure these conditions. Basically, an important warrant for the Broadcast Narration of a letter in the form of Our Tune is the belief that the events depicted therein did actually happen to the Epistolary Narrator in the way described. On the face of it these may seem rather obvious preconditions. Their importance, however, is thrown into sharp relief by anticipating the likely consequences were it to be revealed that a team of professional writers in Broadcasting House (BBC Head Office) were fabricating the materials for Our Tune, so that they had no basis in fact in the ordinary lives of listeners to Radio 1. The whole status of Our Tune as a discursive event would be irrevocably undermined. In this way it can be seen how specific are the generic conventions of Our Tune, as distinct – for example – from even closely related genres with which it shares important formal properties of narrative, such as 'the joke', 'the tall story' or 'the fable'. Even more significantly they highlight how underlying assumptions about the discursive nature of the event are as significant in generic terms as more immanent textual criteria, such as the presence or absence of certain kinds of discursive component.

Such generic conventions imply that when the Broadcast Narrator enunciates events in the following way:

> and at the age of eighteen she left home
> almost immediately she started spending money
> she bought herself a car . . .

there is presupposed a set of statements from the Epistolary Narrator something like:

> and at the age of eighteen I left home
> almost immediately I started spending money
> I bought myself a car . . .

Some of the peculiarities of tone detectable in Our Tune derive from the clash between these two modes of narration. Our Tune charts a personal world of family crises, serious illnesses, break-ups, breakdowns and bereavements. As such they imply an epistolary mode that is confessional – a laying bare of intimate secrets. And, for this very reason of course, transforming them into public discourse routinely requires a change of name. But the further change of the structure of narrative transmission from first to third person radically alters the evaluative economy of these tales. This stems from a basic, if elusive, phenomenon relating to what can be termed (following Pomerantz, 1975) 'assessments'; namely, that 'other-assessments' carry a qualitatively different force from 'self-assessments', even when similar attributions are at stake. Thus, a pair of comparable assessments such as the following do not carry the same weight:

   a. I was out all night with friends; it was stupid of me
   b. She was out all night with friends; it was stupid of her

In this pair the 'other-assessment' (b) seems stronger in force than the 'self-assessment' (a). Similarly, an other-assessment such as

   a. She didn't get on as well as she should have done with her mother

is stronger in force than a self-assessment such as

   b. I didn't get on as well as I should have done with my mother

This differential weighting of self-assessment versus other-assessment produces a potential clash between the evaluation structure of Epistolary Narration and Broadcast Narration. Certainly, any simple transformation of self-assessments from the confessional Epistolary Narration to other-assessments in third-person Broadcast Narration would produce a discourse strong in adverse other-assessment. For this reason, various ways of 'hedging' assessments become built into the Broadcast Narration. A claim, for instance, that:

   she hadn't gotten on as well as she should have done with her Mum

is hedged by 'maybe' and enunciated as follows:

   she hadn't gotten on as well *maybe* as she should have done with her Mum

Assessments, therefore, are often marked with hedges in Broadcast Narration, as can be seen in the following:

   so I *guess* Marianne went a little haywire

   and as a result of that she'd got *a little bit maybe* loose and *a bit* wild

   and *it's fair to say* that Marianne *really* didn't wanna know too much

   now the marriage *as much as anything* was I *guess* two fingers to Mum

   and *I suppose* initially, trying to sort out her
   and trying to check her out
   they gave her a helluva time

It seems reasonable to suppose that the hedged assessments of Broadcast

Narration register the tension between markedly different structure of evaluation. Indeed, there are occasions where the Broadcast Narration does more than merely hedge the assessment but explicitly refers it to the Epistolary Narrator, as may be seen in the following:

> by this time she was realising that she was a bad mother
> *her phrase*
> *not mine*
> to her daughter

Here the tension between the two types of evaluation structure openly surfaces in the narration. The competing pressures of these conflicting structures of evaluation go some way to explain the peculiarities of tone which some listeners find offensive.

Narration and interpolation

If hedged assessments reflect problems in the passage from Epistolary Narration to Broadcast Narration, other features reflect problems in the design of the narration for the broadcast audience. Principal among these is the phenomenon of *interpolation* (see Montgomery, 1986). This refers to the eruption into a clause of elements whose role within the clause is difficult to account for in purely syntactic terms. In traditional grammar these were known as *appositional* items, though Huddleston (1984), in attempting to integrate them more systematically into the structure of the clause, deals with them as *peripheral dependents* (1984: 265). As his term suggests, however, whatever role they have within the clause tends to be marginal to its structure and dependent upon a constituent more fully integrated into the clause's structure. Nor does it seem possible to define the dependency relationship of the appositional item to the clause constituent in syntactic terms. The problem may be briefly illustrated on the following example from Our Tune:

> er the sister
> *the elder sister*
> became the person who looked after everybody

There are three basic clause constituents:

> Subject: 'the sister'
> Predicator: 'became'
> Complement: 'the person who looked after everybody'

How then should the residual element, 'the elder sister', be handled? Is it a second subject or part of the original subject? If 'the elder sister' were coordinated with 'the sister' along the lines of 'the sister and the elder brother', then the separate noun phrases could be seen as built together into a unitary structure. But this is manifestly not the case. And if the 'the elder sister' is treated as a subject in its own right then we are faced with two separate subjects, a claim which is undermined by the relationship of co-referentiality which obtains between the two noun phrases. Thus, grammatical accounts of apposition which seek to place it structurally within the clause run into severe difficulties. It is for this reason that I have adopted for them the term interpolation since they surface within the clause, not to serve a grammatical purpose, but to serve situational and discursive purposes. They seem best understood as ongoing adjustments to the utterance in the light of discursive and situational factors. The discursive dimensions to interpolation may be illustrated by consideration of the following quite typical examples from Our Tune:

er the sister
the elder sister
became the person who looked after everybody

now the two of them
Dad and Joan
were living together

and the husband
Dad
said yes I will try this one out.

all of them
the family
agree that no one could have better parents

but she did the sensible thing and she rang the doctors
doctors again
NHS doctor
a sensible doctor
said listen

As interpolations they display a systematic set of characteristics. They do not seem to function as corrections of the immediately prior phrase. It would thus be an oversimplification to treat them as false starts or self-corrections. It is also noticeable that the interpolated expression does not introduce a new referent into the discourse. Instead, they are co-referential with the expression to which they stand in an appositional relation. There is, however, often some reformulation in the interpolated expression of the appositional expression, so that – while the referent of the two expressions may be identical – the wording of the two expressions is never the same. They provide, therefore, an alternative way of encoding an established discourse referent. In all of the cases above the interpolation has the effect of treating two noun phrases as equivalent expressions for some actant in the narrative. Indeed, designating actants in the narrative constitutes the discursive process which is most susceptible to interpolation. In some cases interpolation follows the use of pronominal reference, as for example:

all of them
the family
agree that no one could have better parents

now the two of them
Dad and Joan
were living together

This provides an important clue to the nature of interpolation as a discursive process. Anaphoric reference by means of a personal pronoun (in expressions such as 'all of *them*' and 'the two of *them*') is essentially a tricky affair, since the hearer has to recover the referent from some place in the prior discourse, and, where several actants have been introduced into the narrative, it may not be immediately apparent which of them are being referred to. Interpolation, thus, may be seen as a way of clarifying which actant is being designated by a particular expression, especially where pronominal reference is involved. Interpolation, however, is not restricted to cases where actants are designated by pronominal expressions. It also includes cases such as the following:

> at this time Mum was
> *that is grandma if you like*
> was gradually bringing the daughter back into the family

> and looking back on it
> Mum was the person
> *that is grandma*
> the older lady
> was the person who was doing all the work

> and the husband
> *Dad*
> said yes I will try this one out.

> er the sister
> *the elder sister*
> became the person who looked after everybody

Thus, interpolation may also be seen to figure prominently in cases where actants are designated by the use of a familial term (Mum, Dad, grandma, sister, husband, etc.). Familial membership terms, in fact, bear some resemblance to deictic items: their field of reference shifts according to their context of use. They are, essentially, relational terms.

Interpolation, familial terms and the naming of actants

Actants within a narrative can be named in an indefinite variety of ways, ranging from proper names (John Brown) through to ascriptions of occupation (the plumber) and national identity (a Frenchwoman). Our Tune is distinctive for the way in which it names actants primarily and routinely in terms of family position: most actants within Our Tune are designated by familial terms (see section 'Actants', p. 170 for further discussion), except for the Epistolary Narrator, who – as we have seen above – is given first name (Penny, Brian, Maxine, Marianne, Marie) early on in the narrative, usually in the opening frame. Otherwise, proper names are used only sparingly, rarely more than twice in any one narrative, probably because extensive use of proper names would generate difficulties for the audience in remembering who was who in narratives involving several actants. However, retrieving the precise referent of any specific familial term depends upon recognizing who the term is being used in relation to; and this can give rise to problems in dealing with certain kinds of family situation. An expression such as 'the Mum' can become ambiguous when dealing with families of more than one generation; similarly, 'the husband' is potentially ambiguous in a case where the Epistolary Narrator has reached her third marriage. Interpolation, therefore, can in many cases be seen as prompted by the problems of using familial terms as referring expressions. In particular, when using such deictic-like terms for the purposes of definite reference (to refer to a unique individual), they presuppose ready access by the audience to the narrative situation even though this may be relatively complex and in flux over the course of the telling of the story. An example such as

> by this time really her daughter had become her mother's daughter
> if you understand what I mean

reflects this difficulty. Family membership terms, therefore, become a not infrequent trigger for interpolation, reflecting the Broadcast Narrator's moment-by-moment assessment of the state of common ground between himself and his audience, which has to be kept in good repair if this kind of definite reference is to succeed. And interpolation itself provides an important resource for accomplishing this repair work.

Other kinds of interpolation

Not all instances of interpolation anticipate difficulties in interpreting who is designated by a particular family relationship expression. They can be used also to particularize the range of an expression, as is the case with 'special treatment' and 'Our Tune' in the following examples:

> she's also been on special treatment
> *radium treatment*
> which is pretty tough

> but the one thing that's pretty apparent from that Our Tune
> *from Maxine's story anyway*
> is the way the family stuck together

Moreover, they can be used as an economical way of introducing an evaluation into the discourse around the use of a specific term as in the following:

> but she did the sensible thing
> and she rang the doctors
> doctors again
> NHS doctor
> *a sensible doctor*
> said listen

Interpolations may also operate in terms of larger units than the phrase. Indeed, there are several instances of not just a phrase being interpolated but a whole clause – for example:

> it was very hard
> *and this is where Marie turns out to be really made of solid gold*
> it was very hard for family and friends because no one knew what to say

A distinctive characteristic of such interpolations is that they involve what Sinclair (1966) has described as a change of discourse plane, or (as Goffman's [1981] more recent formulation has it) a change of footing, where the discourse turns back on itself to comment on or evaluate something as it is being said. They are particularly noticeable in the context of the coda or the moral as may be seen in the following:

and from then on
and this is why it's an ideal Our Tune in many ways
everything's got better

what you have to do is what Marie did
and I just act as a conduit on it
just look inside yourself

if there's a message
and it's Marianne's
it's don't give up on life
it is too hard to come by

In such cases they provide a resource for signalling the status of the discourse at any moment in its production. More specifically, in the context of the moral they are used explicitly to distance the Broadcast Narrator from the moral itself, which is referred back to the Epistolary Narrator. In this respect, the same work may be accomplished as easily by a phrasal interpolation as by a clausal interpolation e.g.:

but the one thing that's pretty apparent from that Our Tune
from Maxine's story anyway
is the way the family stuck together

Generally, however, extended interpolation involving a whole clause differs from phrasal interpolation, in so far as the latter tends to project the interpolated phrase as broadly co-referential to some prior phrase, whereas the former projects not so much equivalence as a change in discursive position or 'footing'. Nonetheless, both types of interpolation may be traced to a similar discursive foundation. In all cases they represent ongoing adjustments to the discourse in the face of possible interpretative difficulties, or in the light of possible misidentification of the status of the discourse. As such, they should be seen as a crucial aspect of audience design, supplied *in situ* and extempore by the Broadcast Narrator. Indeed, they form a significant thread in the weave of Broadcast Narration, a repetitious signalling of the DJ's role as 'honest broker' of the story materials at the moment of presenting them to the public.

Story materials

Chatman (1978) (following Barthes, 1975; Culler, 1975 and others) usefully distinguishes between two basic levels of analysis in the study of narrative: the story material itself, and its mode of discursive presentation. In this account 'events' and 'actants' are located at the level of *story*, whereas selections of first versus third person or spoken rather than written are located at the level of *discourse*. The discussion so far has thus been addressed to this latter level.

But no account of Our Tune would be complete without some examination of it at the level of story itself.

Events

In the discussion above (see pp. 140–3) it was proposed that *events* were realized at the level of discourse by clauses which are distinctive in terms of the tense adopted and in terms of the kind of process encoded by the verb. In particular, clauses dealing with temporally bounded actions, in simple past tense, with verbs of action (met) and cognition (discovered) rather than relation (was, became, had), prove to be a reliable guide to the event-line of the narrative. It was further proposed that the development of the event-line could be understood primarily in terms of complication and resolution as its basic principle of structure. This, of course, is a general property of narrative – particularly narratives of personal experience. Part of the generic specificity of Our Tune lies in the types of events that cohere in this abstract structure.

The background theme music from Zefferelli's film of *Romeo and Juliet* might suggest tales of star-crossed lovers. And there are indeed tales of relationships where the obstacles to marriage prove too difficult to overcome. But these form only a minority of the output. The major class of tales forming over half the current output of Our Tune are stories of life crises within the family, where the integrity of the family unit is threatened by events such as death, sickness, estrangement and divorce. In the context of Our Tune events such as a child falling ill with meningitis, a father dying of a heart attack, a mother dying of cancer, a brother fatally injured in a climbing accident, a husband's affair, are all almost routine complications to the narrative. The basic structure of the tales may be illustrated by three examples:

Tale 1: Marianne's story
  (A happy family initially.)

Complication 1
  1. and then things started to go wrong
  2. and almost inevitably her parents split up
  3. one day Mum just got up and walked out

Resolution 1
  4. after a while ... (Dad) ... met someone else
  5. and brought the lady home for them to meet
  6. and after a while they settled down

Complication 2
  7. and then out of the bushes and out of the blue ... Mum reappeared back on the scene

Resolution 2
  8. and so she (Joan/the lady) left
  9. so Mum came back

Complication 3
  10. and to be honest it didn't work out
  11. divorce proceedings started

Resolution 3
  12. and ... (Joan/the lady) ... reappeared

13. and picked up the pieces
14. and so ... they (Dad + Joan) got married

(and although the family's been hurt
by sticking together
they've won out)

As was noted above the story has a two part cyclical structure in which the situation outlined at the outset is returned to at the end. As the narration informs us in the coda:

everything's got better
all of them
the family
agree that no one could have better parents
Joan isn't a step-mum
she's Mum
simple as that

The overall structure of this story may thus be summed up in the following way:

| *The initial situation:* | *The final situation::* | *The complication:* | *The resolution* |
| 'A happy family': | 'A happy family':: | Mum leaves home: | Dad re-marries |

Although the equilibrium of the family is threatened – in this case by divorce – the trajectory of the narrative works to restore that basic equilibrium at the end.

Tale 2: Maxine's story
   (Dad had died suddenly and tragically; Maxine hadn't gotten on as well maybe as she should have done with her Mum; her father had left her some money.)

Complication 1
   1. at the age of eighteen she left home
   2. almost immediately she started spending money
   3. she bought herself a car
   4. eventually she bought a home

Resolution 1
   5. she got married to a guy called Tom

Complication 2
   6. almost immediately she got pregnant

Resolution 2
   7. well the pregnancy resulted at the age of twenty in a daughter

Complication 3
   8. almost as soon as the daughter arrived the marriage started splitting up

Resolution 3
   9. Mum stepped in and started looking after the daughter

Complication 4
   10. Marianne went back on the juice a bit
   11. and met another fella
   12. fell in love

Resolution 4
   13. almost as soon as they (met she) got married again

Complication 5
14. well two years later the marriage started ... to crack up
15. and one night ... she took half a bottle of pills
16. and she nearly succeeded in killing herself

Resolution 5
17. she was found

Complication 6
18. she found her husband in bed with another woman
19. she discovered that the woman ... was the mother of one of his children

Resolution 6
20. she came through it with a lot of medical help
21. and with the help of the doctors came off the tablets

Complication 7
22. then out of nowhere came the bloke
23. then out of the blue something clicked

Resolution 7
24. the two of them married after living together for a year

Complication 8
25. and then decided that what would make their life complete was a baby

Resolution 8
26. it was Mum that Marianne went to and told about it (when she became pregnant)
27. she gave birth to a son

(just two weeks after her Mum died because Mum didn't make it to the end to see her daughter happy)

Again, the story has a cyclical structure, not only in its repetitive pattern of separation-marriage-divorce-remarriage, but also in the symmetry between the opening situation and its final situation, both of which figure the death of a parent. The overall structure of this story may thus be summed up in the following way:

The initial situation:	*The final situation::*	*The complication:*	*The resolution*
'A parent dies':	'A parent dies'::	'A family unit divides':	'A family unit reconstituted'

From this it may be seen that the trajectory of the narratives is static rather than dynamic. Although they lead to narrative closure it is one in which the disequilibrium of the complicating actions leads finally to a situation not very different from that at the onset so that the integrity of the family is finally maintained. In this respect, it is significant that many of the actions constituting the event-line are presented more in the nature of 'happenings' – as if they were events that supervened upon the life of the central actant, rather than courses of action deliberately undertaken.

things started to go wrong

and then out of the bushes and out of the blue ... Mum reappeared back on the scene

divorce proceedings started

she got married to a guy called Tom

almost immediately she got pregnant

well the pregnancy resulted at the age of twenty in a daughter

almost as soon as the daughter arrived the marriage starting splitting up

well two years later the marriage started ... to crack up

then out of nowhere came the bloke

They are not, therefore, narratives of change and development but narratives whose very event structure encodes a project of surviving, of 'coming through', difficult events. This, of course, is amply reinforced by the overt moral supplied at the level of discourse towards the end of the narration in injunctions addressed to the audience such as 'don't give up on life', 'don't give up on yourself', 'just look inside yourself', 'look deep inside yourself and if you do – if you really do – then you'll find the strength to carry on', 'if you look for a silver lining hard enough you'll find it 'cos it's there'.

Not all narratives situate the protagonist within the family, as may be seen in the following case:

Tale 3: Marie's story
    (After splitting with her husband she lived with her parents for ten months and she finally managed to get a little house, for her son [aged three or four]. One evening at the end of May last year she was in the bath)

Complication 1
    1. and she found a lump
    2. she found a lump on her left breast
    3. now she didn't panic too much at first
    4. but she did the sensible thing and rang the doctors
    5. a sensible doctor said listen come straight in and let's check you out I'm sure it's nothing
    6. when she went in he had a good look and said don't worry a lot of young women find lumps like that are harmless [...] we're going to [...] send you to an expert to a consultant
    7. so the next day she went to see a consultant
    8. he took her straight into hospital for a biopsy
    9. well three or four days after the biopsy she got the results
    10. and she was asked to go and see the consultant
    11. when she went in she was sat down
    12. and she was told that she had a cancerous growth on her breast
    13. and she was told that she would have to have a mastectomy
    14. well she was taken straight into hospital to have an operation

Resolution: deferred
    15. now there's no end to this story

    (because it's still going on, she's now on chemotherapy [...] but it's very hard for Marie [...] and it's even tougher when you haven't got a husband or a boyfriend beside you to help you cope and to make you feel that you are still a woman)

In this case the narrative begins with central protagonist living alone with her child, located on the margins of the family as normatively constituted. She remains positioned in this way throughout the narrative. Although family and friends visit her in hospital

they used to sit by the bed and twiddle their thumbs a little bit

and they bring the things that you take to the hospital like the sweeties and the
grapes
and they'd sit there
and say
well the weather's fine
and Marie would know what they were trying to say
and would know what they were trying to help her feel
and it was only a thing she could understand
not something she could respond to

Her position of separateness remains emphasized throughout and is further
foregrounded in the closing:

but it's very hard for Marie
because she hasn't got a fella to hold her hand at any stage
she's got friends and relatives
and it's even tougher when you haven't got a husband or a boyfriend beside you
to help you cope and make you feel that you are still a woman
it would be nice to think that Marie will find that person and find him quickly

It concludes, therefore, with this basic situation unchanged, despite the
trauma of the illness. Again the mainspring of the narrative is provided not by
intended, purposeful action on the part of the protagonist but by events that
happen to her. Indeed, the primary focus of the narrative is upon what it feels
like to undergo such events – upon reaction rather than action. ('Now she's just
27 years old and so it's a double shock and a double horror.') This incidentally
produces a most marked sense of discrepancy between the Broadcast Narration and the putative Epistolary Narration since Bates classifies the medical
condition under the rubric 'female', but thereby disqualifies himself as a male
from being able to understand it, which leads him into complex empathetic
orientations such as:

no fella can possibly understand what it feels like
what the shock is

it's something that I can't comprehend at all
no bloke could

Even more significantly, however, it is a narrative of complication without
closure ('now there's no end to this story') so that its structure looks
something like the following:

The initial situation:	*The final situation::*	*The complication:*	*The resolution*
Marie alone:	Marie alone::	illness diagnosed:	?(uncertain remission)

The very lack of a cyclical recursion through complication and resolution in
this case only serves to underline the static quality of the narrative in which the
final situation remains little changed from the initial situation. At the same
time it is important to note that, even though this tale deals with a protagonist
located outside the family unit, it does so in such a way as to call attention to it
as a marked case and as, in effect, an absence from the normative order.

Generally, therefore, these tales reproduce in their basic structure the family simultaneously as a unit under threat but also as a unit within which the leading protagonists of these tales have the best chance not only of survival but also ultimate emotional fulfilment.

Actants

Narrative in Our Tune is not concerned with developing character in terms of highly individualized traits. When traits are signalled, it is in a cursory and repetitive fashion so that the same trait surfaces across more than one tale (e.g. 'Marie turns out to be really made of solid gold' and 'Joan [. . .] turns out to be a solid gold lady one helluva woman in fact'). In any case characters are typically identified in terms of their family position and whatever individuality they possess tends to be assimilated with that position ('Dad had been very protective'; 'Joan isn't a step-mum – she's Mum'). *Actants* in Our Tune, therefore, are more significant in terms of *actantial role* than in terms of specified individuality.

At the level of story, narrative theory customarily distinguishes between characters and the role which they occupy in the development of the event-line. Underlying the wide variety of possible individual characters, narrative theory identifies a limited range of roles that they perform. Thus, Propp (1968) identifies for the Russian fairy-tale a recurrent set of roles such as Hero, False Hero, Villain, Despatcher and Donor, dependent upon action within the event-line. In effect, such roles correspond to spheres of action and an individual character may perform more than one role. Similarly, one role or sphere of action may be realized by several characters within a given tale.

In the case of Our Tune, therefore, we may make a distinction between actants (Mum, the brother, a bloke, etc.) that surface in a tale and the underlying actantial roles that they perform. Despite the range of characters that surface in Our Tune there seems – as narrative theory would anyway suggest – only a limited range of roles into which they enter. These seem to reduce to three of particular importance.

The bearer   For any particular instance of Our Tune there is usually one character who occupies a prominent position within the event-line; and this character will figure more frequently in inherent roles in the narrative clauses. In nearly all cases this central protagonist proves to be the putative Epistolary Narrator. (Maxine's story, cited above as Tale 1, proves to be one of the few exceptions to the rule.) However, the sphere of action that they occupy cannot simply be described as that of a hero/heroine. As we noted above, they don't so much undertake actions as undergo them. Things happen to them or around them: 'she got married', 'she got pregnant', 'divorce proceedings started', 'she had totally hook, line and sinker fallen for him'.

The absenter   A recurrent fate of characters in Our Tune is that they become displaced from the family circle in some way. In the Russian fairy-tale, as Propp remarks, 'an intensified form of absentation is represented by the death of parents' – and this forms a recurrent movement in Our Tune. Absentation also occurs, however, through divorce and separation ('Mum just got up and walked out').

The helper   Most of the tales figure a character or characters who perform this role in a variety of ways, supporting *the bearer* through the life crises which they undergo. This role may be realized in narratively incidental ways: the Samaritan phoned by the deserted wife; the sensible NHS doctor in Marie's tale; Chris – the 'true genuine caring guy' in Marianne's tale, who provided support while she 'was going through a fairly traumatic time'. Alternatively, the role may occupy more significant narrative space such as Joan in Maxine's tale who fills the position created by the absence of Mum 'and picked up the pieces [...] and did a great job never giving any thought for the freedom she'd lost by taking on the kids'.

In Marianne's tale Mum dies at the end but not before she has accomplished a crucial role, both in looking after Marianne's child from her first marriage and in preparing for the arrival of the second child, the exemplary nature of whose behaviour is pointed up in series of parallel clauses:

> Mum was the person who was doing all the work [...]
> it was Mum who came round
> her Mum who produced the daughter [...]
> it was Mum that Marianne went to and told [...]
> and it was Mum who said terrific
> now you've got a family
> now have your daughter back
> [...]
> and it was Mum who had been helping her go to Mothercare [...]
> and it was Mum who put the seal if you like on the relationship

The importance of the *helper* is often emphasized in the moral

> don't give up on yourself
> because if you look round you'll notice that there's somebody who will actually give you a boost
> all you have to do is recognise that they're waiting to help
>
> if you look to your family and friends they will rally round
> and they will look after you

In Marie's tale the lack of a fully fledged and prominent helper gives rise to the following closing:

> but it's very hard for Marie
> because she hasn't got a fella to hold her hand at any stage
> [...]
> and it's even tougher when you haven't got a husband or a boyfriend beside you to help you cope and make you feel that you are still a woman
> it would be nice to think that Marie will find that person and find him quickly

Not only the moral but also the *record* helps to emphasize the role of the helper, since the lyric is often situated on an axis between the bearer and the helper. In Marianne's story for instance, the deictic positions ('I' and 'You') of the record *I Can't Live if Living is Without You* are clearly filled by the position of the narrative bearer (Dad) and the narrative helper (Joan).

At the level of story, therefore, it can be seen how the genre of Our Tune replays materials from a simple narrative machine, the parameters of which are set almost exclusively in terms of the family.

Conclusions

By referring from the outset to Our Tune as a 'genre', I did not wish to imply that it constitutes a completely distinct broadcast (or mass-mediated) form. It clearly has links with other genres such as the anecdote, 'true confessions', the record-request, the problem page, the parable or even soap opera. Like all genres, therefore, it feeds upon and overlaps with other generic possibilities (see Bakhtin, 1986). Inasmuch as it does constitute a genre, it does so by virtue of its repeated and predictable recycling of a distinctive cluster of elements at several different levels. It is not that each of these elements in turn is genre-specific; rather, its generic quality lies in the particular configuration or disposition of elements recurring within it, elements that may indeed be found elsewhere but in altered and different dispositions. Our Tune, therefore, as a genre has a particular communicative economy and as such is productive of particular kinds of representation, these in turn being set into a particular kind of relationship with the putative audience (see Volosinov, 1973). When workers organize their morning break in order to listen to Our Tune (see Garner, 1988), they do so on the basis of clear expectations about what will be broadcast within the 7-minute slot, expectations as precise as those brought by a habitual reader to a Mills and Boon romance. In the concluding sections, therefore, I attempt to sum up the basic elements of the generic contract around Our Tune in order to suggest that as a genre it mobilizes particular sets of meanings even if sometimes in a contradictory and uneven fashion. As a discourse genre, of course, it operates in a multilayered fashion (see Berry, 1981) and I trace its distinctive mode of operation separately from one layer to the next, principally from the layer of 'story' to the layer of 'discourse'.

Story, genre and ideology

At the heart of the generic specificity of Our Tune is the simple narrative machine (see Eco, 1981) that daily reiterates recognizably similar stories. The stories generated by this simple narrative machine do not, as we have seen, plot the public world of work, bureaucratic intrigue, personal advancement or exotic adventure. On the contrary they trace the flip-side of this sphere. The crises that central narrative figures undergo are resolved, if at all, within a domestic, familial sphere. The family, in this respect, is often both the ground and the solution to critical problems.

Indeed, the family is a major ideological focus of Our Tune. And whilst it often comes under threat, the threats which are posed to it are primarily of a contingent kind. As often as not they are of an accidental nature and the family finds its own way of coping during which the bearer of the narrative exhibits, with help from others, qualities of honesty, fortitude and courage. Although the family may be destabilized by various life crises in the course of the Our Tune narrative, the narrative trajectory is one which reinstates the equilibrium of the family at the end, so that basically it reproduces in narrative terms the family as a normative order. In the light of current findings that, for instance, one in three new marriages is destined for divorce, that one in five children has divorced parents by the age of 16, and that one in four children is registered at birth to parents not legally married, Our Tune may be seen as performing narrative maintenance and repair work on a troubled institution. But, if the family is often the ground on which the narrative complications of Our Tune arise, it is not easy to see why it should also be simultaneously offered as the solution, particularly when the family in its nuclear form only accounts for something like 25% of households. Part of the answer to this puzzle lies in available ways of 'figuring' the community in contemporary culture. 'The family' as a potent narrative figure seems to survive within our culture precisely because it is the most generally and perhaps the only available way of imagining the small community and so mediating between the individual and society. In the imagining of community, individuals come together in the microcommunity of the family and families come together in the larger community of the nation. (Both terms, of course, are potently condensed in the figure of 'The Royal Family'.) The nation, however, is most particularly potent as a figure for organizing events in the public sphere. In the context of Our Tune, where each narrative trajectory is prompted by a personal and individual life-crisis, 'the nation' is too remote a community to provide a satisfactory resolution. Lacking any other potent figure of community these life crises have nowhere else than the family to go to in their search for narrative resolution. It is thus that the narrative machine of Our Tune – at the level of story – is compelled to traverse the space between two opposing positions – between the family as the ground of problems and as their only resolution.[1]

Discourse, genre and audience: the negotiation of private experience into the public domain

If the story materials negotiate a basic contradiction, related contradictions also operate at the level of discourse or narration. Here, the discourse traverses the space between opposing tendencies: between a first person Epistolary Narrator who changes day by day and the stable Broadcast Narrator – Simon Bates; between a private confessional discourse and a public narrative discourse; between a kaleidoscope of existential dilemmas and a unitary consensual moral; between unique life crises and the durability of everyday life.

The generic specificity of Our Tune lies not only in particular sets of story materials. It also resides in the very discursive conditions that underpin the way these events are narrated. Bates's narration, as we saw above ('Narration and the generic contract', p. 157 ff), proceeds as if:

1 for any Our Tune there exists a letter from a nameable source (the Epistolary Narrator) (e.g. 'this letter... comes from the South of England... from a lady called Marianne'); and that
2 the events depicted in such a letter actually happened to the Epistolary Narrator (e.g. 'now this lady is an honest person'); and that
3 the Broadcast Narrator sincerely believes that the depicted events actually happened to the Epistolary Narrator (e.g. 'so I actually rang Marie this morning'); and that

4   the Broadcast Narrator will have rendered the essential events of the letter
    in a truthful fashion.

These conditions constitute a crucial component of the generic contract that
binds Our Tune to its habitual audience. They do, however, generate a
peculiar frisson in the way the materials are narrated. For one thing, the story
materials are often presented at discursive arms' length. This may be seen in the
act of framing the narrative (as we saw on p. 143, above) where, although the
materials are attributed to a specific source (as in 'this one comes from North
of the border') as a way of authenticating it as a tale of 'real life', it is also
presented with sufficient details of its source withheld to preserve anonymity.
Thus, responsibility for the tale is left to reside ambiguously between the
Epistolary and the Broadcast Narrator. At the same time, the subsequent
focus will commonly point up or foreground the risky dimensions of the
material – as in, for example:

> this one is the kind of letter that's going to get everybody ringing in
> the phones are going to ri light up like Christmas trees
> basically with ladies er ringing into complain that I shouldn't do it

and sure enough the closing begins:

> we've had a few phone calls saying that
> er it's not a subject we should talk about on the radio

The materials, therefore, are often presented as if potentially scandalous or in
some way risky and as if their passage into the publicly broadcast sphere has to
be negotiated with delicacy. It is noticeable, for instance, that – however
contentious the narrative particulars – the outcome or the moral tends to be
consensual: 'don't give up on life'; 'don't give up on yourself'; 'don't give up';
'just look inside yourself'; 'your family and... your friends... will rally
round' (The Moral', see p. 154).

   In preparing for this moral, the discourse works to align the audience with
the bearer of the narrative by various kinds of empathetic orientation. These
play an important role in the handling of the story materials in their broadcast
mode. For one thing they draw the audience itself into the circle of solidarity
and mutual support projected within the tale. But they also help to offset or
pre-empt an adverse judgement at the expense of an actant.

> now unless you've been in that situation of gradually having the panic rise
> inside you you probably can't imagine how she felt

> a::nd ehyou can't make any . accusations . about whose fault it was because
> those things do happen in relationships

   In some ways the presumed delicacy of the materials constitutes a puzzle,
since they are not markedly different from those which surface in documentary form in *Woman's Hour*, or in fictional form in *Afternoon Theatre* or many
TV soap operas (e.g. *Brookside* or *EastEnders*). Their apparent volatility in
Our Tune comes from a tension between different generic antecedents. Not
only do we have a manifest clash between the private confessional letter and
the public narrative (with competing structures of evaluation, as we saw on

pp. 157–60); but at the same time the developed story format and the iterative qualities of the narrative machine are redolent of genres which have an avowedly fictional basis, such as formula fiction and magazine stories. This produces a potent mix. Crossing the boundary from private to public in Our Tune is given an extra frisson by representing – in a generic form more often associated with fiction – the everyday crises of real lives. For a cardinal component of the generic contract which regulates Our Tune, is of course precisely that the material is true ('This story's a long one. It's also a bit like a Russian novel. You almost have to know the cast of characters. But, says Bates, 'It is a true story'; or 'she's honest and that's the reason for using this Our Tune'). Indeed, it is this which provides the avowed warrant for broadcasting potentially delicate material – that it has a basis in the real life of an ordinary listener.

Scannell has argued convincingly that the history of broadcasting from radio through to TV can be read in terms of a search for a voice that replicates everyday conditions of communication – a search that has led to the adoption of 'natural forms of talk and performance in all areas of output' (Scannell, 1988: 18), so that 'amongst the particular pleasures discovered by broadcasting is that of the ordinary talk of ordinary people' (1988: 19). In Scannell's terms, this has been accompanied by a growing celebration of everyday experience skilfully interwoven with the daily routine and carefully adapted to the domestic condition of listening. The most popular programmes 'are precisely those that most fully express the endless continuum of day-to-day life and the interpenetration of the public culture of broadcasting with the private experience of individuals' (1988: 19). More crucially, 'the creation of a public, communicable, pleasurable programme out of the stuff of ordinary life points up the ways in which broadcasting has revalued private experience as it has brought it into the public domain' (1988: 19). And it is certainly the case that Our Tune takes up the lives of ordinary listeners and mediates them back to the public at large. But the ordinariness of Our Tune is not straightforward. As Garner (1988) has remarked of those letters that are chosen: 'for five minutes your private life is more important than that of Boy George'. And the tales that are chosen (one letter out of a hundred or more) consistently chart breaches and disruptions to the everyday continuum of existence. Public space within the discourse of Our Tune is in fact only guaranteed to the ordinary listener by the extraordinariness of the experience which they can offer. And yet at the moment of returning this experience to the public at large it becomes assimilated to the recurring moral: 'don't give up on life'. As Coward points out: 'you are special... but your life experiences are exactly the same as everyone else's' (Coward, 1984: 149).

In this respect, the title Our Tune is significant. As an expression, its field of reference shifts between the narrated story and the requested record. When it refers to the record, the first person plural possessive pronoun (our) narrows in its reference to the actants of the story. The tune or record, therefore, becomes the emotional property of the Epistolary Narrator; and the personae of the performed song – formerly available to diverse interpretations by a listening public – become reinflected in highly particular ways. When, however, the title refers to the story itself (as in 'but she's honest and that's the reason for using this Our Tune'), the field of reference of 'our' expands to encompass the audience as a whole. The story, the experience, comes from us – the audience – as one of 500–800 letters a week, and is relayed directly back to us (as Bates says: 'I just act as a conduit on it') in a subtle blend of institutional and audience voices – private discourses in a public space, public therapy on personal experience. In some respects, of course, this leads to an inevitable flattening out, as the messy contingencies of individual lives are rearticulated into consensual forms. In other respects, however, Our Tune is – as much as anything – about the audience's relation to itself: it affirms the existence of a listening public in a process where that public is itself a most crucial discursive resource. As therapy it works upon precisely that sense of the unspeakable that goes with the profound personal crisis – the sense of separation from the everyday lives of others. In this way, while it may be the case that the story materials foreground the family as community, it is also possible to argue that in the moment of the presentation of these materials to the public another community is being invoked: not the family, or the neighbourhood, or even the nation as such, but rather the radio audience itself.

Note

1. It might be argued that soap opera on British TV provides a further way of imagining the community at a level intermediate between the family and the nation – primarily in terms of the locality or neighbourhood. And it is sufficient to note the titles themselves – *Coronation Street, EastEnders, Brookside, Neighbours,* etc. – to register the force of this argument. But, as many commentators have also noted (see, passim, Brunsdon, 1981, 1984; Allen, 1985; Fiske, 1987) the narrative use of the neighbourhood leads to a characteristic narrative form which is decentred, diffuse and open-ended, with cyclical transitions from household, to shop, to pub, etc. There are clearly problems about utilizing this image of community for the discrete 7-minute confessional narrative of the individual life crisis.

References

Allen, C. (1985) *Speaking of Soaps*. Chapel Hill: University of Carolina Press.
Bakhtin, M.M. (1986) *Speech Genres and Other Late Essays*. Austin: University of Texas Press.
Barnard, (1989) *On the Radio: Music Radio in Britain*. London: Open University Press.
Barthes, R. (1975) *S/Z*. London: Jonathan Cape.
Berry, M. (1981) 'Systemic Linguistics and Discourse Analysis: A Multi-Layered Approach to Discourse Analysis', in M. Coulthard and M. Montgomery (eds).
Brunsdon, C. (1981) '*Crossroads*: Notes on Soap Opera', in *Screen*, 22(4): 32–7.
Brunsdon, C. (1984) 'Writing about Soap Opera', in Masterman (ed.), *Television Mythologies*. London: Macmillan.
Chafe, W. (1980) *The Pear Stories: Cognitive, Cultural and Linguistic Aspects of Narrative Production*. New Jersey: Ablex.
Chatman, S. (1978) *Story and Discourse, Narrative Structure in Fiction and Film*. Ithaca, NY: Cornell University Press.
Coward, R. (1984) *Female Desire: Women's Sexuality Today*. London: Palladin.
Culler, J. (1975) *Structuralist Poetics*. London: Routledge.
Durant, A. (1984) *Conditions of Music*. London: Macmillan.
Eco, U. (1981) *The Role of the Reader*. London: Hutchinson.

Fiske, J. (1987) *Television Culture*. London: Methuen.

Garner, K. (1988) 'Soul Music', in *The Listener*, 26 May.

Goffman, E. (1981) *Forms of Talk*. Oxford: Basil Blackwell.

Greimas (1966) *Semantique Structurale: Recherche de Méthode*. Paris: Larousse.

Halliday, M.A.K. (1985) *An Introduction to Functional Grammar*. London: Edward Arnold.

Hasan, R. (1980) 'Nursery Tale as a Genre' in *Nottingham Linguistic Circular*, 13: 71-102.

Huddleston, R. (1984) *Introduction to the Grammar of English*. Cambridge: Cambridge University Press.

Labov, W. (1972) *Language in the Inner City: Studies in the Black English Vernacular*. Philadelphia; University of Pennsylvania Press.

Martin, J. and Rothery, J. (1980/1) 'Writing Project Reports I & II'. Mimeo, Department of Linguistics, University of Sydney.

Montgomery, M.M. (1977) 'Discourse Structure and Cohesion in Selected Science Lectures'. MA thesis, University of Birmingham.

Montgomery, M. (1986) 'DJ Talk', in *Media, Culture and Society*, 8(4): 421-40.

Montgomery, M. (1988) 'Direct Address, Audience and Genre', *Parlance: The Journal of the Poetics and Linguistics Association*, 1(2): 185-202.

Polanyi, L. (1985) *Telling the American Story*. New Jersey: Ablex.

Pomerantz, A. (1975) 'Second Assessments: A Study of Some Features of Agreements/Disagreements'. PhD. dissertation, University of California, Irvine.

Propp, V. (1968) *The Morphology of the Folk Tale*. Austin: University of Texas Press.

Rimmon-Kenan, S. (1983) *Narrative Fiction: Contemporary Poetics*. London: Methuen.

Scannell, P. (1988) 'The Communicative Ethos of Broadcasting'. Paper presented at the International Television Studies Conference, London (BFI).

Sinclair, J. (1966) 'Indescribable English'. Inaugural lecture, University of Birmingham.

Sinclair, J. and M. Coulthard (1975) *Towards an Analysis of Discourse*. Oxford: Oxford University Press.

Tolson, A. (1989) 'Anecdotes in Interviews'. Mimeo, Queen Margaret College, Edinburgh.

van Dijk, T. (1985) 'Structures of News in the Press', in T. Van Dijk (ed.) *Discourse and Communication*. Berlin: W. de Gruyter.

Volosinov, V.N. (1973) *Marxism and the Philosophy of Language*. New York: Academic Press.

9

Televised Chat and the Synthetic Personality

Andrew Tolson

One of the most interesting, and arguably one of the most influential forms of talk associated with contemporary broadcasting is that produced in the 'chat' or talk show. Loosely based upon a set of protocols for the television interview (see Heritage, 1985; Greatbatch, 1986a, 1986b, 1987) the talk show nevertheless frequently transgresses those protocols and presumes an increasing sophistication on the part of the television audience. The result is a certain ambivalence between forms of talk which are designed both to inform and to entertain; to appear serious and sincere, but also sometimes playful and even flippant. In this article, looking at material from British talk shows in the mid-1980s (*Wogan,* 1984; *The Dame Edna Experience,* 1987), I want to suggest that the 'playful' tendency has now assumed a position of dominance, giving rise to certain effects across the public sphere of broadcast discourse. In particular, the notion of *personality,* frequently associated with the development of television as a medium, is currently undergoing a fundamental transformation.

My argument begins with an insistence on the importance of *genre,* as a concept which is only just beginning to make an appearance in conventional discussions of discourse. Its complexity is evident in one recent discussion (Brown and Yule, 1983) where, on adjacent pages, 'genre' is both a name for the recognition of 'generalized types' – i.e. the classification of 'experiences' into categories like 'fairy stories, chats, news broadcasts, epic poems . . .' etc. (Brown and Yule, 1983: 61–2) – and is a concept which is taken to influence the production and reception of these 'types', by establishing 'norms of expectation' around them (Brown and Yule, 1983: 63–4). In this way, genre is at once an analytical concept, requiring formal demonstration; but it is also operational, at a level of practical knowledge of which speakers themselves may be more or less aware.

However, the phrase 'norms of expectation' is itself ambiguous, in so far as the term 'expectation' seems to carry much less weight as an operational constraint than the concept of 'norms' – 'expectation' seems to open up possibilities for creativity which the concept 'norm' closes down. Perhaps then the most appropriate way to characterize this level of practical knowledge is to talk, not in terms of 'norms' or 'rules', but rather in terms of *conventions.* Furthermore, generic conventions should be seen as socially derived – they are often located in specific institutions, and they undergo historical transforma- tions. The television news interview is a clear example of a genre of this kind.

Brown and Yule are uncertain whether 'norms of expectation' can be specified for 'less constrained' genres of conversation, such as 'chat'. Here, there may be some tension between the analytical concept of genre as defining more generally, has developed its own particular dramatic genres (e.g. constraints may be more variable. A more productive approach to the analysis of generic conventions is, I think, suggested in the sociolinguistic theory of Halliday (1978), who insists that 'there is a generic structure in all discourse, including the most informal spontaneous conversation' (Halliday 1978: 134). Halliday is not suggesting that generic regularities are simply demonstrable in formal descriptions of discourse (at the level of what he calls 'text'); rather discursive genres are located at the point where 'text' meets 'social situation', and more specifically in that dimension of the social situation which he defines as its 'mode' – 'the particular semiotic function or range of functions that the text is serving in the environment in question' (Halliday, 1978: 144). For Halliday, then, the generic identity of 'spontaneous conversation' might be demonstrated in a study of the 'semiotic functions' of 'conversation' in particular environments. It may be difficult to characterize the formal structure of 'chat', but it is possible to study the effects of what may be classified as 'chat' in an environment like broadcast television.

On this basis, I want to suggest that just as television, and broadcasting more generally, has developed its own particular dramatic genres (e.g. situation comedy), so too it has developed certain forms of broadcast talk which have identifiable generic structures. These forms of talk are, in general terms, 'informal and conversational' (Scannell, 1988b), but more precisely, they should be seen as institutionalized variants of 'conversation' as such. Moreover, these forms of talk occur across the different programme formats within which 'talk' predominates. For instance, it would be interesting to undertake a study of the art of 'live commentary' as a speech genre which clearly takes different forms on radio and television, but which occurs across sports programmes, state occasions, live political events and, sometimes, disasters. Live commentary is one broadcast speech genre; and 'chat', I am suggesting, is another. Chat is a form of studio talk, which can be found in all types of interviews, panel discussions, game shows and human interest programmes (e.g. *That's Life!*) – wherever in fact there is a studio.

What then characterizes 'chat' as a broadcast speech genre? In many contexts, to use Halliday's term, chat is apparent in a clear shift of *register* within the programme format where it occurs, such that the primary business of the format is temporarily delayed or suspended. Thus in the context of a game show, chat between participants delays the actual playing of the game (a prime example would be *Blankety Blank* [a celebrity quiz show]); whereas in the context of a current affairs interview chat introduces a suspension within the 'main' discourse, whilst a 'subsidiary' discourse (an aside, a metadiscursive comment) is briefly formulated (cf. Montgomery, 1977). It is this functional contrast between main and subsidiary levels of discourse which frequently allows us to recognize chat when we hear it:

Robin Day.	Mrs Thatcher do you intend to lead the Conservative Party into the next election in say '87?
Mrs Thatcher.	I hope so.
Day.	Because if you do that and let's say that the next is in the autumn of 1987 do you realise then that you would have been, held the office of Prime Minister for a longer, for the longest continuous period this century and possibly long before that?
Thatcher.	Yes.
Day.	Eight-and-a-half-years, and you'll be six...
Thatcher.	Not very long.
Day.	Eight-and-a-half-years.
Thatcher.	Yes it's not very long if you look back to other times.
Day.	And you'll be sixty-two. You still think you want to go ahead at the next election?
Thatcher.	Yes. I shall be a very fit sixty-two. You might be a little bit nearer that than I am, but you feel all right?
Day. (chuckles)	Forgive me if I don't answer that question Prime Minister, towards the end of this interesting interview. (*Panorama*, April 1984).

Actually, I think Brown and Yule have overestimated the difficulties in arriving at a formal definition of 'chat'. There are at least three main identifying features of this speech genre, not all of which may be operating at once. First, there is often a topical shift towards the 'personal' (as opposed to the institutional), or towards the 'private' (as opposed to the public). Secondly, this shift may be accompanied by displays of wit (e.g. foregrounding lexical ambiguities) or humour (double entendres, etc.). But thirdly, and this is the vital point, in any context 'chat' always works by opening up the possibility of transgression. Chat does not simply reproduce norms and conventions, rather it flirts with them, for instance, it opens up the possibility of the interviewee putting questions to the interviewer. Certainly, in the context of a *Panorama* interview, Robin Day must appear to 'manage' this behaviour; but at the same time (as this example shows) it is not simply disavowed. For in this momentary transgression of convention, both Mrs Thatcher, and in his response Day himself, are constructed as 'television personalities'.

Defined in these terms, I would suggest that 'chat' is a central feature of televised public discourse, and I shall return to a discussion of its effects. For not only is chat a ubiquitous and constant possibility for nearly every kind of televised studio talk; it is also, because of the studio's pivotal location in the regime of broadcasting, in a certain position of dominance. However, from a discursive point of view, perhaps the most interesting of all programme formats is the contemporary 'chat' or 'talk' show (I will use the American term 'talk show' to emphasize that 'chat' is a genre which occurs in several formats). In the 1980s, the talk show attained new heights of sophistication, both in Britain and in the USA. In America, David Letterman might be compared and contrasted to the earlier format personified by Johnny Carson; whilst in Britain, the genre dominated in the 1970s by Michael Parkinson (previously, a journalist) was taken over and developed by Terry Wogan (previously, a disc jockey). The talk show is, by definition, devoted to the production of 'chat'; but by the mid-1980s the BBC's prime-time Saturday night show *Wogan* had developed 'chat' to the point where it was virtually an art form.

Television chat and the 'personality effect'

Consider for example the following exchange between Terry Wogan and Shelley Winters (*Wogan,* 10 March 1984):

Winters.	You had to give away my age, huh?
Wogan.	No no.
Winters.	You had to say how old I was. When was it, 1939?
Wogan.	1957 or something, wasn't it?
Winters.	When was *Gone With The Wind* done?
Wogan.	I'm not sure.
Winters.	The only reason I didn't get the part was that I had a Brooklyn accent. Vivien Leigh spoke better otherwise I would have got it.
Wogan.	You would have walked that.
Winters.	*What was that accent, that man, who just talked for fifteen minutes?
Wogan.	What, Terry Venables?
Winters.	Yes.
Wogan.	I'm not sure, a type of East End accent I think. I think he makes it up as he goes along.
Winters.	I did a picture with Michael Caine a while ago called *Alfie* which was sort of a good picture but I never knew what he was saying. Whenever he took a breath I said my line, it was like that.
Wogan.	Many of us have difficulty with Michael Caine, yes.
Winters.	It seems like the same language but it isn't. I mean sometimes you get in a lot of trouble.
Wogan.	*What sort of trouble have you been in?
Winters.	I'm not discussing it.
Wogan.	Come on.
Winters.	There are millions of people watching I mean you say anything on your television . . .
Wogan.	That's what you think.
Winters.	I know er, but you know, no there's nothing. Well you say anything. Last night I watched something on BBC2 about sex.
Wogan.	*Yes we have that over here. What do you call that in America?
Winters.	You don't talk about it you do it (*laughter*). I mean, I never saw a show *Sex Education for Adults*. That's what it was.
Wogan.	Yes, I saw it myself. I learned quite a lot.
Winters.	*It was slides and pictures and diagrams and er, I was, did it shock you?
Wogan.	No, because I know where I'm going wrong now.
Winters.	*Well, listen how long have you done this show, three years?
Wogan.	Feels like it. Only a year.
Winters.	No, you don't.
Wogan.	Still a boy, still a boy at the game. Yes, before I did this there was a very old man who used to do it called Dartington or something.
Winters.	Have you thought, now Saturday nights because of inflation and every-thing, I learned from the crew – I've just been doing a picture called *Always*, and I think it will be done always. It's all about, I play a Russian psychic lesbian I think, I'm not sure.
Wogan.	I'm glad you looked at that sex instruction film.
Winters.	I know er.
Wogan.	I can see the problems you'd have with that part.

Winters.	Well, anyway, it was a sort of weird love story that takes place between 1936 and now and the people they have trouble making out. Do you say making out?
Wogan.	No. Making up? Making it?
Winters.	No, when you do it.
Wogan.	Doing it?
Winters.	Yeah, do you say making out?
Wogan.	No, we say doing it.
Winters.	Well, in the still of the night if you can't sleep do you ever wonder, because people don't go out much on Saturday nights as they used to, it used to be a regular thing.
Wogan.	They do now, look they usen't to, but they do now since we started.
Winters.	*This interview. OK. Now have you ever wondered sort of if people are at home Saturday nights and they're watching you and its warm and they stretch out in the bedroom or the living room wherever the telly is (*TW*: steady, yes). Have you ever thought how many babies you're responsible for?
Wogan.	No, I'm responsible for no babies whatsoever.
Winters.	Well you are though.
Wogan.	No I'm not (*SW*: Yes you are) No, people nod off to me.
Winters.	I didn't nod off last week when Joan Rivers said all those terrible things.
Wogan.	Didn't she, didn't she say some shocking . . . You talk about us saying some shocking things, I mean she really does.
Winters.	We don't let her say those things on television in America.
Wogan.	Yes you do.
Winters.	No we don't. We laugh at night clubs and then we are ashamed we laughed. I mean I'm not exactly a Women's Libber but I mean I get so angry when I laugh at her (. . .)
Wogan.	*You've been a bit of a shocker yourself though, haven't you?
Winters.	Yes, but I put it in print I don't do it on television.

I will begin my formal analysis of this exchange by recognizing that as a species of interviewing, it contains some peculiar, and in other contexts abnormal, features. Just in straight quantitative terms Winters (interviewee) puts nine questions to Wogan, whilst he (interviewer) puts seven questions to his guest. Furthermore, at least four of Winters' questions (marked by asterisks in the transcript) can be counted as major topical initiations, requiring developed responses from Wogan, which Winters then follows up with supplementary questions and comments. Wogan himself makes three such topical initiations, the first of which is rejected by the interviewee ('I'm not discussing it'). Equally, many of the utterances in this exchange are hearable neither as questions nor as answers, but rather as initiating propositions or as contributions to sequences of argument.

Nor is this exactly the intimate and cosy 'fireside chat', casting the audience in the position of 'eavesdroppers' to a private conversation, which some previous forms of the talk show have attempted to simulate (Greatbatch, 1987: 35). Rather, the Wogan/Winters dialogue seems to be much more aware of itself as a public performance: at times it is a kind of double act, with mock pantomimic arguments ('Oh yes you do'; 'Oh no I don't') and with Wogan playing the straight man to Winters' humorous lines. In a word, the talk show interview is now dedicated to *banter*. It is as if the conventions of interviewing have now become a pretext for the development of clever and complex forms of verbal improvisation in which both parties more or less equally participate. Within this space, Winters in particular stretches her position as interviewee to the limit: not only does she ask most of the questions and introduce most of the topics; as she comments on Wogan's introduction and interrogates his career as a talk show host she seems to be highlighting the artificiality of his role.

However, my principal reason for reproducing this extract here is because it provides a particularly rich illustration of my three defining features of 'chat' as a speech genre. First then, in terms of content, there is the characteristic focus on the 'personal', which in *Wogan* was often equated with the sexual, but also was more generally articulated in terms of gossip – both about other stars/personalities (Leigh, Caine) and previous performances on the programme (Rivers). Also at this level a common cultural knowledge is invoked (e.g. the date of *Gone With The Wind*, the joke about 'Dartington' i.e. Parkinson, the BBC's best-known talk show interviewer before Wogan). This is the kind of mass-mediated cultural knowledge which is classified in many contexts today as 'trivia'.

Secondly, and building on this foundation, there is a sustained and highly self-reflexive metadiscourse about television as a cultural institution. Here participants not only invoke the cultural knowledge of the viewer, they also draw attention to the construction of their own performances. It is assumed for instance, that the viewer has a knowledge of the history of television, of its genres and is reflexively aware of the domestic conditions of its reception. Indeed, when Winters refers to these, in her speculations about viewers and babies, she comes very close to transgressing the formal distance between television and its audience – the next step would be to address the viewer directly. It is certainly very far from a realistic simulation, where disbelief is 'suspended', because here the reflexive nature of the talk assumes a viewer who is consciously aware of the forms as well as the contents of television.

In my view, however, it is at a third level that this kind of talk becomes really clever. There is a level at which the dialogic improvisation is somewhat similar to a jazz performance, not only because it is apparently unrehearsed, but also in so far as it involves a play of thematic repetition and variation. In this dialogue the metadiscursive level ('Here we are on television'/'How are people watching this at home?') is articulated to a repetition of two topics (both introduced by the interviewee): i.e. language/cultural difference and sex/the limits of public discourse. A form of *wit* is demonstrated by interweaving these various topics, so that each is inflected in terms of the other. Thus the topic of linguistic difference is inflected into the terminology of sex ('Do you say making out?'), whilst the topic of sexual discourse is inflected into cultural differences in the publicly sayable ('We don't let her say those things on television'). Two or three topics are in the air at once and the skill of the participants consists in their ability to manipulate the dialogue to ensure that the verbal juggling act continues.

And the performance is of course given added impetus by the fact that it is apparently 'live'. Will the participants be able to sustain this spontaneous flow of wit and repartee? In fact, in this case, the programme was recorded, the 'liveness' is an illusion; but an effect of liveness and immediacy is constructed in a number of ways. In this context, with its 'live' studio audience, liveness is an effect of the studio location; but it is also reinforced by deictic features of the reflexive metadiscourse: 'What was that accent that just talked?', 'How long have you been doing this show?' When Shelley Winters talks about the viewer's domestic situation she indirectly refers to immediate conditions of viewing. My point here is that whilst the metadiscourse does, on one level, 'demystify' the institution of television, it also simultaneously contributes to a 'liveness' effect which helps to sustain it. At this level then, the metadiscourse *re-mystifies*: it reaffirms a bond between television performers, studio audience and, by extension, the domestic viewer which implicates all parties in a common and immediate situation.

All of which serves to reproduce a particular kind of 'personality effect'. It is instructive at this point to refer to the discussion of 'personality' in television studies which, in some accounts, has made reference to the effects of televised 'chat'. For instance, John Langer (1981) has defined television's 'personality system' in terms of a 'complex unity [of] heterogenous and multi-faceted codes', amounting to a 'systematic tendency' across many forms of television (Langer, 1981: 352). But after talking in general terms about the effects of 'speaking for oneself' in television interviews, and in close-up, Langer comes to focus specifically on a notion of 'disclosure':

> In the context of the talk-show's carefully orchestrated informality, with its illusion of lounge-room casualness and leisurely pace, the host and guest engage in 'chat'. During the course of this chat, with suitable questions and tactful encouragement from the host, the guest is predictably 'drawn in' to making certain 'personal' disclosures, revealing aspects of what may be generally regarded as the private self, in fact becoming incorporated into television's personality system by disclosing for the purposes of television, one's 'personality'.
> ... What prevails in the end is not the talk show's diluted hucksterism and commercial 'hype' but its capacity to provide a special setting for personal disclosure where guests appear to be showing us their 'real' selves, where they can discuss how they 'feel' and reflect on their private lives with impunity. If these guests are among the great and powerful or are well-known celebrities, which is most frequently the case, this is the place where the cares and burdens of high office or public life can be set aside, where we can see them as they 'really are', which in the end after all, as these programmes set out to illustrate, is just like us, 'ordinary folks'. (Langer, 1981: 360-1)

On this basis, Langer goes on to attribute an ideological effect to this discourse of personality, in so far as it displaces social and political criteria. But perhaps his frequent recourse to inverted commas ('real' selves, etc.) already begins to suggest some doubts about the sincerity of personal disclosure in the contemporary talk show. In fact, what Langer really seems to be describing here is an earlier form of 'human interest' interview programme, of which John Freeman's *Face to Face* (BBC, 1959-62) would be an exemplary instance, where indeed a populist personality discourse was frequently reflected in the open and apparently sincere disclosure of 'real feelings'. In these programmes, Freeman's interviewing technique might certainly be characterized as a strategy of 'tactful encouragement', allied to a rigorous, probing use of the camera. But today, I would suggest, this kind of transparent populism appears old-fashioned. Although its rhetorical structure (i.e. public/private persons; apparent/real selves, etc.) persists as a generic formula for the talk show, it seems to me that a fundamental shift has taken place in the way this formula is reproduced.

Increasingly, as the Winters interview illustrates, 'personality' now appears not in transparent revelation, but in the interviewee's capacity to negotiate the terms of 'disclosure'. This is precisely not the context for a 'true confession' (as Winters herself indicates) and so part of the pleasure for the audience in this speech genre consists in working out the different degrees of truth/untruth in what is then spoken. A certain level of complexity, which implicates the 'knowingness' of the viewer, is related to a form of speaking from 'experience' where *the experiences may or may not be real.* I return to this point later; but clearly at this level 'personality' is no longer reducible to 'people as they really are'. Rather, it seems to me that the personality effect now consists in the willingness of stars and celebrities, like Winters, to take the risk of playing this kind of public verbal game. In the contemporary talk show the interview is explicitly and transparently a *performance* of 'chat' – that is its *raison d'être* – and there are moments in this performance when the very concept of 'personality' is up for discussion.

Personality as performance

In the *Wogan* series, regularly and in various ways, the whole notion of 'personality' was called into question. But it was not that the populist personality discourse, with its emphasis on sincerity and authenticity, was entirely redundant; rather the earlier formula was now explicitly interrogated, and other rhetorics of 'authenticity' were on display. Consider, first of all, the following dialogue between two established television 'personalities':

(*Terry Wogan interviewing Bob Monkhouse, 10 March 1984.*)

Wogan.	You've done your chat show series for BBC 2. How do you like being an interviewee rather than an interviewer?
Monkhouse.	I found being an interviewer very very difficult. I have watched this series of course I have, and the last one and the previous one. And I think you are, I hate to do this, I think you're very good (*laughter*). I really do ... I found it very difficult. I find the biggest problem for me is, that my admiration for my guests, because they were all comedians, is so considerable that I can't disguise it, I can't hide it, and therefore it's possible to appear erm obsequious and er over-enthusiastic about a guest when that is a genuine emotion, and that's been criticised. I noticed er (*W*: Yes). Well I should develop the same contempt that you obviously have for your guests.
Wogan.	No, only for some of them.
Monkhouse.	(Laughs) Adsum.
Wogan.	Do you think then that erm, being honest or showing honest emotions on television is not a good idea, if they could be misinterpreted, as they have been in your case, they're called smarm which is genuine admiration?
Monkhouse.	(*Laughs*) Yes, er I don't think er, television is a place for me to show

my genuine emotions. I think it's a place for, I would rather, I'm much happier, er Joan Rivers when you interviewed her the other week so, so excellently said the cabaret stage was her psychiatrist er that she regarded her job as to entertain, to get laughs. And that's the way I feel I, I came into the business in eighteen hundred and forty five in order to get laughs but that meant inventing a persona, offering something which is not necessarily me, it's an invention, it's a construction.

I, I've known you long enough to know that there are er, inconceivably deeper parts of you than are actually visible on the TV screen. There are parts of you which have never been seen on the TV screen (*audience laughter*). I for one hope that they will never be seen.

Wogan. You nearly got into a compliment there. And you decided to duck out of it. Because a little bit of the real Bob came out there and you quickly shoved it back again.

Monkhouse. Yes, yes I don't really want to, no, exposing myself on the TV screen is not my idea of fun.

In a previous article (Tolson, 1985) I have analysed another extract from this interview in which Monkhouse tells a couple of very funny anecdotes about a television programme he used to compere, *The Golden Shot*. The aim of that article was to highlight certain similarities between the formal structure of the anecdote and the regime of broadcast television – arguing that the rhetoric of much contemporary television can be characterized as 'anecdotal'. However, that discussion also makes a further point which is more immediately relevant to this extract, where Monkhouse and Wogan are directly discussing the activity in which they are simultaneously engaged. This point is again that increasingly, talk on television is self-reflexive. It is not only talk, but also talk about talk: that is 'metatalk', and talk about television in general (Tolson, 1985: 23).

Moreover, I think it is very significant that some of the talk about television in the contemporary talk show, now extends to the notion of 'television personality' as such. There now seems to be a space for Monkhouse to engage in what is effectively a *critique* of his own television personality. In the light of Langer's account this is a very interesting discussion: for Monkhouse is now saying that his television personality is a 'construction' – and that the same point applies to our host, Wogan himself. Not that this critique is particularly disturbing, however – for somehow Monkhouse appears as an even more authentic and sincere personality ('the real Bob') in so far as he admits that his television personality is a sham.

Also, of course, Monkhouse is making an attempt to inject some (not very subtle) humour into the discussion. Again, in comparison with *Face to Face* (recall Freeman's interview with Tony Hancock) the rhetoric of personality has changed. The terms of an acceptable talk show performance now extend to an ability to play with conventions of sincerity and personal disclosure, and to develop jokes at their expense. Joan Rivers herself is particularly adept at this kind of strategy:

(*Terry Wogan interviewing Joan Rivers, 3 March 1984.*)

Wogan. You do chat shows yourself I know in the States. You sit in for the biggest

	chat show they have there, *Johnny Carson*, and he hates you because you're more popular than he is.
Rivers.	No no he loves me. He found me, he found me. He's my mentor.
Wogan.	So you're his protegee.
Rivers.	I'm his protegee.
Wogan.	Mm. And when you hosted that show you had a bit of a run in with one of our own lovely ladies Joan Collins, didn't you?
Rivers.	The best, she's the best. She's the best because she's bitchy back. Do you know what fun it is, Joan Collins is so ... 'Cause that's what television should be, it should be fun. And she gets on, and I'll be bitchy to her. It's like a tennis match and she goes whack back. I said to her, you know 'cause we call her the British Open, I mean she's just had everybody, so but (*laughter, applause*)
Wogan.	But did you say that to her face?
Rivers.	Yes, so I said to her, you know 'who is the best man you ever had?' And she said to me 'your husband'. (*laughter*) Well, that's great. You just want to say that's what television should be.

Of course, not everyone tells them like Joan Rivers, and in fact when the Rivers talk show was shown subsequently on British television it was not particularly successful. But in both content and form I think this exchange with Wogan is indicative of a transformation in the talk show genre, and its attendant concept of 'good television', as compared for instance to the kind of talk show interview which Langer has described. Two essential points can be made. First, the grounds for speaking from 'experience' have changed. In so far as personal experiences still remain the focus for such interviews, and in so far as they are 'disclosed', they may be recounted sincerely (Monkhouse), but equally they may be represented as constructions, even fabrications (Rivers) for the 'game' which is 'good television'. But, secondly, the reason why the grounds for disclosure have shifted is that a key generic development has taken place in the history of the talk show interview. The Rivers interview (and there were several similar interviews in the 1984 series of *Wogan*) is in fact indicative of an institutional 'mixing' of genres, where the talk show interview meets stand-up comedy. The interview provides a vehicle and the interviewer poses as the straight-man, for an established and rehearsed comedy routine. Thus 'chat' may still be serious, or it may be comic; but more often than not it has now become a complex and entertaining mixture of the two.

The Dame Edna Experience

I now propose to illustrate this last point, and to consider some of its more general implications, in a brief examination of what is perhaps the most extreme example of generic transformation in the talk show interview to have been produced in Britain. In the autumn of 1987 the most popular talk show on British television was hosted by a theatrical dame, Edna Everage, played by the Australian comedian, Barry Humphries. *The Dame Edna Experience,* produced by LWT (London Weekend Television), occupied a prime-time slot on Saturday evenings, and in terms of ratings regularly outscored the BBC's *Wogan*, which had by then assumed a more conventional weekday format. For those who did not see it, or perhaps have never observed a Dame Edna performance, it is not easy to summarize the show's appeal. As one rather sycophantic newspaper article claimed 'in *The Dame Edna Experience* . . . Humphries in fact, destroys the chat show as a form, replacing it with a freak show' (Lewis, 1987: 62). But the point is that for the most part, these 'freaks' were internationally famous celebrities, leaving at least one TV critic (Patrice Chaplin in *The Listener*) thoroughly bemused:

> The chat show guests, the TV and home audience, never know what will come next. Does Barry Humphries? . . . This week, behind a foreground of celebrities, Charlton Heston appeared in wheelchair. Dame Edna with a cry, 'Chuck, for a minute I thought you'd brought your chariot', sent a nurse to help him down the stairs. In the process he fell and wasn't seen again. Was his exit real? Or part of the game? Apparently this wasn't the first time Dame Edna has 'aborted' a star interview. So presumably it's just a joke. But it was thoroughly mystifying. Of course Dame Edna isn't what she seems. Anything could be going on under the make-up. (Chaplin, 1987: 34).

Clearly, this kind of commentary begins to locate *The Dame Edna Experience* within the broad generic transformation of the talk show which I have described. Here again, the celebrity interview meets stand-up comedy, and the distinction between what is serious and what is a game becomes very blurred indeed. The 'experience' of this show was all about ambiguity – and as Chaplin herself recognizes, this leads to interesting questions about the position and potential response of the television audience. But is the viewer really 'thoroughly mystified' by such developments? I would suggest that Chaplin is writing from a position of (perhaps mock) innocence, and that the contemporary television audience has access to various kinds of knowledge through which to make sense of this show. Indeed, it is in its appeal to such knowledge, in its construction of a position of 'knowingness' for the viewer, that many of the pleasures of *The Dame Edna Experience* can be located.

Consider, for example, the following extract, taken from the show in which Charlton Heston made his wheelchair appearance. This programme was introduced by Humphries/Dame Edna, in a elaborate gynaecological metaphor, as 'woman oriented', and it began with an interview with Germaine Greer:

Dame Edna.	I want to take you down memory lane. (*turns to direct address*) Viewers, when I was just a young and prematurely intelligent housewife in Melbourne (*laughter, turns to guest*) in my home town of Melbourne, and you were just a little schoolgirl, I had a kitchen, I suppose it seemed to you then a very, very big kitchen.
Germaine Greer.	Laminex.
Dame Edna.	It was, it was a huge kitchen. And there was a lovely smell of cooking there and sponge fingers and Lamingtons and vanilla slices. And these little kiddies from the neighbourhood and from other neighbourhoods used to come along and they'd pop in, and sit around the table and they just – well I suppose they were looking to me for help and advice. And you were one of them. It was a Catholic home you came from, wasn't it?
Greer.	No, it was mixed, my father was a Calethumpian.
Dame Edna.	Oh was he, well I knew there was a problem of some kind. (*laughter*) But, darling, think of the other children who sat

	around my kitchen table. There was that little boy with hair all over his face, rather stunted, who used to trace some of the little Donald Ducks on the TV. Who was that, Rolf was it? *(laughter)*
Greer.	He wasn't called Rolf then though was he?
Dame Edna.	No, no, he was little Mrs Harris' boy anyway. That funny boy from Sydney who I always thought was a little bit c-o-double m-o-n. Clive, he's done well for himself *(laughter)* hasn't he? You remember little Rupert who delivered the papers? *(laughter applause)*
Greer.	He was very shy though.
Dame Edna.	He was. But you got a lot of advice in those days, posture I used to advise you on ...
Greer.	Well er,
Dame Edna.	and dress. If only you'd sought my advice this evening. *(laughter)* However, no no it's lovely, it's lovely, it is, it's ...
Greer.	I know I've let you down that's why I'm nervous.
Dame Edna.	No it's practical. It's ... it'll see you out anyway darling. *(laughter)* But Germaine, a magical thing happened which thrilled us all. You wrote *The Female Eunuch* which is a classic of its kind. I know Madge loved the book, didn't you *(turns to Madge)* oh ... she did. Didn't – Germaine my bridesmaid was a pioneer of New Zealand feminism, she was, that's why it never took off. *(laughter)* She didn't burn her bra, the neighbours did. *(laughter)* Tell me how did the book, the success of *The Female Eunuch* change your life, because it must have, money rolling in.
Greer.	I don't think it's been very er influential at all. I think you've been more influential. I mean Mrs Thatcher is someone who's learned every lesson you had to teach. She's going to turn England into Moonee Ponds. That's her stated objective: everybody in their own home, making new surrounds for the fireplace, and mowing the nature strip and polishing the car. It's going to be just like Moonee Ponds.
Dame Edna.	There's nothing wrong with those activities Germaine, please, you're talking about your background now. *(laughter)*

In the context of this article, my interest in *The Dame Edna Experience* is that it directly engages with the two main points about 'chat' as a form of broadcast talk which I have been principally concerned to establish; i.e., (a) it has a complex and flexible generic structure which (b) is related to television's obsession with the display of 'personality'. In *The Dame Edna Experience*, Humphries is exploring both areas simultaneously, in such a way that the viewer is involved in a complicated de-coding procedure. And the pleasure and popularity of the show lies in this very complexity, which leads to further questions about the contemporary television audience and its relation to broadcast talk.

For instance, with its previous familiarity with developments in *Wogan*, etc. the audience can already be presumed to have some orientation to the talk show's flexible and cross-generic structure. *The Dame Edna Experience* now takes these generic developments some stages further, to the extent that aspects of the celebrity interview/comic routine are clearly shown to have been rehearsed (Greer in fact brings a gift of Lamingtons on to the set, and produces a 'scone' which she claims to have baked in Dame Edna's kitchen all those years ago). Furthermore, it is also assumed that it is the guests, and not the interviewer, who will play the 'straight' role. Indeed it is the interviewer who is the principal celebrity on this show, which is reflected in the fact that Dame Edna herself produces most of the talk. But again this is all clearly foregrounded to the audience from the start, where, in introducing her first show of the series, Dame Edna announces her 'wonderful new concept':

It's a *form* of a talk show. It's really a monologue interrupted by total strangers.

A second, related generic development in the contemporary talk show which is taken to new levels by Dame Edna, concerns the behaviour of the interviewer. We have come a long way from the days when interviewers simply confined their activities to 'probing' the interviewee on behalf of the audience. Certainly Dame Edna does do this, for example in her question about how the publication of *The Female Eunuch* changed Greer's life, but this doesn't lead to a sustained exploration of that experience. Rather, as an interviewer, Dame Edna seems more concerned to 'probe' the conventions of interviewing. Traditionally, it is assumed that the interviewer will preserve a neutral posture, and will refrain from making direct comments or expressions of disaffiliation towards the responses of interviewees. Dame Edna, however, is particularly adept at verbal 'put-downs' – making negative comments on both the appearance of her guests and the limitations of their answers ('please, you're talking about your background now'). Since the show is dedicated to confirming the celebrity status of the interviewer, the interviewees can expect a rough, and occasionally humiliating, ride.

Thirdly, I also think this extract illustrates an interesting series of variations on what, according to Heritage (1985), is the defining feature of interview talk; that is, its orientation towards the audience. In some respects, as I have suggested, this orientation is conventional – as Dame Edna turns to the camera, directly to address the audience as 'viewers', before proceeding to question the interviewee on its behalf. At another level, it is also clear that the entire exchange, as a 'double act' between the participants, is designed as a performance for the audience – as a piece of comic theatre. But I think it is most significant that this performance, in its public context, parodies a type of discourse which is more characteristic of a private, interpersonal reminiscence ('Clive, he's done well for himself . . . hasn't he? You remember little Rupert who delivered the papers . . .'). This exchange has the *form* as well as the content of private gossip, which is visually reinforced by an extensive use of reaction shots which show Greer nodding, smiling, etc. as if in direct acknowledgement. The general point is that Dame Edna not only manipulates the conventions of interviewing, she also manipulates the audience's relationship to those conventions. The distinction between what is public and what is private begins to appear ambiguous.

But all this is simply at the level of formal generic variation. The play with conventional roles, with politeness and with the boundaries of public discourse, is made intelligible and pleasurable, rather than simply 'destructive', at a second level of viewer involvement. As Patrice Chaplin recognizes, and as the audience knows, this is indeed all a 'game'; but it is not quite reducible to the Rivers metaphor of a 'tennis match'. Obviously the entire exchange between Dame Edna and Germaine Greer mobilizes the viewer's prior knowledge of Greer's (real) and Dame Edna's (spoof) biographies. On this basis, the possibility of a transgression into private reminiscence is mitigated by the knowledge that the kitchen in Moonee Ponds is *fictional*.

Indeed, in the light of previous discussions, the 'personality' of Dame Edna is absolutely fascinating. It is an extremely complex creation, in which there are at least three interconnecting dimensions. First, as a character in a fictional world, Dame Edna is explicitly paradoxical, as reflected in her description of herself as a 'prematurely intelligent housewife': that is, she is the housewife who is also a 'megastar', the suburban colonial who is now a jet-setting celebrity. Much of the explicit wit relies upon a play between these possibilities. Second, however, Dame Edna is also, of course, an impersonation. At this level, the humour is often implicit (though obvious) rather than explicit: for it is clear for instance that when, later in this programme, Dame Edna talks about exchanging 'women's talk' with Zsa Zsa Gabor, what we are in fact watching is a man dressed up as a woman. On this basis, Dame Edna undercuts any suggestion that the function of the talk show is to probe the 'real person' behind the public mask. And when in her introduction to the series, in typically exaggerated style, she does in fact make this suggestion – we know, because of who she is, that the 'real person' on this show is always a construction.

But it is the third dimension of Dame Edna, which is not always immediately apparent in her comedy, that I particularly want to emphasize here. For although on one level, Dame Edna is a character in a fictional world; on another, particularly in this chat show, she is a television 'personality'. This creates an extremely complex web of multiple identities in which Dame Edna's *personality*, as manifested in her wit and repartee, establishes a knowing and ironic distance from her identity as a *character*. What she is now mocks what she was before – her spoof biography – even though what she was before is a constant reference point. So in *The Dame Edna Experience*, it is not simply that 'personality' has displaced 'character' as the dominant criterion for interview talk (cf. Tolson, 1990): rather it is that the former reflects back on the latter and humorously deconstructs it.

And what is being deconstructed in the world of 'Moonee Ponds'? The viewer who is familiar with this Barry Humphries creation already has extensive knowledge of this world and some of the characters who inhabit it. There is Dame Edna's visible depressed, silent, spinster companion 'Madge' (her 'bridesmaid', who sits beside Dame Edna on the TV show). There are constant references to 'Norm', Dame Edna's absent and permanently disabled husband. Now, it seems, this fictional world is to be extended to absorb the biographies of other eminent, and real, Australians. In this piece of theatre, Germaine Greer herself bears witness to the 'reality' of Moonee Ponds. It is crucial, I think, that this world is suburban, homely, domestic, lower middle class and, above all, 'typical'. That is, although set in far-off Melbourne, this is precisely the kind of world, with a certain range of petty-bourgeois values, with which the domestic television audience can be presumed to be familiar. This is the world which Dame Edna reveals to be a construction, and which she mocks. Her 'personality' thus establishes the grounds for an extensive critique of lower middle-class culture.

I think it may be true to say that Dame Edna belongs to the 'burlesque' tradition of 'mass middlebrow laughter' which David Cardiff (1988) argues is central to the history of broadcast comedy. For on one level, *The Dame Edna Experience* is indeed a parody of a talk show – with its highly spectacular set (a long staircase down which the participants descend, dominated by a hugh pair of Dame Edna spectacles), its trick devices (an ejector seat with which Dame Edna can automatically remove boring guests) and its large and visible orchestra (Laurie Holloway and the Holocausts). To this extent the show is a modern version of the genre of comedy which Cardiff describes, characterized by 'everyday modernism, self-reflexiveness and cultishness'; addressed to the prime target for such comedy, the 'knowing viewer'. However, in his discussion of mass middlebrow laughter, which he locates in the development of a lower middle-class audience for public service broadcasting, Cardiff emphasizes a certain kind of satirical stance, in which the middlebrow consensus makes fun of extremes:

> The 'knowingness' on which so much of this comedy depended was not restricted to a familiarity with the kinds of culture which were being parodied. As it began to approach satire it also involved a stolid, worldly assessment of human nature. This was a satire whose objects were always the extremes of social, cultural or intellectual life – extravagance in manners, intense sensibility, rarefied ideas. At worst it was crude debunking. At best, by the artistry with which it achieved its effects, it could persuade the audience that it was witnessing something shocking and iconoclastic or that it shared with the author a subtle and perceptive laughter. But the laughter was always the same laughter for it always emanated from the same standpoint of decent conventionality and commonsense. (Cardiff, 1988: 49–50)

Cardiff refers to *The Young Ones* as a contemporary TV comedy show which follows this kind of tradition; but perhaps *Monty Python's Flying Circus* is its apotheosis. Clearly, Dame Edna is also indebted to it: the 'stolid, worldly assessment of human nature'; 'sharing with the author a subtle and perceptive laughter'. But now, I think, there is a crucial difference. For whereas the kind of comedy described here makes fun of alien eccentricities (cf. Monty Python's 'Ministry of Silly Walks', etc.); the eccentricities derided by Dame Edna are precisely located in the suburban, lower middle-class audience itself. Here the satirical and parodic middlebrow tradition has turned on itself: it no longer mocks extremes; rather it now mocks the supremely ordinary, as symbolized by Moonee Ponds, to which Dame Edna's celebrity guests, no matter what their fame or status, are reduced. Furthermore, Dame Edna mocks the very possibility of that key suburban concept, the 'real person'. For the ordinariness of the celebrity is of course precisely not real – it is fictional. In *The Dame Edna Experience*, it seems to me, the whole concept of 'personality' has begun to self-destruct. 'Personality' is achieved at the expense of there being a 'real person', with real experiences; and the suburban world which these so-called 'persons' inhabit is reduced to a fictional fabrication, 'Moonee Ponds'.

So it is entirely consistent that having deconstructed its suburban reality, the kind of comic vision presented by this talk show should also turn its attention to the politics of 'mass middlebrow' culture. Of course, in this kind of game, no political perspective can be taken seriously, including Greer's feminism. As we might expect, feminism is equated with the character of Madge; but (and perhaps I am guilty of a value judgement here) it seems to me that the really witty development in this dialogue is Greer's own equation of Moonee Ponds with Thatcherism. This develops to a point where a sexual political perspective is recruited back into the humour:

Dame Edna.	I just want to know though when the money flowed in, how did you spend it? Now come on.
Greer.	Well I, I needed your advice Edna. I didn't find a tax...
Dame Edna.	Stop fiddling with that kleenex too, Germaine (*laughter*)
Greer.	I didn't find a tax haven.
Dame Edna.	You didn't find a tax haven.
Greer.	No, I paid it all to the Government sooner or later.
Dame Edna.	Well, that's what we all have to do, we have to pay our dues my darling.
Greer.	Then they bought a polaris. (*laughter*)
Dame Edna.	With the proceeds of *The Female Eunuch*, (*direct address to audience*) isn't that spooky? (*laughter*) Big long pointed things (*laughter*).

Again, this extract clearly illustrates Humphries' ability, as Dame Edna, to shift discursive registers – from the 'character' (who offers her own brand of banal, 'worldly wise' advice) to the 'personality' (who engages the audience with her 'knowingness'). But also, I think, there are moments when this 'knowingness' is extended, beyond the level of mere mockery of the common-sensical world which it invokes. Here, a kind of camp sensibility is developed, which is rooted in a recognition of its own theatricality, but which also lays claim to an alternative logic, a perception of contradictions in the 'mass middlebrow' world. At the outer limits of the talk show genre, and exploiting 'chat' to its full potential, *The Dame Edna Experience* just begins to hint at an alternative kind of 'common sense' which lies beyond the taken-for-granted, suburban perspective so characteristic of popular television.

Broadcasting's public sphere

Of course, I have to admit that in many respects Dame Edna is unique. This is certainly not the standard talk show – nor, with such shows still, 3 years later, occupying their regular place in the British TV schedules (*Wogan*, BBC 1, weekdays: *Aspel*, LWT, Saturdays) can the talk show format be said to have been finally 'destroyed'. However, what this programme does offer, I submit, is a kind of exemplary (and clearly very deliberate) crystallization of tendencies in broadcast discourse which are more widely apparent. What I now, finally, want to offer are some speculative suggestions as to why such talk might be increasingly prevalent on broadcast television, which is indeed, at the present time, undergoing a major institutional transformation.

Briefly, by way of summing up, let us remind ourselves of three symptoms of the phenomenon. First, in all types of television interview, there is some

space for interviewees to negotiate their role. This space does vary with the
format of the programme: whether the interview is live or recorded, and
whether it takes place in a studio or is part of an edited film – such factors are
crucial. Nevertheless to a greater or lesser extent in every context we can
observe interviewees challenging the presuppositions in interviewers' questions; displaying their wit and verbal dexterity sometimes at the expense of the
interviewer; and shifting to metadiscursive commentary on the strategies of
the interviewer, on the format of the programme and on the institution of
television itself. Moreover, although in certain contexts such behaviour by
interviewees would seem to be 'violative' (Greatbatch, 1987), it is by no means
always 'sanctioned' or edited out. I have suggested that this is because the
priorities of the institution are themselves ambivalent – as between 'probing'
interviewees on behalf of the audience, and constructing some interviewees as
'television personalities'.

My second point then concens the apparent complicity of the institution
itself in creating spaces for such forms of verbal display. I think it is
particularly interesting to observe the historical transformation of the 'straight'
celebrity interview (*Face to Face*) into the kind of 'camp' performances
frequently apparent today. Presumably a detailed history of the British talk
show could trace this process of transformation through key instances like the
Simon Dee Show (late 1960s) and *Parkinson* (1970s) to *Wogan* (c. 1983–4). But
the two general points I have tried to establish are: (a) that in such developments the role of the interviewer becomes increasingly variable, which is
related to (b) an institutionally validated experimentation with the mixing of
formats (talk, variety, comedy) and their associated speech genres. However,
this cross-generic activity is not restricted to formats normally classified as
'entertainment' – for it extends into the discourse of news and current affairs
as we have seen.

So, the third area of questions concerns the audience for these developments. What does the television audience make of them? For a terrain is now
established where: (a) the function of the interview is constantly shifting
between soliciting information on the audience's behalf and alternatively
providing them with forms of verbal entertainment; which means (b) that
the audience cannot possibly know at times whether the talk is serious
or sincere; and (c) this whole ambiguity is explicitly related by the participants
in interviews to the fact that they are performing on television. There is here, I
submit, the clear basis for an audience research project which would seek to
establish, not simply the decoding procedures adopted in interpreting the
meanings of talk on television, but also the very credibility of that talk, and of
the television institution itself, as perceived by different audience groups. But
in conclusion to the present discussion, let me now turn to some of the wider
questions and speculative connections which I think might be involved.

For in so far as the credibility of some forms of interview talk would now
seem to be at stake, I think this connects with more fundamental questions
about the purposes of interviewing as such. As I have argued elsewhere
(Tolson, 1990), interviewing is essentially a genre of public speaking, in which
an individual, under cross-examination, produces certain forms of speech

which are appropriate for public circulation. In the process of speaking in this way, an individual takes on a public identity, a form of 'subjectification', in so far as he or she then becomes recognizable as a certain kind of subject. Increasingly, in contemporary broadcast discourse, the 'witnesses' and 'experts', the social 'types' and 'characters', constructed in other public contexts, now appear as 'personalities'. This is the form of subjectification which is overwhelmingly characteristic of mass-mediated forms of publication. So my wider question now concerns the type of 'public sphere' in which the 'personality system' is in dominance.

As developed by Jürgen Habermas (1974), the critical potential of the concept of the public sphere lies in its 'double function'. That is to say, 'it provides a paradigm for analysing historical change, whilst also serving as a normative category for political critique' (Hohendahl, 1979: 92). My discussion here continues in this vein, although I think closer attention needs to be given, than is evident in most accounts of the public sphere of broadcasting, to the *historical* dimension of the analysis. The basic problem for historical discussions of the public sphere seems to stem from Habermas himself, and specifically from his normative equation of a 'classical public sphere' with the age of Enlightenment in the eighteenth century. Here, supposedly, a model for the liberal and rational exchange of opinion was realized in the free circulation of newspapers and journals through democratic networks which were independent of state intervention. As soon as large-scale commercial interests in publishing began to develop, together with appropriate forms of state regulation, the classical public sphere was, in Habermas' view, fundamentally compromised; it passed 'from a journalism of conviction to one of commerce', and from the exchange of reasoned opinion to a more cynical institution for publicity (Habermas, 1974: 200). Interestingly, the precise historical moment for this shift, the mid-nineteenth century, is also the moment when interviewing emerges as a pervasive genre of public speaking. For public speech is now necessarily regulated, mediated and, in Habermas' view, homogenized in the manufacture of 'public opinion'.

In this way, Habermas' argument seeks to unify the normative and the historical – indeed to make the latter subservient to and proof of the former. It is interesting that exactly the same approach has been taken in current debates about the future of broadcasting, and the apparently imminent demise of the 'public service' tradition. For both Garnham (1986) and Robins and Webster (1986) suggest that the concept of the classical public sphere might be mobilized today against a shift towards increasing consumerism, commodification and the international trade in 'information'. However, these writers differ in their attitudes to public service broadcasting as an embodiment of the classical public sphere. For Garnham 'the great strength of the public service model', which was realized in principle in Reith's original vision for the BBC, lies in its 'noble effort to address listeners as rational political beings rather than as consumers' (Garnham, 1986: 45). In his argument, it is this tradition which requires defence today against the encroachment of market forces. But for Robins and Webster, even the pre-commercial public service tradition is dismissed as an inauthentic compromise. So pure is the normative concept here that any kind of mass-mediated public sphere must appear as 'spurious':

> Participation was vicarious and remote, with the citizen as spectator consuming images of the political process. Radio, and then television represented – in both senses of that word – the political interests of social groups. Acting as the brokers and traffickers of public opinion, these broadcasting media established their own (mediated) community of para-social interaction. It was a process through which audiences were apparently unified around a spurious collective and national identity, while, in reality they experienced an increasingly fragmented, privatised, and serialised social existence. (Robins and Webster, 1986: 33)

Where discussions of the history of broadcasting continue, in this way, to mobilize an idealized notion of a classical public sphere, it seems to me that two sorts of problems are apparent. First, within the perspective of Robins and Webster, it simply becomes irrelevant to distinguish between different types of mass-mediated public sphere and their associated forms of broadcast talk. But rather than simply contrasting a debased 'pseudo public sphere' to an ideal, it seems to me to be more productive to talk in historical terms of a series of transformations in the mass-mediated public sphere, evident in the changing forms and genres of broadcast discourse. For instance, it may be difficult to date this shift, but it does seem feasible to differentiate between 'paternalist' and 'populist' public spheres, characterized by different forms of mass-mediation and changing modes of address. A new lease of life was given to the populist public sphere by independent television; but, as the work of Cardiff (1980) has shown, the development of populist forms of talk can be traced to the 1930s, as in BBC radio the 'straight talk' gave way to new or revived forms of mediation, including the interview.

So I am arguing that a detailed, historical analysis of the contemporary public sphere should in effect precede its normative critique. And my second point is related to this. It seems to me that the more this history is understood, the more its shifts and developments cannot be dismissed as 'spurious'. Indeed the distinction between 'spurious' and 'real' identities for media audiences makes very little sense in the light of Paddy Scannell's recent work (1988a, 1988b, 1989) concerning the impact of broadcasting in modern public life. I return to certain problems in Scannell's argument in a moment, but basically its great contribution to the debate about public service broadcasting lies in its detailed account of the specific kind of public sphere which broadcasting has developed. There are perhaps two key dimensions to this 'distinctively modern' public sphere. Firstly, in the daily consumption of broadcast discourse, the public and private are increasingly interconnected (for instance, in the organization of domestic routines around schedules – see Scannell, 1988a). But secondly, diverse public spaces and activities are now articulated to each other, in national networks, so constituting the audience as a *general* public:

> Thus the particular publics who hitherto had enjoyed privileged access to such events [state occasions etc.] now had grafted onto them a *general* public constituted in and by the general nature of the mixed programme service and its general, unrestricted availability. The fundamentally democratic thrust of broadcasting lay

in the new kind of access to virtually the whole spectrum of public life that radio first, and later television, made available to all. By placing political, religious, civic, cultural events and entertainments in a common domain public life was equalised in a way that had never before been possible. Moreover, whereas previously such events had been quite discrete and separate, they took on new meanings as they came in contact with each other in common national broadcast channels. (Scannell, 1989: 140)

Now as Scannell himself argues, as a form of speaking in which public figures could be made 'answerable and accountable' to the audience, the broadcast interview became a central and crucial technique in the formation of this 'democratic' public sphere. In fact, Scannell recruits a familiar argument about the pioneering work of ITN (Independent Television News), and its presenter Robin Day. In my view, however, the problem with this account of the development of the public sphere for broadcast talk remains a commitment to an idealized notion of its 'communicative ethos'. To be sure, in his latest paper (1989) this commitment is explicitly qualified, in two ways. First, Scannell is not now suggesting that the general accountability of broadcast talk necessarily entails that such talk will appear 'rational'; rather the emphasis is now on 'reasonableness': 'in this context reasonableness has the force of mutually accountable behaviour; that is, if called upon, individuals can offer reasons and accounts for what they have said or done' (Scannell, 1989: 160). Secondly, Scannell further recognizes the possibility that some behaviour (e.g. of interviewees) may in this context appear as unreasonable, where for instance such accounts are not forthcoming: 'the extent to which politicians can refuse to be answerable and accountable marks the boundaries of open, reasonable and informative discussion on radio and television' (Scannell, 1989: 162). Perhaps. But my argument would be that reasonableness in this sense is not the only criterion which is applicable to broadcast interviews. As the recent history of the talk show clearly indicates, it is possible to be evasive and insincere and at the same time entertaining.

I am suggesting then, that the popular public sphere which broadcasting has constructed is not in fact unified around a single 'communicative ethos'. On the contrary, the popular public sphere has always been potentially contradictory, vacillating between its two demands for information and for entertainment. Perhaps in the 1950s, as a succession of commentators on that period have claimed, the notion of a sincerely informative public discourse was in dominance, both in political and celebrity interviews. Sincere opinions were expressed and interrogated, sincere experiential disclosures were made. Going by what I have seen of the early ITN, of social documentaries produced in the 1950s (cf. Corner, 1988), and of the celebrity interviews in the BBC series *Face To Face*, I would say that these do seem to be orientated towards a concept of the popular audience which is very much as Scannell has described. A populist form of public accountability holds sway and there is an attempt to construct a commonality around 'what most (reasonable) people might think'.

This, I would suggest, is the high moment of the post-war populist consensus, at least as reflected in broadcast talk. But some 30 years later, this 'popular public sphere' is not quite what it was. The basic formats of broadcast television, pioneered in the 1950s, are still with us; as, of course, is the public service tradition. But judging by the interviews I have presented here, the popular public sphere now appears increasingly ironic about itself, reflexive about the forms in which it presents itself, and at times totally ambiguous in its ability to differentiate between sincere and insincere talk. In *The Dame Edna Experience* the suburban constituency which is the focal point for the popular public sphere is remorselessly deconstructed. The show is, in this sense, 'post-populist'. And in particular, what is now apparently open to question, is that lynch-pin of the popular public sphere, its ultimate epistemological guarantee: the so-called 'real person' who *speaks from experience*.

So there is now the question of what we might make of these developments. I am not going to argue here that, with *The Dame Edna Experience*, we have moved into some kind of 'postmodern' world where people no longer speak honestly or sincerely, or where experience is no longer taken to be a source of truth. Again I want to stress that, at least in the first instance, I am describing a very specific generic shift in one particular kind of broadcast talk ('chat'), which takes its most developed form in some late-night talk shows (not only Dame Edna, but also in the late 1980s, David Letterman, Jonathan Ross, Max Headroom). Also, given their 'camp' appeal, there is probably a very specific audience for such programmes, which may be generationally specific – and as I have suggested there is the basis here for some interesting audience research. It would be too much to argue then, in apocalyptic fashion, that a few talk shows are symptomatic of a total collapse of the Western 'experiential episteme'.

Nevertheless there are some particular points which this analysis raises for Scannell's discussion of the contemporary public sphere, and I now try to clarify these, in reaching a conclusion. The first two points have already been made, but when taken together they produce an interestingly paradoxical situation. On the one hand then, if broadcast talk does constitute a distinctive field of discourse, it becomes possible as I have shown to recognize inter-generic developments, and cross-generic effects, within this field. It is not necessary to maintain a rigid distinction between the 'serious' and the 'popular', despite the official ideology of broadcasters. On the other hand, however, if that point is granted, then the paradoxical outcome seems to be that the audience for these developments and effects becomes increasingly fragmented. It is no longer the general 'popular' audience (targeted by mass advertising) but rather it is diversified into cults and cliques, characterized by different kinds of 'knowingness'. The paradox, at least for Scannell's argument, is that developments in the public sphere of broadcast discourse may be starting to undermine the very notion of the 'general public' which broadcasting itself has constructed. That is how I would define the basic instability of the contemporary 'popular' public sphere.

But now a third point, which will become more speculative, picks up on Scannell's discussion of the centrality of broadcasting in modern Western cultures. For if the discourses of broadcasting are so influential, and if they are also paradoxically unstable, what are the wider implications of these instabilities. In Foucauldian terms this is a question about the 'discursive formation' within which broadcast statements are circulated – an analysis of which is clearly beyond the scope of this article. However, I offer two limited speculations, which do seem to connect with this analysis of television talk shows. First, talk shows are not the only context in which there has been some displacement of 'social-democratic' criteria in public discourse, particularly during the 1980s. Secondly, if there is a tendency to address more specific target audiences, away from the notion of the 'general public', then this would certainly harmonize with current commercial and political influences for change in media institutions. In other words, on both these counts, *The Dame Edna Experience* is consistent with certain aspects of the dominant political philosophy.

But, as we have seen, that philosophy (like all philosophies) is itself grist to the Dame Edna mill. My conclusion then, must be inevitably ambivalent. In some contexts today, the transformation of the talk show, with its associated 'personality effects', has reached a point where the very credibility of the 'real person' is open to question. Coincidentally, in his recent discussion of interviewing as a 'discourse technology', Norman Fairclough (1989) has located its effectivity within a general cultural development which he defines as 'synthetic personalization'. This is a 'major strand in the systemic re-structuring of the societal order of discourse' (Fairclough, 1989: 213), which involves the manipulation of the personal, the subjective, etc. for institutional ends. It is identified by Fairclough in fields as diverse as advertising, social skills training and political discourse, so much so that:

> ... it may be difficult to prevent even the most genuine of relational and subjective practices being open to synthetic interpretation. When we are surrounded by synthetic intimacy, friendship, equality and sympathy, could that not affect our ability to confidently recognize the real article? (Fairclough, 1989: 218)

Clearly the tendencies I have pointed to in contemporary broadcast discourse are equally 'synthetic' in this sense. Indeed they are self-consciously, triumphantly so. I agree then that the 'synthetic personality' may well be a pervasive contemporary phenomenon, supported by a major restructuring of 'the societal order of discourse'. This chapter gives further support to that argument. But it also, I think, finally points to another conclusion. For given that the societal order of discourse was itself an institutional product, and given that, in this context, public speaking was never simply the sincere and authentic practice it was sometimes assumed to be, at least the playful and camp performances of some television personalities now draw attention to its discursive construction. They also, as we have seen, draw attention to the construction of other 'synthetic personalities' – politicians, for example. Could it be then that here we have a popular context in which a long taken for granted claim to truth is interrogated, denaturalized, and so made available for critical reassessment? That at least is the other side of the coin of 'synthetic personalization'; it exposes the artificiality of the 'human interest' which has dominated popular broadcasting for the last 30 years.

References

Brown, G. and G. Yule (1983) *Discourse Analysis.* Cambridge: Cambridge University Press.

Cardiff, D. (1980) 'The Serious and the Popular: Aspects of the Evolution of Style in the Radio Talk, 1928–1939', *Media, Culture and Society*, 2(1): 29–47.

Cardiff, D. (1988) 'Mass Middlebrow Laughter: The Origins of BBC Comedy', *Media, Culture and Society*, 10(1): 41–60.

Chaplin, P. (1987) *The Listener,* p. 34.

Corner, J. (1988) 'Looking in on Life – The Social Relations of Documentary Television in the 1950s'. Paper presented at the International Television Studies Conference, London (BFI).

Fairclough, N. (1989) *Language and Power.* Harlow: Longman.

Garnham, N. (1986) 'The Media and the Public Sphere', pp. 37–53 in P. Golding et al. (eds), *Communicating Politics.* Leicester: Leicester University Press.

Greatbatch, D. (1986a) 'The Management of Disagreement between News Interviewees'. Offprint, University of Warwick, Department of Sociology.

Greatbatch, D. (1986b) 'Aspects of Topical Organisation in News Interviews: The Use of Agenda-Shifting Procedures by Interviewees', *Media, Culture and Society*, 8(4): 441–55.

Greatbatch, D. (1987) 'A Turn Taking System for British News Interviews'. Warwick Working Papers in Sociology, University of Warwick, Department of Sociology.

Habermas, J. (1974) 'The Public Sphere', *New German Critique*, No. 3. Reprinted pp. 198–201 in A. Mattelart and S. Siegelaub (eds), (1979), *Communication and Class Struggle I: Capitalism, Imperialism.* New York: International General.

Halliday, M. (1978) *Language as Social Semiotic.* London: Edward Arnold.

Heritage, J. (1985) 'Analysing News Interviews: Aspects of the Production of Talk for an Overhearing Audience', in T. van Dijk (ed.), *Handbook of Discourse Analysis Vol. 3: Genres of Discourse.* New York: Academic Press.

Hohendahl, P.U. (1979) 'Critical Theory, Public Sphere and Culture. Jürgen Habermas and His Critics', *New German Critique*, 16: 89–118.

Langer, J. (1981) 'Television's "Personality System"', *Media Culture and Society*, 3: 351–65.

Lewis, R. (1987) 'Barry Humphries Comes out of the Closet', *Sunday Times Magazine*, Nov. 29.

Montgomery, M. (1977). 'Discourse Structure and Cohesion in Selected Science Lectures'. MA thesis, University of Birmingham.

Robins, K. and F. Webster (1986) 'Broadcasting Politics: Communications and Consumption', *Screen*, 27(3–4): 30–44.

Scannell, P. (1988a) '*Radio Times*: the Temporal Arrangements of Broadcasting in the Modern World', pp. 15–31 in P. Drummond and R. Paterson (eds), *Television and its Audience.* London: British Film Institute.

Scannell, P. (1988b) 'The Communicative Ethos of Broadcasting'. Paper presented at the International Studies Conference, London (BFI).

Scannell, P. (1989) 'Public Service Broadcasting and Modern Public Life', *Media, Culture and Society*, 11(2): 135–66.

Tolson, A. (1985) 'Anecdotal Television', *Screen*, 26(2): 18–27.

Tolson, A. (1990) 'Social Surveillance and Subjectification: The Emergence of "Subculture" in the work of Henry Mayhew', *Cultural Studies*, 4: 113–27.

10

Talk, Identity and Performance:
The Tony Blackburn Show

Graham Brand and Paddy Scannell

I

Erving Goffman has shown the constructed nature of identity, the self as a presentation or performance designed to be appropriate to the circumstances and settings in which it is produced in the presence of others (Goffman, 1969). This self is not the privileged possession of its owner-presenter. It is not an essential, inalienable quality of an individual – it is not the soul – but intrinsically social, sustained in relationships with others. If human beings are sacred objects, they can be desecrated, the territories of the self invaded and, in 'total institutions', stripped away and destroyed (Goffman, 1970). The self is, from moment to moment, perishable, dependent on others who, since their self-projections are vulnerable too, have a common interest in collaborating to sustain the general character of the performance in most mundane social settings.

Goffman's early work was subject to two criticisms: the first concerning the nature of the relationship between the individual and his or her projected self, and the second concerning the episodic nature of the social settings he took for consideration. One strong inference from *The Presentation of Self in Everyday Life* (1969) was that the self was a mask behind which lurked an unknowable individual possibly manipulating the performance for undisclosed ends – 'there is no art to read the mind's construction in the face'. Such a 'naughty' view – as Harold Garfinkel calls it – suggests that individuals may be radically disaffiliated from their performance, and Garfinkel wished to show that most individuals in most contexts are committed to their performance, that they play themselves 'to the life', that the self projected is offered as a case of 'the real thing' (Garfinkel, 1984: 116–85).

A non-committal stance in relation to self is more likely to seem plausible when social situations are treated as discrete events or episodes with no before or after – as in the theatre where the actor assumes the role for the duration of the play and quits it when the curtain falls. In such an instance we are inclined, like Hamlet, to ask of the actor, 'What's he to Hecuba or Hecuba to him That he should weep for her?' But in real life we cannot walk away from the part(s) we play. The crucial issue of continuity – of the management and maintenance of self through a lifetime – was examined by Garfinkel in the case of Agnes, an intersexed person who wished to discard her biological maleness and become a natural, ordinary 100% female. Agnes displayed, by a perspective of incongruity, what for 'normals' is profoundly taken for granted – the effortless production of a sexed identity. A major crux for her was the lack of a plausible and consistent feminine biography for use in appropriate circumstances. How to produce 'girl talk' with other girls, for instance, is dependent on the incremental accumulation of know-how from such experiences which accrue to the individual through time:

> The troublesome feature encountered over and over again is the cloudy and little known role that time plays in structuring the *biography and prospects of present situations* over the course of action as a function of the action itself. It is not sufficient to say that Agnes's situations are played out over time, nor is it at all sufficient to regard this time as clock time. There is as well the 'inner time' of recollection, anticipation, expectancy. Every attempt to handle Agnes's 'management devices' while disregarding this time, does well enough as long as the occasions are episodic in their formal structure; and all of Goffman's analyses either take episodes for illustration, or turn the situations that his scheme analyses into episodic ones. (Garfinkel, 1984: 166 [emphasis added])

The same problem arises in relation to Goffman's last published work on forms of talk (Goffman, 1981). Goffman is concerned to dissolve the unitary categories of 'speaker' and 'hearer' and in so doing opens up issues of fundamental importance for the analysis of the construction of self, social interaction and the role of talk. The complexities of the relationship between speaker and utterance and between speaker and addressee begin to emerge in the essays on 'Footing' and 'Radio Talk'. Both are richly suggestive and their ideas, as will be apparent, have been absorbed into the bloodstream of this article. Nevertheless, what is missing still is attention to the problem of long-term continuity in time, the reproduction of identity and the way that this is accomplished through talk.

Routinization is the basis of continuity. As Anthony Giddens puts it: 'Routine is integral both to the continuity of the personality of the agent, as he or she moves along the paths of daily activities, and to the institutions of society, which are such only through their continued reproduction' (Giddens, 1984: 60). Routines have a double articulation: they have a structure and content that is produced across a single episode. But this structure and content is formatted so that it can be reproduced again and again, thereby achieving the recursive effect of 'things as usual', familiar, known from past occasions, anticipatable as such now and in future. To study the double articulation of routine requires attention to Goffman's concerns with self-presentation in episodic social settings, and to Garfinkel's with the continuing maintenance, on all occasions, of 'the self same identity'.

The study of such issues in relation to broadcasting is particularly interesting because routinization is at the very heart of programmes and programming. An individual programme is the briefest of ephemerides that perishes in the moment of its transmission. As such its identity is so transient as to be unnoticeable. Broadcast programmes build identity through repetition and regularity via formatting and scheduling. The art of scheduling was, in Britain at least, not immediately obvious and was something learnt, through trial and error, by the programme planners of the pre-war National Programme. Crucially it involved 'locking' programmes into regular time slots so that they recurred, from week to week on the same day and at the same time. Thus what began to be established was a familiar, regular pattern of daily output, reproduced through the weeks and months of the year that meshed in with the day-to-day routines of the population (Scannell, 1988). Once this basic principle was accepted – and it encountered stiff opposition from certain areas of programme output – the more subtle arts of continuity between programmes began to be discovered, and of positioning and sequencing them in the schedule to attract specific or more general audiences.

The routinization of programming went hand in hand with the routinization of programmes, and here the key discovery was seriality (Scannell and Cardiff, 1991: 377-9). The problem of production in broadcasting is, more exactly, that of reproduction. The magnitude of broadcast output is obscured by over-familiarity, but continuous, unceasing production day in day out can only be sustained, in the long term, by formatting. This involves the creation of a template for the production of a programme whose basic structure and content remains the same but which varies in its particularities from one episode to another. Once, say, the format for news as a programme or for a situation comedy (a form invented for radio and television) has been laid down the programme can last indefinitely. On British radio, as is well known, there are programmes that have run continuously now for well over 40 years; *Desert Island Discs, Woman's Hour* and *The Archers* are famous instances.

How is a format created? Key elements include the use of signature tunes, programme presenter(s), standard sequences for the programme material (lead with the big news story and end with a human interest one), techniques of 'anchorage and relay' for moving through the sequence and maintaining continuity (Brunsdon and Morley, 1978), standardized beginnings and endings. The combined effect of such techniques is to create, through time, a familiar, recognizable programme identity that is perceived as such by audiences. When the BBC's newly established Listener Research Unit began, in the late 1930s, to investigate the impact of serialized productions in regular time slots they found that 91% of respondents to their questionnaire favoured the increasing use of serial formats for drama, entertainment and talks, and 85% assured them that the BBC was not overusing the format (Scannell and Cardiff, 1991: 378).

II

Certain kinds of career are histrionic. Teachers, preachers, politicians and media entertainers all make a living that is, to a greater or lesser extent, dependent on performing in public. This may involve the projection of a carefully crafted public identity and the maintenance of that identity in and through time. One such class of performers on radio is the disc jockey. It is an unremarkable feature of the job of being a DJ that, like most jobs, those that take it up as a career often stick at it. Terry Wogan, for instance, did the early morning show on Radio 2 for 10 years before switching to hosting Britain's best known television chat show. John Peel has been doing his kind of music for many years on Radio 1. And Tony Blackburn is one of the longest-running DJs in the business with a career going back to the mid-1960s – a 'living legend' in his own eyes at least.

Most pop music programmes are known by the name of their DJ, and they make use of recurrent devices for reiterating the identity of the station, the programme and the presenter. Institutional identity is mediated through that of the show's host, and his or her identity is mediated very largely through talk. In the accounts that follow we wish to show how the production and maintenance of programme/presenter identity is routinely accomplished through the talk of the DJ. We wish to bring out the double articulation of identity as routine by highlighting the discursive formats recursively deployed across particular morning transmissions of *The Tony Blackburn Show* and repeatedly across a 10-week recorded sample of the programme.

We offer an account of the discursive world of *The Tony Blackburn Show* with a view to displaying its communicative ethos, its expressive idiom. With the concept of a discursive world we draw attention to the *limits* of discourse to what is ruled out (what can *not* be said) in order to maintain the consistency of the programme's 'line' or identity. As such it has an inside and an outside which is known and understood by the audience who demonstrate, when they phone in, their knowledge and competence as they routinely reproduce not merely a particular discursive content but a communicative manner and style that embodies the show's ethos. That ethos, is, as we shall see, defined and firmly controlled by Blackburn himself through his 'philosophy' of radio and his expressive idiom which embodies it.

Blackburn is well aware that 'behind a microphone you can become exactly what you would like to be' and, from the beginning of his career, he worked hard to carve out an identity for himself that would make him familiar to and popular with radio audiences. That identity is part of the 'personality system' of broadcasting (Langer, 1981; Tolson, Chapter 9 in this collection). What is on display is 'Tony Blackburn' as a public institution rather than Tony Blackburn the private individual. Up to a point. For Blackburn, as we shall see, routinely draws on his own past – his career in broadcasting and his private life – in his talk on the programme. He has, in fact, produced an account of this career, 'as told to Cheryl Garnsey', in *Tony Blackburn, 'The Living Legend'. An Autobiography* (Blackburn, 1985), and we offer a thumbnail sketch of that biography as part of the texture of relevances that make up Blackburn's self-projection in *The Tony Blackburn Show*.

III

Tony Blackburn began broadcasting in 1964 as a DJ on the offshore pirate ship, Radio Caroline, and quickly established himself as the station's best known and most popular broadcaster. From the start he appreciated the importance of creating an identity that would distinguish him from the other DJs and make his audience remember him. He was the pioneer of those 'identity marks' that have become the DJ's stock-in-trade. The corny gag for instance:

> On board Caroline I began to tell jokes as something to say between records, but then I made my great discovery. My jokes marked me out. The public became aware of me because of them ... I was on my way to achieving the crown as the king of corn. Love me or hate me, the public would never in future be indifferent to me. My jokes are my way of seeing the public doesn't forget me. (Blackburn, 1985: 19)

Or the personalized jingle. These were already in use as identity devices by the pirate stations and one day Blackburn noticed a driver listening to Caroline's rival, Radio London, and singing along with the station's jingles:

> In a sudden flash of inspiration it came to me that if a radio station could brainwash an audience, why not a DJ? So I booked a studio and musicians in Tin Pan Alley and had them make up my own personalised Tony Blackburn jingles. Every DJ in the country now has his own jingles of course, but I was the first. (Blackburn, 1985: 35–6)

Other innovations included 'Arnold the Dog', a 'woofing' sound effect that also became part of his studio identikit.

In 1966, Blackburn jumped ship and joined Radio London. It was a short-lived move, for the following year the Marine Broadcasting (Offences) Act was introduced which, in effect, ended the pirate radio era. But the pirates had shown there was a huge audience for pop music to which the BBC responded by setting up, in 1967, Radio 1 – Britain's first, legal pop music station. Blackburn was recruited to host the peak-time Radio 1 breakfast show and felt he was offered this plum job because of the success of his already established broadcasting style. He was the first voice to be heard on the new station when it went on air, greeting the new audience with 'Welcome to the exciting sound of Radio 1'. Later he would construe this distinction as giving him general warrant and authority to comment on Radio 1 and pop radio in general. In his own mind he was 'the voice of Radio 1'.

When he joined the BBC Blackburn brought with him, as his dowry, Arnold the dog and his stock of jingles. 'Tony Blackburn is Number One!', he informed listeners after every record, convinced that when they voted for their favourite DJ in the popularity polls, listeners would remember that it was Tony Blackburn who was number one. Blackburn's marriage, in 1972, to the actress Tessa Wyatt and the birth of their son, brought a new dimension to his radio performance as he began to talk about his personal life on his radio programme. To the performed personality of 'Tony Blackburn', the chattering DJ, was added the 'real' Tony Blackburn, the private individual. The dividing line between a professional and a personal identity began to erode.

Blackburn and Wyatt divorced in 1976, Blackburn experiencing a nervous breakdown in the process. This too became part of his on-air talk:

> I eased my suffering by sharing my pain with the listeners. Where once I had regaled them with stories of my happy home life with Tessa and Simon, now I told them about my broken marriage. I played a love song by R. and J. Stone called 'We've Thrown It All Away' and dedicated it to 'the person who will always be very special

to me'. I followed that with a 1964 hit by Peter and Gordon called 'A World Without Love'. That should have been enough but once the dam of misery broke I found I couldn't stop. I bored the listeners to death with details of my sorrows. I gave interview after interview on the subject of man abandoned by wicked woman. (Blackburn, 1985: 121)

This collapse signalled the start of a disastrous period with the BBC. It was not so much the public airing of his private misery that brought Blackburn into conflict with BBC policy, as the gradual intrusion, in his on-air talk, of his views on social and political issues. Blackburn's sister, Jackie, had been unable to walk from infancy and his experiences of, for instance, trying to take her in her wheelchair to a West End show, showed him how little provision was made in Britain for handicapped people. In 1976, when the government decided to stop the issue of special cars to the handicapped, Blackburn read out a letter from a disabled listener and congratulated him on his demonstration against the decision. The provoked a letter of complaint to the BBC from an MP and a warning from the Controller of Radio 1.

But having started Blackburn was not going to be put off airing his views on issues that included strikes, Northern Ireland, racism, blood sports and the divorce laws. He was warned again, taken off air for a 2-week spell and finally threatened with the sack. That did not happen, but he was shunted from the morning to the afternoon and then from one show to another, finally ending up with *Junior Choice* on Saturday mornings and *The Top 40 Programme* on Sunday afternoons. Neither of these allowed any opportunity for venting views and feelings on air and in 1984, after 17 years with Radio 1, he moved to BBC Radio London to present *The Tony Blackburn Show*.

The programme ran for 5 years as Radio London's morning show from 9 a.m. to noon, Monday to Friday. In the space of 3 hours Blackburn would play between thirty and thirty-five records punctuated by news and weather reports on the hour, and travel and traffic updates approximately every half-hour. In the first 10 minutes Blackburn performs a number of ritual introductions. Listeners are welcomed to the show and offered a run-down of features to come. Listeners' messages are read out. He may comment on newspaper stories, usually of the jokey or human interest variety or to do with TV soap operas. These will serve as topic initiators for the programme's first phone-in.

Every day there are two or three phone-in features. The first one or two are flexible, though often focusing on Blackburn's preselected newspaper topic. The last, which always comes in the final 20 minutes of the show is for birthday and anniversary dedications. There are special phone-ins on particular days of the week: Dial-a-Date is on Wednesdays and Sex and Sympathy on Fridays. Midway through each programme there is a 'teabreak' of about 10 minutes in which Blackburn reads out listeners' letters, chats to them and offers his beliefs and opinions on this and that. There may be competitions which are usually included at the expense of the third phone-in. In the last quarter-of-an-hour Blackburn produces ritual closing-down signals. The next day's programme features will be mentioned and farewells and renewals offered. The routine, recursive character of all the elements of the show is endlessly, unobtrusively underlined:

> It's birthdays and anniversaries time. That time has come round again. (12 September 1986)

> We will be having, as always, birthdays and anniversaries. (1 August 1986).

> And we'll have all the regular features for you at the same time as well. (16 July 1986)

> And that tune tells us once again that it's time for Sex and Sympathy. (18 July 1986)

IV

Blackburn's past diffusely pervades his Radio London show and helps to 'make sense' of his performance. The weight of experience, and its claims to authority, may be invoked both in respect to his career in broadcasting and his personal life:

> National radio is in a terrible state. Believe me. I've been in broadcasting for 22 years. On the pirate ships, on Radio 1 and now here on Radio London. I've seen it all. I know what I'm talking about. (21 July 1986)

> Radio 1 is a station that is regrettably out of touch and one that I opened up many years ago. It plays naff music and is filled with banal characters. My ambition is to close it down and to get the radio system working. (30 July 1986)

> (*TB is advising a teenage on a personal problem.*) As you get older, Nicola, and I'm speaking from experience . . . (18 July 1986)

> (*To caller.*) Don't worry about being yourself Lorraine. It's great. I've had ten years of divorce and it's wonderful. (19 August 1986)

The troubled past is often referred to and, on occasion, assumes an epic dimension as an aspect of Blackburn's heroic self-thematization:

> I have never been a yes man. The BBC hierarchy don't like people speaking their minds. They play safe with rather banal and inane characters. I'm not safe. I speak my mind. That's why I left Radio 1. They couldn't cope with my not being safe. I was always in trouble. (19 August 1986)

> Your Leader loves you. A man barely alive. A man who refuses to be beaten by the establishment. A man who wouldn't go away. A man who refused to shut up and, though half dead, refuses to die. (25 July 1986)

The mythification of the past is encoded in frequent self-reference to 'The Living Legend' and in jingles such as 'Tony Blackburn. Older and Bigger than Stonehenge' or 'Tony Blackburn. Preserve your National Heritage'. If the thrust of Blackburn's thematization of his biography is his 'struggle' for broadcasting freedom, then his arrival at Radio London is the victorious triumph.

> You know something, gang? One great thing about working here at Radio London is I pick all the music for you. But for 22 years I've been with you and now this is the very first programme where I can literally come on the air in the morning and know that I definitely have the best music for you. And it's really terrific for me to know

that and to know that I'm bringing you the very best in music. There is no better music I can bring you. It's taken me 22 years to be able to do that. I tell you. (17 July 1986)

Part of this new-found freedom finds expression in the free play of his opinions. Of course, as he admits, 'radio is not a platform for a DJ's political beliefs. But we are frequently criticized for being inane and if we are forbidden to talk about life around us, what is there left?' (Blackburn, 1985: 140–1):

> There must be room on radio for a bit of serious discussion. If we can't talk about life around us, and people's problems and the real world what is there left? I mean, you can't have people coming on the whole time and just saying 'Isn't the weather wonderful' and 'I went out and I've got some blue socks on today and I've got a great big medallion dangling round my neck' God Almighty. We must have come on a little bit from there. (12 August 1986)

The following are a representative sample of Blackburn's views on political and social matters, and his way of expressing them:

> I think the divorce laws are mad. (27 July 1986)

> I think people who resent other people because of their colour are just being ignorant. (18 July 1986)

> Politicians are all a load of old fools who don't know what's going on. (1 August 1986)

> Fool's Paradise. A good name for the Houses of Parliament. (25 July 1986)

> Here's a message for you Mrs Thatcher. When the hell are you going to introduce sanctions? (16 July 1986)

Whenever Blackburn reads from newspapers he invariably quotes from the *Daily Mirror* or the *Sun* (which wrote an editorial lamenting his departure from Radio 1 – Blackburn, 1985: 159), and the way in which he delivers his opinions echoes their editorial style. His philosophy of radio is entirely consonant with the ethos of the tabloid press:

> If I was asked about broadcasting, my philosophy on radio would be ... it's very Americanized really ... it's fun radio. It's creating a Disneyworld for everybody that they can escape into. It's creating a nice atmosphere for people to have fun in. (BBC Radio 1, *The Broadcasters*, 15 November 1985)

In the same radio programme Blackburn said that he saw his Radio London show as being the radio equivalent of a holiday camp (though in his autobiography, speaking of his time at boarding-school, he says 'My idea of hell is a holiday at a Butlins camp and school gave me the same feeling of organized fun', 1985: 7). Throughout each morning run the show is permeated with a variety of audio images – jingles, sound effects and slogans – that emphasize the values of fun and entertainment. This melange of sound creates a specific audio environment of 'fun' which Blackburn himself endlessly reiterates:

> Good morning, gang. This is where the fun begins. (15 July 1986)

> Welcome to Fun Radio. (1 September 1986)

> The Tony Blackburn Show. Pioneering new parameters of fun. (27 August 1986)

Within this world of fun radio, Blackburn has strong views about the kind of music that is appropriate for it.

> I'm the one DJ who actually *does* listen to the music. (1 August 1986)

> Let me give you a word of advice. Stick with me and not the inferior rubbish like Radio 1. We only play the best in soul music, the type of music that we like. You won't hear bland rubbish like on the other stations. You'll only hear proper music. (18 July 1986)

'Soul music is fun music' (25 July 1986) and embodies the Blackburn notion of fun radio. Soul music is sexual and, in an interview in *Melody Maker* (22 November 1986: 21), Blackburn declared that the show 'is geared around "sex and soul"'... All the lewd connotations go along with the music which is very sensual and suggestive.' Those lewd connotations are another pervasive feature of every show – 'the show that's proud of its naughty bits and at every opportunity flaunts it' (25 July 1986):

> What's the weather like? Never mind the thermometer. Let's do the nipple test. Thrust your breasts out of the window and if the nipples are erect, then presumably it's chilly. (16 July 1986)

> (*Jingle: Sexy female voice.*) The Tony Blackburn Show. The only programme that asks 'When was the last time you got it?' (30 July 1986)

> (*Jingle.*) Tony Blackburn plays great soul music to bonk to. (1 August 1986)

The discursive world of Blackburn's show in multiple ways – his 'editorial' comment, his preoccupation with sex as fun, his phone-ins, dating service (London Love) and competitions – creates a tabloid radio equivalent of the *Sun*.

V

Within this world Blackburn thematizes himself in a number of different ways, but always quite self-consciously. On a Radio 1 documentary programme Blackburn admitted that behind a microphone you can become exactly what you would like to be. 'If I'm talking to a microphone and I want to be a macho, butch Sylvester Stallone type, I can be that person. If I want to be a buffoon talking nonsense, I can be that person. I can be a giant-sized person, or what I want to be' (BBC Radio 1, *The Broadcasters*, 15 November 1985). In *The Tony Blackburn Show* he can, within minutes, assume totally opposing identities:

> I'm a big, butch and magnificent macho man. (9 July 1986)

> I'm wearing my pink frock today and carrying a matching handbag. (9 July 1986)

Lest anyone should mistakenly take this kind of thing at face value Blackburn is at pains to spell out the nature of his performance.

> You may have noticed that most of the things I do actually say are meant as a send-up. And, er (pause) I don't mean a lot of what I say, I talk a load of nonsense, I'm aware of that. (15 July 1986)

Send-up, particularly of himself, has been part of Blackburn's style from the start. On Caroline, lying in his bunk, he would jot down his corny gags in a notebook and not a few of them were turned against himself:

> My mother had me at home, but when she saw me they had to rush her to hospital.
>
> My parents never really liked me. When I came home from school they moved.
>
> Even my mother rejected me. She always wrapped my sandwiches in a roadmap. (Blackburn, 1985: 20)

If Blackburn's performance is intended to be recognized by listeners as a performance, what are the markers that might make his intentions apparent? One crucial resource is voice, and it is not difficult to hear several different voices routinely deployed by Blackburn to signal momentary changes of footing in his own discourse or in his interactions with audience members on the phone.

Changes of voice are heard as motivated departures from the base-line of a standard, or 'natural' voice that is returned to when speaking 'normally'. The *standard voice*, though seemingly natural, can be modified or adjusted to achieve particular effects.[1] Mrs Thatcher, early in her premiership, adjusted her voice to a lower pitch, at the same time slowing down her rate of speaking, to sound less shrill and 'bossy' (Atkinson, 1984: 112–14). Blackburn, at an early point in his career, decided to adjust his 'normal' voice after being teased, by fellow pirates on Radio London, for having a voice that was 'too high pitched':

> After a night of being sent up in the mess with doubts being cast on my sexuality, I disappeared from the studio and recorded myself just to check that my hormones weren't playing tricks on me. I decided my voice was a bit high, so after that I worked to lower it to the warm attractive tone listeners hear today. (Blackburn, 1985: 39)

Blackburn's ordinary speaking voice is heard both in monologue chat – during 'tea-breaks' for instance – and in telephone conversation. It tends to merge at times into his *DJ voice*, characterized by a tendency to end an utterance with a rising pitch where a falling pitch would normally be heard. It is common, in performing professions (singers, clerics or actors, for instance) for performers to have a distinctive professional voice as a trade mark. The hyped-up, upbeat DJ voice is used routinely for station and self-identifications, for record introductions, competitions and announcements of future programme events. An occasional *authoritative* voice is used to assert technical knowledge (of radio or music in particular) or to reassert distance in telephone conversations with audience members (if they are tending to get out of control) or for giving advice or instruction either in monologue or in conversation with audience members. In telephone conversation Blackburn will often switch to an *empathetic* voice that imitates the voice of the other speaker in order to establish intimacy or shared point of view. Finally, Blackburn has a number of *camp* or *send-up* voices that may signal a switch to macho man, transvestite queen, Casanova or whatever.

The following bit of telephone talk illustrates some routine voice changes (*TB* stands for Tony Blackburn and *C* stands for Caller):

1	*TB.*	You could always come on holiday with me Sandra.
2		I'd look after you.
3	*C.*	I have to stay at home to look after the kids.
4		They're a problem.
5	*TB.*	Us mums have got our hands full haven't we?
6		Hubbies don't understand our problems.
7		(*pause*)
8		Never mind. Hope you have a nice day, Sandra.

A favourite Blackburn gambit with callers is to pursue a line of humorous 'slightly risqué' chat' (Blackburn, 1985: 141). This is usually underlined by a 'chat-up' voice which is here turned on for Sandra (lines 1 and 2). She, however, refuses to enter the fantasy game and instead asserts the mundane reality – her kids. Blackburn, as we will see later, persistently filters out of his world the problems of day-to-day life and, when they are introduced by callers, he will ignore or bypass them in a variety of ways. Here he turns it into a game – his empathy game in which he identifies with the caller and changes his voice again to register the positional shift (5–6). But again Sandra refuses to play along (perhaps she doesn't know how. We will see, in a moment, how listeners show they know the rules of the game). The pause (7) is an invitation to make an appropriate response but it is declined. Blackburn, realizing he is not going to get anywhere with this co-conversationalist decides to close it down. Reverting to his 'normal' voice (8) he briskly wraps the call up.

In a rather more complex case Blackburn has one conversation nested in another and, in the middle of this, an address to the general listening audience.

1	*TB.*	[1]→	You went to a screening did you, Suzanne?
2	*C.*		Yeah.
3	*TB.*		I see. What was the film?
4	*C.*		Erm, What was it? *Girls Just Want to Have Fun.*
5	*TB.*	[2]→	We are taking people to a screening on Monday, is
6			that right, Ms Garnsey?
7			(*pause*)
8			I wonder if I can get a little reaction here.
9			Are we going to a screening on Monday?
10			(*pause*)
11		[3]→	We have a screening on Monday.
12			We're going to be taking everybody too and we're
13			giving away the tickets on Monday. Alright?
14	*C.*		Mmmm.
15	*TB.*		So we're going to do that. So if you want to come
16			along and see a film with me on Monday
17	*C.*		Mmmm.
18	*TB.*		Er, not you Suzanne, because you've been to one,
19			alright?
20			But I'm just saying to everybody listen out on Monday
21			morning and we'll be giving away tickets, alright?
22			(*pause*)
23		[1]→	OK, Suzanne. Who did you ring up for?

Blackburn is in his usual chat-up mode on the phone with Suzanne who offers him (4) a classic opening to develop a line of lewd chat. This, however, is not pursued and, quite unpredictably, Blackburn switches (5) to a backstage conversation with his producer Cheryl Garnsey. Evidently the caller's talk of the screening she went to see courtesy of *The Tony Blackburn Show* (cf. 18) reminds Blackburn to check if he can announce that there are tickets available for a screening next Monday. This is confirmed by the studio in the pause at line 10 (there is a muffled, off-mike 'yes'), whereupon Blackburn, now switching to his professional DJ role, goes into an announcement, directed at the listening audience in general, that tickets *will* be available on Monday (12–16). Suzanne, still on the line and under the impression that Blackburn is talking to her, produces response tokens at lines 14 and 17. Blackburn overlooks the first but, interpreting the second as a personal acceptance by her of a general offer he is making to listeners, clarifies for Suzanne in the first place (18–19) and then everybody else who's listening (20), just who it is that he's talking to at this point. Finally, after a brief pause (22) he returns to Suzanne and their telephone chat.

Here we have Blackburn shuttling in and out of three different roles: chat-up artist on the phone with Suzanne, professional broadcaster consulting the studio and DJ showbusiness presenter to the listening audience. The switches between these front- and back-stage roles are cued by modulations in voice tone that indicate changes of footing from talking to a caller in voice [1], to conversation with the studio in voice [2] to an address to listeners to voice [3] and finally back to voice [1] and the original caller and conversation.

VI

It is routinely made explicit that this programme exists for its audience:

The Tony Blackburn Show. The show that makes *you* become part of the programme. (8 August 1986)

This is your programme, gang, and you can choose the records. Let's open up the Power Line for your Power Line requests. (27 August 1986)

Blackburn, however, is in charge of his gang, as he makes plain in a variety of ways.

How's everything in the furthest corners of my kingdom this morning? What's it like out there in Wimbledon, or Bromley, or Deptford? Good morning to you wherever you are. (25 July 1986)

Good morning gang. Your leader loves you. (8 July 1986)

Power, in this kingdom, is sometimes exercised with ruthless authority.

(*Caller tries changing topic.*)
TB.　Hang on a minute Susan. This is *my* programme.
　　　I'll decide what we talk about. (1 August 1986)

(*Caller is talking. Blackburn cuts in.*)
TB.　I'm getting bored with you Paul (*cuts her off*).
　　　Jonathan is in Willesden.
　　　(*Continues conversation with Jonathan.*) (27 August 1986)

(*Blackburn has been talking to caller for nearly
a minute about EastEnders.*)

1	TB.	OK Mandy. So you think it was stupid of the BBC
2		to kill off Andy?
3	C.	Yes I do. Can I say hello to a few people?
4		I'd like to say
5	TB.	Hold it. Hang on. You're not going to do
6		a load of boring dedications are you?
7	C.	I just
8	TB.	We only allow dedications at the end of the show and
9		then only birthdays and anniversaries. OK?
10	C.	Yes. I'm sorry.
11	TB.	OK.
12		(*pause*)
13		So you think it was wrong of the BBC...(*Conversation continues.*)
		(9 July 1986)

This is a show for its audience so long as audience members remember that Tony Blackburn is in charge and play along with the rules of the game in his world of fun radio. One basic rule is to confirm Blackburn's own frequently asserted self-assessment that he is 'the best'.

TB.	There's no other good broadcasters around, are there?
C.	No that's true.
TB.	I suppose there's Robby Vincent, but he's not such a genius, is he though?
C.	No, you're the genius.
TB.	Exactly. I'm the best.
C.	You are the best, Tony and we wish you were on the radio all day. (11 September 1986)

This caller, who we may infer is a regular listener, knows how to play the role of courtier. Note caller's assumption of a plural mode and a presumption to speak on behalf of a community of listeners ('*we* wish you were on radio all day'). Callers who know the game may begin their conversation with supportive remarks such as 'Hello Leader' or 'This is a thrilling honour to talk to you Tony.' Such remarks may be seen as sacrificial offerings to win acceptance and entry into Blackburn's discursive kingdom. Those who fail to sustain such a line are usually summarily dispatched.

1	TB.	[1]→	Why don't you leave him for me. He sounds miserable.
2	C.		Well maybe when I've finished with him I'll come to see you.
3	TB.		Oh thanks. Treating me as second best now, are you?
4	C.		Well you are a bit.
5	TB.	[2]→	Thanks! Oh thank you very much. Thank you ve- so much!
6		[3]→	Joy's on the line from Streatham.
7	TB.	[1]→	Hello Joy.
8	C.		Hello Tony.
9	TB.		Did you hear that?
10	C.		I did.
11	TB.		How insulting. You're not going to give me any of
12			that are you?
13	C.		On no, you are the best Tony.
14	TB.		Well exactly, Joy. You're on the same wave length as
15			me. (*Conversation continues.*) (18 August 1986)

Blackburn as usual, is in his chat-up mode (1, Voice [1]), but caller isn't exactly playing along. Blackburn tries to sustain his line and offers (3) another chance to play the game by affirming that he's the best, not second-best. This gambit is refused and Blackburn now switches to a voice (5, Voice [2]) of heavy irony, immediately drops the caller and switches to his professional voice (6, Voice [3]) as he announces the next caller to listeners. Assuming an outraged voice (9), he makes it plain (11) that Joy had better play along and, when he receives her ritual unction (13, 'You *are* the best.'), conversation continues in the normal chat-up mode. How much this is all a game is hearably uncertain. It seems that Blackburn is put out of face by first caller's putdown at line 4, and momentarily loses fluency as he stumbles, a trifle incoherently, in his heavily ironic response (5). But the flow is quickly restored and the indignation is hearably put on.

Only rarely does the Leader lose control, and that is when the talk goes seriously off course. The following is from a call during a Birthdays and Anniversaries phone-in. Blackburn has been chatting to caller for about a minute:

1	C.	I'm not at all shy Tony. Can you do me a quick
2		favour?
3	TB.	No I can't (*knowing laugh*) I wouldn't have time.
4	C.	Oh go on.
5	TB.	I have more (*laughs*) staying power than
6	C.	Just a quick favour. Just say hello to my
7		boyfriend, Brian.
8	TB.	Oh, why?
9	C.	Well, because he's been acting very funny lately.
10	TB.	He's been acting very funny! Has he been
11		wearing women's clothes or something?
12	C.	I think I might be pregnant.
13	TB.	Has he, err (*nervous giggle*)
14		I was just err (*inaudible mumble*)
15		(*nervous giggle*) I bet he does wear women's clothes.
16	C.	He doesn't.
17	TB.	He's probably a transvestite who's kept it from you.
18		That's why he's been acting strangely.
19	C.	He's not talking to me very nicely.
20	TB.	Well. It's his tendencies.
21		Anyway Simone I hope very much indeed that everything
22		turns out alright.
23		OK. John's in Tottenham. (17 July 1986)

This caller's request to say hello to someone is not immediately put down as the hapless Mandy's was. For one thing it is OK, as Blackburn made clear to Mandy and everyone listening, to do 'boring dedications' in the appropriate slot – and this is a Birthdays and Anniversaries phone-in. Moreover rather than barging in with an unsignalled topic-change as Mandy does, and without waiting for permission, Simone begs her favour three times (1, 4, 6) before proceeding to name it. In this she shows her understanding of the rules of the game and ostensibly appears to be providing Blackburn with the cues he likes for his line of innuendo. The asked for 'favour' is glossed by Blackburn as sexual (3, 5) and he is momentarily disconcerted (8) when it turns out to be a request for him to say hello to Brian. Caller's response ('because he's been acting very strange recently ' [9]) is again interpreted by Blackburn as an offering to continue his line of lewd chat, so that caller's next utterance (12) is devastatingly unexpected.

At first Blackburn continues with his line, and the beginning of another jokey question overlaps caller as she says 'be pregnant'. When Blackburn catches up with what she has actually said he is quite unable to assimilate it into his performance and, after a lapse into mumbled incoherence and nervous laughter, all he can do is cling to his line (15). That, however, is simply refused by the caller (16) and, when Blackburn repeats his line for a third time ('he's probably a transvestite'), caller continues with her own line by offering a gloss on Brian's strange behaviour ('he's not talking to me very nicely'). At this point all Blackburn can do is offer a feeble explanation of Brian's behaviour, a feeble hope that it will all be alright and escape to the next caller. It should be noted that Blackburn has a regular phone-in slot, Sex and Sympathy, for talking about callers' sexual problems. The point here is that Simone's mention of her possible pregnancy is situationally inappropriate and, as such, derails the conversation which, up to this point, has developed along the usual lines of chat in the Birthdays and Anniversaries slot. Blackburn's talk collapses *not* because he cannot handle the topic, but because he cannot handle it in this particular context. His conversational collapse demonstrates the extent to which the talk in all the phone-ins is organized into routines that sustain their particular topical and relational identities.

VII

We began by considering two sociological views of self-identity, the cynical and the serious. A third possibility has emerged, namely the playful self. The notion of playfulness retains the dramaturgical echo of Goffman and the spontaneity (sincerity) of Garfinkel: its differential characteristic is self-reflexiveness, that is, awareness of the performed nature of the displayed self. Such self-reflexiveness is hidden in the cynical performance (which is thereby manipulative or instrumental), repressed in the sincere performance (no this isn't a performance, it's the real me) but manifest in playful performances. A playful identity involves a momentary going out of character. It is less likely to be a career unless that career is, as in the case of DJs, a performance.

Garfinkel has argued eloquently that there is no time out from the burden of responsibility for the management and maintenance of identity. Nevertheless, there are, as Goffman shows us, all kinds of occasional opportunities for stepping outside of self: that is one major way in which we relax or have fun:

> When an individual signals that what he is about to do is make believe and 'only' fun, this definition takes precedence; he may fail to induce the others to follow along in the fun, or even to believe that his motives are innocent, but he obliges them to accept his act as something not to be taken at face value. (Goffman, 1974: 48)

Having fun involves pretending, putting temporary brackets round reality, a momentary suspension of the ordinary daily round. We have tried to bring out, in our presentation of *The Tony Blackburn Show* not only how fun is defined, organized and projected as such, but also how it is bracketed out from ordinary reality, how it deliberately refuses to be serious.

It is clear, from the strips of conversation considered above, that the participants in the fun – Blackburn and callers – do not stand in the same relationship to each other. Broadcasting is an institution – a power, an authority – and broadcast talk bears its institutional marks, particularly in the way that it is not so much shared between participants as controlled by the broadcasters. Because the institution is, ultimately, the author of *all* the talk that goes out on air (it authorizes it) it is responsible for the talk in a way that those invited to speak are not. If an invited participant should transgress the norms (by saying 'fuck' for instance) it is the broadcasting institution rather than the transgressor who will be held accountable (cf. Lewis on 'referable words', Chapter 2). Thus control and management of all talk in broadcasting must rest, first and last, with the representatives of the institutions, that is, the broadcasters.

Blackburn's control of the talk – in terms of topic management and closure – though idiosyncratic in its manner, is not in any sense particular to him. Broadcast telephone conversations, while sharing many characteristics of private phone calls, have some that mark them out as public displays produced for a listening audience. Blackburn shows this awareness routinely and it is manifest whenever he switches from talking to callers to talking to the studio or the listeners. When he pulls the plugs on a 'boring' caller this may be (subjectively) intended and heard as impolite. It may also be (objectively) intended and heard as dramatic, as 'livening things up a bit' – not so much for the caller, of course, as for other listeners for whom there may be the added frisson that – if their turn should come – they too might provoke, deliberately or not, the same rough treatment.

It is, from moment to moment, from one day to the next, week in week out, Blackburn's responsibility – and no one else's – to maintain the fun. For listeners and callers the fun is optional: for its presenter it is not and this is why Blackburn patrols its boundaries so carefully, since he alone must manage and maintain the show's expressive idiom. To do so he has devised – formatted, we would say – an identity for the programme and himself that is routinely talked into being by himself and others. The talk is the routine, the routine is the identity. Goffman, in a particularly suggestive passage, discusses how talk routines are produced on radio. It may seem as if what he calls 'fresh talk' is constantly produced in unscripted radio talk:

> But here again it appears that each performer has a limited resource of formulaic remarks out of which to build a line of patter. A DJ's talk may be heard as unscripted, but it tends to be built up out of a relatively small number of set comments, much as it is said epic oral poetry was recomposed during each delivery. (Goffman, 1981: 324)

Goffman has in mind the work of Milman Parry (1971) and Albert Lord (1960) who demonstrated how it was possible for the ancient oral tradition to produce such heroic tales as *Iliad* and *The Odyssey*. The problem they addressed was, simply, how did the old tellers of tales know and remember such lengthy narratives which, when transcribed, were thousands of lines long. Since each retelling in the oral tradition must be a fresh version of the tale, what are the techniques that enable them to be learnt, stored and reproduced afresh in each retelling? By a study of the still living tradition of oral epic in Southern Yugoslavia Parry was able to show, as Goffman puts it, how 'prose narratives, songs and oral poetry can be improvisationally composed during presentation from a blend of formulaic segments, set themes and traditional plots, the whole artificially tailored to suit the temper of the audience and the specificities of the locale' (Goffman, 1981: 228).

The production of the same kind of smoothly continuous talk, day in day out, on every broadcast occasion, over a 3-hour stretch poses similar problems for today's DJs. It is not difficult to show that much of Blackburn's monologue talk is a patchwork of formulaic utterances woven into set routines:

		(music fades)
1	TB.	Paris and *I Choose You*.
2		It's now seven minutes before eleven o'clock.
3		Your main funking funketeer.
4		Your Boss, with all the hot sauce.
5		Your Leader ... *(pause)* ... Me.
6		Right. Now Dave in Greenford says 'Drive safely 'n
7		love you' to wife er Jill who's on her way to Radlett
8		at the moment.
9		Mark in Bermondsey sends all his love to fiancée Sally
10		Ann.
11		And also Rachel or – yes it is – Rachel in Barnet
12		says 'Love you' to husband Peter who's working at
13		Shenley Hospital hrhmm oh dear must clear my throat.
14		Right. Now, Em Garry's in Camden. Hello Garry.

(1985 Polytechnic of Central London tape)

This strip of talk is embedded within a larger half-hour formatted section of the programme called London Love in which listeners are invited to 'show you care for the one you love' by phoning in if, for instance, they have just got engaged or are getting married or are back from a honeymoon or want to make up a quarrel. The phone calls are taken in pairs between suitably romantic soul 'twelve inchers' and the methodological problem for the presenter is to get from the music to the calls to the music always with an eye on the studio clock to keep to the overall format of the show and the scheduled number of plays within it. Here three routines are displayed: a) Continuity talk (1–5), b) Audience message (6–13) and c) Telephone chat (14). Continuity routines generally contain three elements in sequence: i) record identification, ii) time check, iii) programme-presenter identification. There is more scope for variety in the third than in the first two elements. A jingle may be used or, as here, a few formulae – 'your funking funketeer', 'your Boss with all the hot sauce', 'your Leader' – from Blackburn's stock of stock phrases.

The switch from one routine to another is succinctly signalled by 'Right. Now ... (6) which indicates ending (Right.) and beginning (Now ...). The next routine, audience messages, has its standard format: A in X → 'message' → B in Y. The message may be quoted or reported. There are usually three messages, as there were three components of the preceding routine and three in the programme-presenter identification. Triads are, as Max Atkinson has shown, an extremely useful and common rhetorical device for packaging memorable and memorizable utterances (Atkinson, 1984). This routine too is closed down and the next introduced in the same way as the preceding one: 'Right. Now . . . (14)' and into the phone-in routine.

Blackburn brings off these routines with effortless ease, including the self-monitoring utterances ('Oh dear must clear my throat') that repair momentary disruptions of the flow (cf. Gottman, 1981: 290). This is the mark of his professionalism, and if lay speakers were suddenly given the DJ's talk tasks they would doubtless be dumbstruck. But this, Goffman suggests, is more for a want of tag lines than for a want of words (Goffman, 1981: 325). Regular listeners, however, know the tag lines and their appropriate usage of them and show this knowledge in conversation when they go on air in phone calls with the programme presenter.

VIII

In his concluding remarks on broadcast talk, Goffman compares it with 'everyday face-to-face talk' without, however, commenting on or distinguishing between monologue talk (with which he has been, in fact, very largely concerned) and talk as social interaction between two or more participants. The absence of such a distinction suggests that is not significant in Goffman's terms of analysis and indeed he concludes that DJ monologue is basically the same as 'what the speaker is engaged in doing' from 'moment to moment through the course of the discourse in which he finds himself'. If face-to-face talk then is something a (male) individual 'finds himself in' he makes the best of it by selecting that footing 'which provides him with *the least threatening position* in the circumstances, or, differently phrased, *the most defensible alignment* he can muster' (Goffman, 1981: 325, our emphases). Talk appears, in Goffman's terms, as yet another threat to face, as a kind of external imposition, to which the individual must respond self-defensively. In this curiously grim view of talk there is no perception of it as sociable interaction, as something collaboratively produced by two or more participants which, at best, is what it is mutually and enjoyably achieved in Tony Blackburn's radio show:

14	*TB.*	Right. Now, Em Garry's in Camden. Hello Garry.
15	*Garry.*	Hello Tony.
16	*TB.*	(*chat up voice*) Hello. I gather you're getting
17		married tomorrow.
18	*Garry.*	Oh yeah 'n I'm really scared I tell you.
19	*TB.*	After all – I'm not surprised – after all you 'nd I
20		have meant to one another as well.
21	*Garry.*	I know but (?) my Leader what can I do. We tried to
22		get down 'nd see you last night as well.
23	*TB.*	Really?
24	*Garry.*	Yeah we couldn't. We wanted to see your twelve
25		incher but –

26	*TB.*	I'm – Garry!
27	*Garry.*	Ahh.
28	*TB.*	I'm amazed you're getting married. All those times
29		that we spent in the sand dunes in Swanage together.
30	*Garry.*	Ah d'you remember that time in the Bahamas?
31	*TB.*	Yes.
32	*Garry.*	On the beach just me 'nd you.
33	*TB.*	When you used to whisper and nibble my ear.
34	*Garry.*	Ahhh.
35	*TB.*	Underneath the coconut trees.
36	*Garry.*	And you you used to show me your twelve incher.
37	*TB.*	And you threw it all away and you're getting married
38		tomorrow. Don't you think you should reconsider this?
39	*Garry.*	I think I should Tone, I think I should mate.

In analysing this strip of talk we wish to bring out how the two participants collaborate to co-produce talk that is 'in frame', as Goffman would say, i.e. within the terms of the discursive world of *The Tony Blackburn Show*.[2] In this respect we attend both to the content (what the talk is about) and the style (how it is talked about). We further show how both speakers, in working to produce appropriate talk, draw upon their knowledge of what Garfinkel calls 'the biography of the present situation' that we have sketched above, and thereby how identities are routinely reproduced and reaffirmed by talk.

> Hello Garry
> Hello Tony
> Hello

An exchange like this is so utterly familiar that its oddity escapes us, for the fact is that neither Tony nor Garry know each other, nor have they ever met or spoken to each other before this moment. How then can they hail each other as familiars? We must assume, as must they, that – if not familiar with each other – they must be familiar with the programme and that this is a common knowledge and thereby a shareably relevant resource for the production of talk, both in content and manner. Thus the embedded implicatures, as working conversational hypotheses initially made by each speaker, can be posed as follows:

> *TB*: Hello Garry [I have not spoken to you before, have never met you and don't know who you are, but I take it that you have listened to this programme before and to that extent know me, and I let you know that I make these assumptions in calling you Garry]

> *Garry*: Hello Tony [I have not spoken to you before, we have not met and you don't know me but I have listened to this programme before and I confirm your assumptions in calling you Tony, thereby displaying knowledge of the programme]

If TB starts with this assumption it enables him to mobilize a routine without further ado, because he can reasonably assume that caller will recognize the routine-to-be-initiated as such. One of the most economic ways of getting into a routine that Blackburn uses is voice change, which simultaneously indicates both a change of footing and the character of the new alignment. We have discussed above, in relation to several data samples, Blackburn's voice as an aspect of his chat-up routine with callers. Blackburn's repeated 'Hello', here said in a lower pitch and with a softer inflection than the first 'hello', hearably implicates intimacy. This change of voice accomplishes a number of things: first it shifts out of the first paired greetings exchange which is a display for the general audience into particular conversation with this displayed caller. The change from DJ voice to intimate voice 'keys' the tone of the talk to be initiated, it sets the frame. Note, at this point, that an intimate tone of voice is being used with a male caller (Garry's voice, like his name, is hearably masculine).

'I gather you're getting married tomorrow' is said in the same intimate tone. Let us deal first with the technical question – how does TB know this? – before attempting to account for why he says it here in this tone of voice. Callers to this, as to other radio shows with phone-ins, get through to a switchboard in the station that handles the calls. The operators will ask callers for their names, where they come from, their telephone number and if they have anything special they want to say. These bits of information are written down on paper and handed to Blackburn in the studio who is cued, by the producer, as to who is next in the bank of callers on hold to talk to him. 'I gather' implies that Blackburn's source for the statement-query that follows is not directly Garry – by inference, then, the station – and requests confirmation which Garry immediately produces (18).

But what is the object of this utterance at this point? Consider the predictable conversational lines that might be taken by recipients of the information that the person to whom they are speaking is to be married next day. A next turn might be to ask 'to whom?' – a question not posed until line 55 – and certainly the offer of congratulations should be forthcoming very soon, but these are not offered by Blackburn until line 96. Garry's marriage – which is topically relevant *today*, in programme terms, by virtue of being tomorrow – serves as the envelope for the conversation as a whole. It is the first thing referred to after initial greetings exchange and the last thing referred to before final thank-yous and good-byes:

106	*TB.*	Be happily married Garry.
107	*Garry.*	Thank you very much.
108	*TB.*	Thanks very much indeed for phoning.
109		Jill's in Woodford. Hello, Jill.
		(Continues conversation with Jill.)

The introduction of Garry's marriage at the beginning of the conversation serves not so much as a topic to be sustained in its own right, but as a foil for the routine that Blackburn wishes to establish.

What that routine is is not apparent at this point and Garry, after confirming Blackburn's statement-query, produces a response – 'nd I'm really scared I tell you – that keeps up the topic of marriage-as-an-imminent-prospect. Blackburn's next turn (19–20) is, for anyone unfamiliar with the biography of the occasion, downright peculiar or 'weirdo!' as Blackburn would say (73), but in context it is routine and indeed only makes sense as a routine. It does not at first attend to Garry's response but builds on Blackburn's opening move and begins to reveal how he wants to use Garry's marriage as a conversational resource. 'After all . . . after all you'nd I have meant to each other' is said in a hearably reproachful voice that continues and makes explicit the claims to intimacy implicated in the tone of voice adopted in Blackburn's preceding turn. His interpolated reaction to Garry's response – 'I'm not surprised [you're scared]' – is a rapid change of footing, a 'normal' response in his 'normal', slightly jokey voice, a return to the real world from which the conversation is beginning to depart if Blackburn can establish his routine.

That depends on Garry's support, and that depends on Garry recognizing and keying into the fantasy routine. Garry is not in the least fazed by Blackburn's line, 'I know but . . . what can I do?' (21) acknowledges the line of reproach and plays along with it. The playfulness is underlined by the smoothly interpolated 'My Leader', said in a tone of mock deference, which claims membership of 'the gang' and displays knowledge both of the content of the discourse of *The Tony Blackburn Show* and of its jokey, 'send-up' style. Garry has now shown to Blackburn his understanding of the rules of his conversational game and a general disposition to play it. But it is not yet clear, to Garry, that Blackburn wishes to sustain his line, so Garry continues with a bit of real-world chat – 'We tried to get down 'nd see you last night as well'.

A notable feature of the way *The Tony Blackburn Show* reaches out to its audience, attempts to create a listening community, is the Soul Night Out that Blackburn regularly announces on the show.[3] This is a disco, presented by Blackburn often with a guest soul artist, in a venue somewhere in London, to which fans of soul music and Tony Blackburn are invited. It is this that Garry tried to attend, presumably with his bride-to-be, and which he offers here as a topic (it is one that often crops up in phone-in talk on the programme). In referencing it Garry further displays his membership of the programme's listening community, but his object in introducing it here is not yet clear. Blackburn's response token – 'Really?' (23) – is a pass that allows Garry to continue, and to make explicit what was implicit in 'We *tried* to get down' – 'we couldn't' (24). A reason is produced for wanting to get to the show, namely the desire to see Blackburn's twelve-incher. As heroes in the old sagas have their trusty weapons – Achilles his spear and shield, Beowulf and Arthur their swords – so Blackburn has his tool of heroic proportions which he may offer to show to callers on the programme. Garry's use of the formulaic phrase – like 'my Leader' – shows his familiarity with the programme's word-hoard. More particularly, it switches from real-world talk back to fantasy-world talk, keying in to Blackburn's general line though not yet his particular tune.

Blackburn now, taking up the talk after a slight pause after 'but', tries to re-play that tune, having momentarily given way to Garry, 'I'm – Garry! – [. . .] I'm amazed you're getting married. All those times that we spent [. . .] together' (26–29) repeats the pattern of the first effort: 'After all – I'm not surprised – after all you 'nd I meant to each other' (19–20). The interpolated 'Garry!' (26), however, is in a tone of mock reproof (for mentioning Blackburn's unmentionable) that is consonant with the rest of the utterance whereas the interpolated 'I'm not surprised' (19) required a momentary change of footing back to the real world. Garry's production of Blackburn's twelve-incher helps to retrieve the tone of the talk which the introduction of the Soul Night Out seemed temporarily to have abandoned. But why the sand dunes in Swanage (28) of all places? Well, the young Tony Blackburn grew up in that part of the world, his father being a doctor with a practice in Poole (Blackburn, 1985: 4–13).

Garry's response (31) tunes in to Blackburn's line and now the conversation has clicked. Both will collaborate in the game of Let's Pretend to produce an imaginary relationship with an imaginary past, places and memories. The account we have offered of the talk thus far has attempted to show how it gets to this point where both participants have sought and found an agreed conversational framework and a shared attitude towards it. That they *can* get to this point depends, from moment to moment, as we have tried to show, on mutual knowledge and understanding of the programme's content and manner. Such knowledge is incremental. It accumulates in time as it is reproduced through time. The past of the programme is not the dead past. It is a pervasively relevant resource for renewing its identity in the particularities of the present. That identity is not wholly constructed and mediated by Tony Blackburn. Listeners, like Garry from Camden, playfully interact with the show to keep up the fun.

IX

It remains to link the biography of the occasion to the 'geography of the situation' (Meyrowitz 1985: 6). A broadcast programme has two spaces: that from which it speaks and that within which it is heard. Evidently programmes may be more or less oriented towards one or other of these two spaces depending on the overall communicative intentions and strategies of the programme. In hosted game shows and quizzes, for instance, the fun is visually and audibly organized in the studio before a participating studio audience. Listeners and viewers are invited to participate, *in absentia*, in the staged events taking place in the public space of the studio.

Martin Montgomery has shown how DJ talk is pervasively audience oriented: that is, its talk is directed outwards from the studio into the imagined spaces within which it is heard (Montgomery, 1986). Audiences do not eavesdrop on someone in the studio seemingly talking to himself. The modes of address routinely deployed by the DJ speak to an audience 'out there' which may be 'hailed' in many different ways. At the same time the talk of the DJ intermittently acknowledges the gap between speaker and listeners by references to the studio itself and what is going on in it. Montgomery restricts himself to DJ monologue and its attempts to simulate co-present conversation with the imagined audience. We have included, in our account, direct interaction between the DJ and those self-elected audience members who call in during the regular phone-in slots that are a feature of every programme.

This two-way talk underlines the ways in which the identity of the programme and its presenter are in part interactively sustained by a dialogue between institution and audience. Programme identity can thus be thought of as a relationship that lies across the public institutional space from which

Blackburn speaks and the private, domestic or work spaces from which callers speak. And if that identity is perishable, the threat is likely to come less from faulty DJ talk than from caller talk that is out of frame. This can readily enough be understood in terms of the differences between the diverging circumstances of the studio and its geography, on the one hand, and that of the household or workplace, on the other.

The radio or television studio is a public space into which people come to take part in a wide variety of political, cultural, educative or entertaining programmes. In all events to enter the studio is to cross a threshold, to enter a social environment that creates its own occasions with their particular situational proprieties, discursive and performative rules and conventions. To enter this space is to assume, for the duration, a role and identity appropriate to the particular communicative event that is being staged: thus interviewers and interviewees in political news interviews display, as several chapters in this book make plain, an orientation to the character of the event by sustaining the part they are called upon to play. To be physically present in the studio, whether as programme host, participant or audience member, is to be inescapably aware of the broadcast character of the event for the technology and personnel of broadcasting – cameras, microphones, lights, production staff – are pervasively evident. The design of the setting – whether for a political interview, a chat show or a game show – structures the communicative character of the event and orients all participants (including studio audiences) to the roles and performances they are expected to produce for absent viewers and listeners. In short those in the studio are committed to the communicative situation and their part in it.

Audience members who elect to take part in phone-ins enter the discursive space of the programme but not its physical space. They remain in their own place while dialling into a public discourse. That discourse may be defined in the first instance either by the studio or the caller. In phone discussion programmes, such as that analysed by Ian Hutchby (Chapter 7), it is the callers who are normatively expected to define the topic of their call. In *The Tony Blackburn Show*, however, callers elect to enter a conversation in which the tone and topic of the talk will be defined by Blackburn not themselves. They must enter a predefined discursive space with tightly defined boundaries. Those boundaries are liable to be transgressed, as we have seen, by callers introducing into the fantasy discourse coming from the studio their own immediate everyday problems or worries – the difficulties of obtaining a baby-sitter or an unexpected pregnancy, for instance. Fun is easier to sustain in a space (momentarily) dedicated to it, than one in which it is circumscribed by mundane realities.

There is, then, an inescapable lack of fit between the institutional spaces from which broadcasting speaks and the domestic and working spaces within which it is heard. If in the first place broadcasting has had to learn to adjust its discourses to fit its audiences it simultaneously requires those audiences to adjust to its discourses. Broadcasting does not, as Joshua Meyrowitz suggests, enter into the spaces of everyday life 'like a thief in the night' (Meyrowitz, 1985: 117). The flaw at the heart of his critique of television as having 'no sense of place' is that he nowhere recognizes that television has its own institutional spaces – above all the studio – which contribute to defining the character of broadcasting's communicative interactions. There is nothing furtive or hidden about this. The spaces of radio and television manifest themselves as public and as oriented towards particular kinds of public in the nature of the events there taking place and in their manner and style. Access to the public culture of the studio is open to all and voluntary. But once that domain is entered audience members must measure up to institutional expectations. In the case of *The Tony Blackburn Show* it is to maintain the fun. And if you don't like it, you can go elsewhere. As Tony Blackburn says

> If you're offended by sex I advise you to turn to another station. There's plenty of children's programmes around. We have an adult programme going on here. (25 July 1986)

Notes

This article is an extensively edited and rewritten version of a Polytechnic of Central London Media Studies undergraduate dissertation (Brand, 1987).

1. Any change of voice from a speaker's base-line, 'normal' voice will be treated as intended, more exactly (following Grice) as intended to be recognized as intended and hence as giving rise to inferences (implicatures). Voice is a fundamental resource for generating communicative implicatures in talk.

2. A full transcript of the conversation is given in the Appendix.

3. For a vivid account of a Blackburn Soul Night Out and its audience, see Brand (1987), pp. 70–3.

Appendix

15	*Garry.*	Hello Tony.
16	*TB.*	*(chat-up voice)* Hello. I gather you're getting
17		married tomorrow.
18	*Garry.*	Oh yeah 'n I'm really scared I tell you.
19	*TB.*	After all – I'm not surprised – after all you 'nd I
20		have meant to one another as well.
21	*Garry.*	I know but (?) my Leader what can I do. We tried to
22		get down 'nd see you last night as well.
23	*TB.*	Really?
24	*Garry.*	Yeah we couldn't. We wanted to see your twelve incher
25	*TB.*	I'm – Garry!
26	*Garry.*	Ahh.
27	*TB.*	I'm amazed you're getting married. All those times
29		that we spent in the sand dunes in Swanage together.
30	*Garry.*	Ah d'you remember that time in the Bahamas?
31	*TB.*	Yes.
32	*Garry.*	On the beach just me 'an you.
33	*TB.*	When you used to whisper and nibble my ear.
34	*Garry.*	Ahhh.
35	*TB.*	Underneath the coconut trees.
36	*Garry.*	And you used to show me your twelve incher.
37	*TB.*	And you threw it all away and you're getting married
38		tomorrow. Don't you think you should reconsider this?

39	*Garry.*	I think I should Tone, I think I should mate.
40	*TB.*	You'd have made me such a lovely wife as well.
41	*Garry.*	Huh huh
42	*TB.*	The way you swing that little hand-bag Garry
43	*Garry.*	heehh
44	*TB.*	And you look so nice in a cocktail dress as well
45		in the evening
46	*Garry.*	You remember when we met in the bar?
47	*TB.*	Ahh
48	*Garry.*	Ahhh
49	*TB.*	Those were the days, weren't they?
50	*Garry.*	Oh, you're telling me Tone.
51	*TB.*	D'you remember when I bought you a cocktail
52	*Garry.*	Yes yes
53	*TB.*	And the remark afterwards? Well, it's unrepeatable heh
54	*Garry.*	Hehheh
55	*TB.*	Hehheheh, Heheh who'y're getting married to Garry?
56	*Garry.*	Ah Kerry Robertson.
57	*TB.*	Kerry.
58	*Garry.*	Yeah.
59	*TB.*	*(Miffed)* Huh. How did you meet *her?*
60	*Garry.*	Ohh
61	*TB.*	I s'ppose it was on that holiday together wasn't it?
62	*Garry.*	Oh well
63	*TB.*	When you went off by yourself wandering along the
64		seafront. I know Garry. I always had my suspicions
65		about you.
66	*Garry.*	Oh well (?) you give the cocktails didn't you
67	*TB.*	Well that's what it was
68	*Garry.*	'n that's it 'nd I went to the toilet to have
69		relief 'nd I went in the gels toilets
70	*TB.*	Absolutely you well you were always a bit strange and
71		now ehheh you're getting married
72	*Garry.*	Ah
73	*TB.*	You weirdo!
74	*Garry.*	Ah
75	*TB.*	You real weirdo you heheh
76	*Garry.*	Actually now she's done she's going to two-time me
77		for you Tone
78	*TB.*	Absolutely
79	*Garry.*	Ohh I dunno
80	*TB.*	Well, it doesn't matter Garry cos when you're married
81		I can be your little bit on the side.
82	*Garry.*	Alright
83	*TB.*	You can call me up in times of need
84	*Garry.*	Ahh thank you Tone
85	*TB.*	Hehh
86	*Garry.*	We're coming up to see you next weekend is it, next
87		Thursday is it the day? Well we're gonna try
88	*TB.*	You're coming up – but you're getting married
89		tomorrow
90	*Garry.*	I know, doesn't matter does it?
91	*TB.*	Hehhh hehh
92	*Garry.*	Well we're going out tonight. I'm goin' to get my
93		last fling tonight
94	*TB.*	You're the last of the romantics you are aren't you?

95		Heheh so you're getting married tomorrow
96		congratulations
97	*Garry.*	Thank you Tone
98	*TB.*	Hope you'll be very happily married 'n you're going
99		on honeymoon anywhere?
100	*Garry.*	Er well we're going to stay over here a little while
101		'nd we're waiting till next year see we're going to
102		see Mum in Jamaica
103	*TB.*	Great. Well I hope that you er come and see us at the
104		Soul Night next Thursday
105	*Garry.*	Will do Tone
106	*TB.*	Be happily married Garry
107	*Garry.*	Thank you very much
108	*TB.*	Thanks very much indeed for phoning.
109		Jill's in Woodford. Hello Jill.

(*Continues conversation with Jill.*) (Polytechnic of Central London Collection)

References

Atkinson, M. (1984) *Our Masters' Voices*. London: Methuen.

Blackburn, T. (1985) *Tony Blackburn, 'The Living Legend'. An Autobiography. (As told to Cheryl Garnsey)*. London: W.H. Allen.

Brand, G. (1987) 'Tony Blackburn. The Construction and Maintenance of a Broadcast Identity and a Broadcast Universe'. Media Studies dissertation, Polytechnic of Central London.

Brundson, C. and D. Morley (1978) *Everyday Television: 'Nationwide'*. London: British Film Institute, TV Monograph 10.

Garfinkel, H. (1984) *Studies in Ethnomethodology*. Cambridge: Polity Press.

Giddens, A. (1984) *The Constitution of Society*. Cambridge: Polity Press.

Goffman, E. (1969) *The Presentation of Self in Everyday Life*. Harmondsworth: Penguin Books.

Goffman, E. (1970) *Asylums*. Harmondsworth: Penguin Books.

Goffman, E. (1974) *Frame Analysis*. Harmondsworth: Penguin Books.

Goffman, E. (1981) *Forms of Talk*. Oxford: Basil Blackwell.

Langer, J. (1981) 'Television's "Personality System" ', *Media, Culture and Society*, 3(4): 351–65.

Lord, A. (1960) *The Singer of Tales*. New York: Atheneum.

Meyrowitz, J. (1985) *No Sense of Place*. New York: Oxford University Press.

Montgomery, M. (1986) 'DJ Talk', *Media, Culture and Society*, 8(4): 421–40.

Parry, A. (ed.) (1971) *The Making of Homeric Verse. The Collected Papers of Milman Parry*. Oxford: Oxford University Press.

Scannell, P. (1988) '*Radio Times*. The Temporal Arrangements of Broadcasting in the Modern World', pp. 15–31 in P. Drummond and R. Paterson (eds), *Television and its Audience*. London: British Film Institute.

Scannell, P. and D. Cardiff (1991) *A Social History of British Broadcasting*, Vol. I, 'Serving the Nation, 1922–1939'. Oxford: Basil Blackwell.

Index